LAKE TROUT

North America's Greatest Game Fish

ROSS H. SHICKLER
EDWARD M. EVELAND

THE DERRYDALE PRESS
Lanham and New York

THE DERRYDALE PRESS

Published in the United States of America
by The Derrydale Press
4720 Boston Way, Lanham, Maryland 20706

Distributed by NATIONAL BOOK NETWORK, INC.

Library of Congress Cataloging-in-Publication Data

Shickler, Ross H.
Lake Trout : North America's greatest game fish / Ross H. Shickler and Edward M. Eveland.
p. cm.
Includes bibliographical references.
ISBN 1-58667-062-X (cloth : alk. paper)
1. Lake Trout. 2. Trout fishing—North America. I. Eveland, Edward M., 1927– . II. Title.
QL638.S2 S485 2001
597.5'7176'097—DC21

2001028656

∞™ The paper used in this publication meets the minimum requirements of American National Standard for Information Sciences—Permanence of Paper for Printed Library Materials, ANSI/NISO Z39.48-1992.
Manufactured in the United States of America.

CONTENTS

TABLES

ACKNOWLEDGMENTS

A number of people, including the authors, wondered at times if this book would ever be completed. During the nearly eight years it took to research and write, we were obliged to a great many kind individuals in Canada and the United States for competent assistance. Enthusiasm, cooperation, and generosity were exhibited by all those contacted for scientific information, Arctic exploration literature, lake trout records, angling knowledge, lure history, references, referrals, brochures, articles, books, photographs, and answers to a myriad of other questions.

We are particularly indebted to the six experts selected for their invaluable contributions to lake trout lore:

- Curt Bilbey, a Vernal, Utah, oilfield pipe inspector who claimed a record Utah Mackinaw at Flaming Gorge in 1988;
- Lloyd Bull, a retired owner of a petroleum products distributorship and upstate New Yorker or Floridian, dependent upon season. Bull holds current all-tackle records for lake trout from the International Game

Fish Association, National Fresh Water Fishing Hall of Fame, and Canadian National Fish Registry with a 72-pounder (32.65 kg) caught at Great Bear Lake, Northwest Territories, in 1995;

- Bret Everson, a retired New York State teacher and veteran West Virginia, New York, and Ontario angler;
- Rodney Harback, operator of an auto body shop in Harriman, Tennessee, and previous owner of the all-tackle lake trout record. Harback's trophy, scaling 66.5 pounds (30.16 kg), was lifted from Great Bear's frigid waters in 1991;
- John Herrmann, a Los Angeles, California, security consultant, who boated the largest gray trout at Nueltin Lake, Manitoba/Nunavut, in 1991; and
- John Rickett, an Orangeville, Idaho, dentist, whose family has owned for years an island cabin at Saskatchewan's excellent laker fishery, Lac la Ronge.

Particularly helpful were the following Canadian sources:

ALBERTA. Richard Pallister, President, Len Thompson Lures, Lacombe.

MANITOBA. Marvin Benson, owner/operator, Nejalini Lodge, Nejanilini Lake; Garry and Lois Gurke, owners/operators, and Shawn Gurke, Operations Manager, Nueltin Fly-In Lodges.

NEW BRUNSWICK. W. Bev Scott, Ph.D., co-author, *Freshwater Fishes of Canada,* and Senior Scientist, Brandy Cove, St. Andrews.

NORTHWEST TERRITORIES. Ron and David Frederickson, owners/operators, North of Sixty Fishing Lodges Ltd.; Howard French, angler and Manager, Community Development Corporation, Deline, Great Bear Lake; Irene Landry,

Secretary, and Chummy Plummer, President, Plummer's Lodges.

ONTARIO. Casey Creber, charters and guiding, Lake Simcoe; Lee Gerrish, Information and Planning Supervisor, Ministry of Natural Resources, Red Lake; Walt Jones, northwestern Ontario fishing expert and former owner of Snake Falls Flying Service and Trailer Park, Pakwash Lake; Ontario Federation of Anglers and Hunters, Peterborough; John Power, Lake Simcoe fisherman and outdoor writer, Beaverton; Claire Quewezence, Assistant Superintendent, and Al Theiss, Superintendent, Woodland Caribou Provincial Park, Ministry of Natural Resources, Red Lake; Bruce Ranta, Field Editor, *Ontario Out of Doors*, angler, and area biologist, Ministry of Natural Resources, Kenora; Rob and Nancy Rowe, owners/operators, Snake Falls Camp and Airways, Pakwash Lake.

QUEBEC. Jean-Paul Daigle, Vice President, sales and marketing, and Sharon Gautrey, Controller, Breck's International Inc., Sherbrooke.

YUKON TERRITORY. Susan Thompson, Fisheries Technician Supervisor, Department of Renewable Resources, Whitehorse.

We are grateful to these persons in the United States for their assistance:

CALIFORNIA. Rick Edmisten, angler, antique lure authority, and co-author of *Fishing Lure Collectibles*, North Hollywood; Dean Lester, photographer, Long Beach; Jon Meyer, fly fisherman, Long Beach; John Roush Jr., lake trout angler and author of *Enjoying Fishing Lake Tahoe, the Truckee River, and Pyramid Lake,* Kentfield; Russ Wickwire, Fishery Biologist, Department of Fish and Game, Tahoe City.

FLORIDA. Jim Brown, Assistant to the President, and Michael Leech, President, International Game Fish Association, Pompano Beach.

MAINE. Bob Lawrence, owner/operator, Lawrence's Lakeside Cabins and Guide Service, Moosehead Lake, Rockwood.

MICHIGAN. Harry Gunter, Marketing Director, Eppinger Manufacturing Company, Dearborn; John Rustowicz, President, Lake Products Company, Imlay City.

MINNESOTA. Dan Gapen Sr., tackle company owner, angler, and outdoor writer, Big Lake; Craig Weber, Communications Director, Normark Corporation, Minneapolis.

NEW YORK. Norman Gauch, Staff Adviser, Red Eye Tackle Company, Elba; Richard Preall and Bill Schoch, Senior Aquatic Biologists, Department of Environmental Conservation, Ray Brook and Saranak Lake, respectively; Helen Wirt, Communications Coordinator, Lake Placid/Essex County Visitors Bureau.

OHIO. Beulah Kiel, Administrative Assistant, Fred Arbogast Company, Akron; Dick Wilson, angler, lure historian and collector, Kent.

OREGON. Hobart Manns, angler and antique lure authority, Portland; Barry Ternahan, Media Liaison, Luhr Jensen & Sons, Hood River.

UTAH. Steve Brayton, Project Leader, Flaming Gorge/Green River, Division of Wildlife Resources, Dutch John; Glenn Davis, Fisheries Program Coordinator, Salt Lake City; Dale Hepworth, Aquatics Program Manager, Cedar City; Kreig Rasmussen, Wildlife Biologist, Fishlake National Forest, Richfield; Roger Schneidervin, Project Fisheries Biologist, Flaming Gorge, Dutch John; Kent Traveller, Supervisory Landscape Architect, Fishlake National Forest, Loa.

WASHINGTON. Pam Burton, Marketing Director, and Roy Houle, Field Researcher, Worden's Lures/Yakima Bait Company, Granger.

WISCONSIN. Ted Dzialo, Executive Director, National Fresh Water Fishing Hall of Fame, Hayward.

WYOMING. Dave Balford, Fisheries Biologist, and John Kiefling, Regional Fisheries Supervisor, Game and Fish Department, Cheyenne.

Janet Dominger, executive secretary, deserves special recognition as a capable keyboarder for considerable portions of this volume; early drafts found her laboring to decipher the authors' sometimes illegible handwriting. Noteworthy appreciation is expressed to Diane Gleason, a supervising school secretary, who computer-processed the final manuscript. We are thankful to Merrie Lyn Shickler for exceptional editing skills that helped to provide a more presentable text. Finally, we are especially grateful to our wives, Marilyn Eveland and Merrie Lyn, for expressing patience throughout the lengthy project and encouragement when undisguised disagreements periodically arose between fishing friends of disparate writing styles and temperaments.

INTRODUCTION

This is an adventure book, a lake trout journey of personal experiences—along with those of others—described by coauthors who have fished together more than thirty years. We were close friends, angling companions, and fellow educators before becoming lake trout fishermen. While we love to catch and release forktails, it is the breathtaking beauty of the Canadian north country that entices us to return repeatedly. In North America, it could be argued with considerable justification that lake trout and extraordinary scenery go together. When fishing for lakers in such gorgeous surroundings, we delight in serenity, solitude, and wonder. This profound appreciation of a wilderness lake trouting experience is our passion, an enthusiasm the writers desired to share with others.

Biology, geology, geography, and history are integrated in the text. While gray trout are quickly associated with the first three disciplines, the historical connection—other than lure chronology—may not be so clear initially. Early in our literature review, we discovered brief mention of Samuel Hearne's captivating, eighteenth-century account of a lake trout feeding frenzy at Snowbird Lake in the Northwest Territories (see bibliography, "Snowbird Lake Lodge . . . " *North of Sixty News, 1988*). Further map study of northern Canada revealed lakes, rivers, bays, and islands named for Franklin, Back, Richardson, or Hood. Who were these men, and what were they doing in this part of the world at various times from 1770 to 1850? W. B. Scott, co-author of the bible of Canada's inland fish, *Freshwater Fishes of Canada*, directed us to studies of Arctic exploration and the hunt for history commenced. Particularly enchanting were the numerous references to lake trout in the detailed journals of these courageous seekers of a western passage. Like most adventure travelers today, we wanted to get behind the history of what we saw. Mankind's record in upper Canada, the gold mine of laker fishing, is a truly fascinating story. In a sense, titanic lake trout are unwitting participants in history. Indeed, the longevity of these revered giants of the Arctic often exceeds that of the anglers who seek them.

In the notes, we have employed a method that we hope will be least distracting to the reader. Instead of notes positioned at the bottom of pages, abbreviated chapter sources and comments appear in a special section at the end of each chapter. Those interested in additional research can find complete references in the bibliography.

ONE

EVOLUTION OF A LAKE TROUT FISHERMAN

The gods do not subtract from the span of a man's life the time spent in fishing.

—Ancient Assyrian scroll

This is an account of how one of the authors, Ross Shickler, nurtured a boyhood dream to fish for lake trout and to catch them in beautiful and ruggedly exotic surroundings. It also tells how the co-authors, of disparate backgrounds, combined a love of fishing and the outdoors to focus on a common purpose—to catch the often elusive laker. It is also the story of why we wrote this book: To share what we've learned from personal experience, expert laker fishermen, and the literature about this lovely, strong, distinctive, enigmatic, and largest member of the char group, Salvelinus namaycush.

Toward the end of August, 1945, my dad returned empty-handed from a lake trout expedition to northern Ontario, Canada. He told me of putting in long hours of deep water trolling employing huge reels filled with copper line, and dragging big, wobbling spoons in his quest for hefty trout. As a youngster and hard-working muskie fisherman living on the shores of western New York's Chautauqua Lake, I could well understand the fruitless attempt to catch challenging fish that knew how to play tough to get. But a laker, I thought, must be something special to cause fishermen to travel long distances and struggle with such heavy equipment to boat one. A trout like a laker seemed to be far more exciting than the seven- or eight-inch (17.8–20.3 cm) brook trout that I'd caught with worms up until that time. I wanted to learn more about forktails and how to catch them. My budding interest in lake trout was to be heightened further two years later.

The family album displays photos of two young brothers and their dad at Golden Beach, Raquette Lake, during a camping trip to north-central New York State's sprawling Adirondack Park in early July 1947. Dad had told me before we left that picturesque Raquette held smallmouth bass and lake trout. I recall casting for bass from a bouldered shoreline, but a swarm of the region's infamous black flies caused me reluctantly to abandon the project. Later, we saw a fisherman with a stringer of nice, dark-hued smallmouths, but no lake trout. As a result of these two experiences, a seed of laker lore had been planted in a boy's mind.

Gray trout were again in my thoughts when I next visited the pristine Adirondacks, this time as a part of a group of eager Explorer Scouts on a canoe trip near the head of the Fulton chain of lakes in July 1951. A buddy and I had secured permission to break off from the rest of the intrepid Scouts for a few days to work on survival skills requirements, necessitating some serious fishing. While we caught some scrappy bass in the Raquette River and Forked Lake, I looked forward to trying for lakers while paddling through scenic Raquette Lake. However, Raquette, a deep body of water, was too rough for canoe fishing the day we arrived, and it was all we could do to negotiate the big waves safely and ultimately catch up with the rest of the group.

Our family vacationed frequently near North Bay, Ontario, from the late 1940s through the 1950s, but lakers were not among the many bass, northern pike, and walleyes caught. During my college years in the 1950s, nearby Lake Erie's lake trout fishery was very much in the news. It was discouraging to learn of the laker's decline there because of commercial overfishing, pollution, and the lamprey eel (and later gratifying to find out that the historic efforts of science, industry, and community had combined to save and enhance game fishing in the Great Lakes).

My first opportunity to fish for forktails came at the end of June 1960. I was included among a foursome—Bret Everson, one of the best fishermen I've known; Louie Mangano; and Jim Concilla—to drive to Hollow Lake, located in the Huntsville-Dorset area of southeastern Ontario. Upon reaching Hollow, my excitement rose when I saw a mounted Saint Bernard-sized lake trout displayed over the Mountain Trout Inn's fireplace at Russell Landing. Surely other magnificent lakers like this one swam in the depths of this picturesque lake. All one had to do was know how to catch them! While we worked hard and trolled for miles over a long weekend using lead-core line and an "Abalone Killer," a no-longer-manufactured small, thin spoon, the four of us caught less than ten fish in the three- to-five pound (1.4 to 2.3 kg) category. However, far from discouraged over the results, I was impressed by the fighting quality and otherwise enigmatic nature of these beautiful fish.

I had an unforgettable experience during this brief trip. Bret told us that a smaller body of water, Round Lake, above Hollow and requiring only an easy portage, could be reached by boat through connecting Bear Lake. Round reportedly held lakers, brook or speckled trout, and splake (a hybrid of speckled and lake trout). An adventurous spirit prompted me to ask that I be dropped off at the mouth of a stream which flowed from Round into Bear and which marked the portage. Then, while I took the short walk to Round Lake and fished both stream and lake for a couple of hours, my buddies could try their fortunes elsewhere. Bret, Louie, and Jim graciously agreed. Equipped with a light spinning rod and a small box of spinners, I began the trek upstream. My recollection some forty years later is that I reached Round, observed the beauty of this seldom fished little lake, took a few unsuccessful casts from shore and headed back downstream.

It's what happened during the walk upstream to Round that remains a vivid memory. The stream was fairly large, perhaps ten to fifteen feet wide (3 to 4.6 m). It had that color of weak tea that characterizes so many rivers and lakes of the North. I tested a riffle or two with a spinner and felt some hard strikes from what were probably brookies. Then I came upon a shaded, clear pool fed by a small waterfall. I approached on my hands and knees so as not to startle what fish, if any, might be in this quiet place, some three or four feet deep (.9 to 1.2 m) and about twenty feet wide (6.1 m). When close enough to observe the pool in its entirety, I blinked in disbelief. There, right in front of me, were a half dozen four- to five-pound (1.8 to 2.3 kg) lakers finning lazily near the middle. I could readily note the light spots against the background of their darker bodies and large forked tails.

My strategy to catch one of these impressive fish unfolded. A spinner was arched from a sitting position into the tail of the water pocket. Nothing happened. Successive casts moved up the pool. No interest shown. I changed spinners. Still the grays remained indifferent to my offerings. Near the waterfall a big brookie grabbed a Mepps Black Fury and the resulting fight scattered the lakers.

Ultimately, I had to give up on the pool and the fickle forktails it held. "How did they get there?" I wondered. "Were the lakers temporarily trapped after the spring high water?" I breathlessly related this experience to my friends when they returned to pick me up at the outlet into Bear Lake.

My respect for these seemingly tough-to-catch members of the char family only increased as a result of this encounter. While not realizing it at the time, I had been part of a most unusual and rare occurrence—that of closely observing lake trout for a lengthy period in their natural habitat. Bret Everson reminded me years later that he had visited the mouth of the same stream a few weeks prior to this trip, in mid-May, and had caught and released several two- to four-pound (.9 to 1.8 kg) lakers while spincasting from shore with an Abalone Killer. Spring, Bret told me, always proved his favorite time to pursue grays since they were still in shallow water after ice-out and therefore could more easily be taken. I couldn't help but note the big difference in fishing techniques for lakers between the middle of May and late June!

I relocated from New York to southern California in the fall of 1960 to take a teaching position in the Golden State. I now had new places to fish and different fish to catch. My trips to eastern Canada became less frequent, although vacations were taken in New York and Ontario during the summers of 1961 and 1962. In both years, Bret, his brother, Hobart, Jim Concilla, and I visited Mud Turtle Lake and the Crowe River, a terrific smallmouth bass, walleye, and muskie fishery northeast of Peterborough, Ontario, in the Kawartha Lakes chain.

Co-author Ed Eveland and I hooked up as southern California fishing buddies in the mid-1960s and have fished locally for trout and largemouth bass ever since. My adventurous sons, Mike and Matt, and daughter, Suzanne, joined me in hiking Yellowstone National Park's crystal clear streams for scrappy cutthroat trout and exploring Montana's blue-ribbon trout rivers, the Gallatin and Madison, for big rainbows and browns in the summer while growing up in the 1970s and early 1980s. In August 1982, we caught colorful golden trout in stunning high country lakes of the majestic Gallatin range southwest of Bozeman, Montana.

The lure of Canada's great fishing continued to tug at me over the years. I clipped, saved, and studied literature on lake trout, such as John Fowler's piece in the July 1960 issue of *Outdoor Life*, "You Should Know About Lakers"; A. J. McClane's February 1963 *Field and Stream* account of dry fly-fishing for lakers at Great Bear Lake, "Topside Togue"; and "We Caught 'Em by the Ton," an article by Homer Circle on Saskatchewan's Churchill River area in the June 1963 issue of *Sports Afield*. A story by Tom Opre in a Lou Eppinger publication in 1969, "Great Bear's Great Fishing," described an encounter with a lake trout by a nineteenth century explorer, Colonel La Nauze. The colonel related how one of Great Bear's ravenous lakers struck his oar and was nearly drawn into the boat. I eagerly read and reread Ray Bergman's chapter on lakers in his classic book, *Trout* (reprinted by The Derrydale Press, 2000). These fascinating articles, among the first that I located on the subject, helped keep alive the idea of a return trip to Canada someday. Most of these stories were fly-in ventures, something I'd dreamed of since boyhood. Copies of these and other magazine accounts were shared with Ed over the years. We had frequent discussions about Canadian fishing, especially in Ontario, during our many trips together. We agreed that someday we'd make the trip, even though Ontario was a long way from southern California.

During the summer of 1969 our family passed through Utah's Capitol Reef National Park while on vacation. As I looked at a rack of postcards during a stopover at a souvenir shop, my eye was attracted by a photo of a fisherman holding a large Mackinaw trout taken in nearby Fish Lake. Following our return to southern California, I showed the postcard to Ed. It didn't take us long to plan a trip to Fish Lake, a beautiful, natural reservoir at an elevation of 8,700 feet (2,652.4 m) in south-central Utah, for the closing days of June 1970.

Shortly after we arrived, rangers described local laker lore, including that of big fish observed in the shallows along the south shore during fall spawning. We hit the water at five o'clock the next morning with less than total confidence. It was bitter cold, with 20-degree F (-7°C) temperatures accompanied by strong, icy winds. Ed used a weighted Dave Davis lake troller with a large Flatfish and I tried the trusty Abalone Killer with lead-core line to take the lure down. While a half day's trolling yielded only a small rainbow, the results probably reflected our expectations. We didn't know the lake, at what depth the fish were to be found, the best lures to use, and were generally inexperienced in laker fishing techniques.

Overall, however, the venture was a success. Since our families were with us, the remaining few days were spent catching lots of rainbows while still-fishing the picturesque lake and landing some cutthroat on spinners from sparkling feeder streams. I suppose we were somewhat discouraged that we didn't experience a laker strike while trolling. But we felt there would be another time and place for that to happen. What we didn't realize was that it would be nearly twenty years before we would have another opportunity to fish for lake trout.

Co-author Ed Eveland, who had moved to Long Beach, California, from Mason City, Iowa, as a youngster during World War II, didn't take up fishing as a sport until he was nearly thirty years old. And, like virtually everything else Ed does, he soon became very successful at his new hobby. When Ed used the weighted Luhr-Jensen Dave Davis lake troll with a large Flatfish for Macs at Fish Lake, he was using a deep trolling technique perfected over a ten-year period through the mid-1960s at Convict Lake, a small water-body in the Sierra Nevada range just east of the southern portion of Yosemite National Park. The flashing, rotating blades of the troll served to attract fish and set off vibrations. The Flatfish did the rest. Ed was able to consistently catch hefty browns and rainbows at Convict using this method, outfishing others. He also learned a lot about trolling during this period, noting the effectiveness of tracing figure eights, *S* curves, and zig-zag patterns to vary the depth, speed, and action of the lure.

Ed has experienced some excellent saltwater fishing, too. Since 1980, he has taken many San Diego–based long-range fishing trips off the Pacific side of the Baja California peninsula, including journeys to the Alijos Rocks and Cabo San Lucas. He has caught big fish in these waters: a 150-pound (68.2 kg) marlin in the Sea of Cortez, Dorado (dolphin-fish) as large as 60 pounds (27.3 kg), grouper over 100 pounds (45.5 kg), a 190-pound (86.4 kg) giant (black) sea bass, pargo of 30 pounds (13.6 kg), yellowfin tuna of 150 pounds (68.2 kg), and wahoo of 90 pounds (40.9 kg). Ed, however, prefers freshwater fishing, and, in particular, trolling for gray trout.

By the mid-1980s, Ed and I were ready to take that Canadian fishing trip. A school district colleague, Eloise

Thompson, recommended that we fly to Larry and Mary Rowe's Snake Falls Camp on Pakwash Lake in northwestern Ontario, 25 miles (40 km) southeast of Red Lake, where her family had enjoyed good walleye, northern pike, and bass fishing for years. The camp brochure revealed an outpost cabin at Meandrine Lake, 140 miles (224 km) northwest of the Snake Falls base. Easily reached by portage from Meandrine, an excellent walleye and northern lake, was Cherrington Lake, which held lakers. The package looked ideal, so we made arrangements to fly from Pakwash to Meandrine for a week's stay in late July 1987. The bush pilot was one of the Rowes' sons, Rob, who, along with his wife, Nancy, ran Snake Falls Airways. We found the Rowe family to be friendly, hard working, generous people who managed a superb base camp operation and fly-in service.

During our visits to the outpost in 1987, 1988, and 1989, Ed and I spent most of our time at Meandrine Lake, catching and releasing hundreds of walleyes and northerns. We fished Cherrington for only a few hours each trip and had only modest success with forktails there, probably because we fished relatively late in summer, when the trout were in deep water, and we lacked the equipment to reach them. We knew, however, that the lake trout were there. Wall graffiti at the outpost cabin bragged of a 26-pounder (11.8 kg). A veteran Cherrington fisherman whom I consulted about how to fish the lake had caught suspended grays (fish holding at various depths) as large as 18 pounds (8.2 kg) jigging in mid-June. The same angler told me that he spent most of his time at Cherrington since members of his fishing party weren't much interested in Meandrine's big northerns.

In mid-July 1989, Robbie flew Ed and me into Sturgeon Lake (also referred to as Upper Kilburn), a seldom bothered laker fishery 50 miles (80 km) west of the Snake Falls base camp in the southeast corner of newly created Woodland Caribou Provincial Park on the Ontario-Manitoba border. We had an eventful day at Sturgeon, catching about 30 four- to six-pound (1.8 to 2.7 kg) fish while trolling medium-sized Thompson spoons.

Since Rob Rowe, in expanding his outfitting service, had built a new cabin at fly-in Cleveland Lake, an excellent catch-and-release, barbless hook laker water 110 miles (177 km) north of his base, Ed and I decided to try this lovely lake for a week in early July 1991. We were not disappointed. We boated a batch of good-sized lakers while trolling moderate depths with large Thompson Five-of-Diamonds spoons. It was during the trip that we decided to write this book, a research project that would serve to inform others—and ourselves—of the vagaries of laker fishing.

As part of our preparation for this volume, we returned to Cleveland Lake in late September 1992. Accompanied by Roger Cronin and Ron Tessada, school business administrators in Long Beach, our goal was to analyze laker fishing just prior to spawning. We found the fish to be real fighters in the fall, grabbing spoons and plugs on light tackle in the cool surface waters. It was during this particularly memorable trip that we encountered an indelible event: a surprise snowstorm.

Ed and I revisited northwestern Ontario's Sturgeon Lake during a fly-in in July 1993. Outfitted by bush pilot Rob Rowe with a comfortable Zodiac inflatable boat and outboard motor, we found while trolling that the laker's preferred temperature zone was a tad deeper than four years earlier. We again caught some 35 nice lakers using lead-core line or monofilament, one or two ounces (31 or 62 grams) of weight, and large spoons. A few days later, we fished Cherrington Lake, reached by short portage from Meandrine where our outpost cabin was situated. The screen of our portable Humminbird fish/depth finder displayed big, bottom-dwelling forktails at depths of 70 to 80 feet (21.3 to 24.4 m). However, deep trolling and vertical jigging failed to stir any interest. So, in less than a week, our level of angling success had gone from the penthouse to the basement. Such is often the nature of lake trout fishing![1]

The foursome that visited Cleveland Lake during the first week of July 1994 included second timer Ron Tessada and newcomer Frank Thometz, a Long Beach architect. Since we looked forward eagerly during each trip to a day's fly-in laker fishing at Sturgeon, our travel agent, as usual, had scheduled an itinerary that put us into Red Lake on a Wednesday evening. Friday was the fly-out day for Cleveland, so Thursday was slated for the much-anticipated Sturgeon visit. However, for the second time in four trips, a rainstorm moved in Wednesday night and continued the next day, grounding Rob Rowe's de Havilland Beaver float plane at Pakwash. Along with other anglers who had driven to Snake Falls Camp for a day's fly-in to a different lake, we exhibited the keen disappointment and angry impatience of little boys denied their outdoor play. The four of us spent the gloomy day in Red Lake, picking up our groceries for the Cleveland stay, and browsing local gift shops. We knew that we had to develop an imaginative strategy to allow more flexibility in working out a fly-in to this fruitful lake. Scheduling this side trip for a specific day proved just too risky.

During our journey to Cleveland Lake in late June and early July 1995, we finally devised an alternative plan for reaching Sturgeon (or Upper Kilburn) despite unstable weather conditions, although it turned out to be a close call. After our usual Wednesday evening arrival, the temperature dropped suddenly during the night, with rolling gray clouds and driving rain greeting the visitors to Rowe's Snake Falls Camp on Thursday. Huddling with our grounded bush pilot, we learned that the reservation for the week following our stay at Cleveland had been cancelled, so Robbie didn't need to fly the following Friday to pick us up and drop off the incoming party. In other words, by cutting short our stay at Cleveland, Robbie could fly us back to Pakwash on Wednesday, freeing up Thursday or Friday for the fly-in to Sturgeon Lake. (Our departure for the return trip to Los Angeles was scheduled for Saturday morning.)

This looked like an ideal solution to a frustrating problem, but as things developed, we weren't out of the woods yet. Meanwhile, we enjoyed a delightful stay at Cleveland, catching many nice forktails. We were thrilled to be just the second group to fish a small lake to which Robbie and other family members had hacked a short trail and dragged a boat only a few weeks before. The pretty, ribbon-shaped lake—unnamed—about a mile (1.6 km) in length and no more than 300 feet (91.5 m) wide, yielded a pile of sturdy walleyes and northerns as we slowly trolled the rugged, tree-strewn shoreline with floating Rapalas and Rebels. All were released. A member of the initial party to test the lake's virgin waters had caught and released a ten-pound (4.5 kg) walleye two weeks earlier.

Those familiar high cloud signals of an approaching storm—mare's tails and a mackerel sky—were evident on Tuesday, the day prior to our Cleveland departure, and we groused aloud that yet another Sturgeon fly-in attempt would be washed out. Rain was beginning to fall when Robbie picked us up the next day, and we landed at Pakwash some forty-five minutes later in a downpour. (On the return flight, our pilot pointed out the shoreline of former glacial Lake Agassiz, which once covered a large portion of Canada and the United States.)

No bush flying was possible on Thursday, as the storm plodded across northwestern Ontario. However, the skies cleared later that night and a beautiful, clear day dawned on Friday, with only small patches of fog hugging the Pakwash shoreline. The thirty-minute flight was perfect and we splashed down on Sturgeon's mirror-like surface at about seven-thirty. Within twenty minutes, the Zodiac was properly inflated, fitted with a motor, and filled with gear. We netted our first laker of the day just as Robbie's plane, taking off, cleared the treetops at the east end of the lake. When he returned at four o'clock to pick us up, we had thoroughly enjoyed a superb day of fishing, photography, and exploring. Trolling large Doctor and Thompson spoons all over this three-mile-long (4.8 km) lake, we caught nearly 40 scrappy forktails, drank in the magnificent scenery of the Canadian north, and even nosed around an abandoned Indian trapper's cabin nestled in a thick stand of jack pines on the north shore. Back at the Pakwash base camp that night, Ed baked a big Cleveland laker he had caught, stuffed with shrimp, crab, and walleye, placed on a generous bed of celery and onions, and gently basted with wine and chicken broth. Other camp visitors joined us for the gourmet dinner. It was an elegant meal in a wilderness setting that capped an exceptional lake trout fishing trip.

In the latter part of June 1997, Rob Rowe flew us, for the first time over a six-day period, into three separate gray trout lakes—Cleveland, Trout, and Sturgeon. Despite showery conditions throughout this period, laker fishing proved to be superb, with the fish found consistently within 20 feet (6.1 m) of the surface. Trout and Sturgeon represented one-day fly-ins, with a guide hired at Trout Lake. In only five hours of leisurely trolling at Sturgeon, we boated over 40 black-bodied, spotted scrappers.

Two years later, during the last week of June, we again planed to three lakes, but with one change from the 1997 visit. This time Trout Lake was replaced by Dragon, a water body with only lake trout and northern pike in Woodland Caribou Provincial Park. Fishing proved excellent overall, despite alternating periods of bright sunshine and severe storminess. Dragon's fighting forktails outweighed those at Cleveland and Sturgeon on this trip.

The preceding account, covering more than fifty years, reflects the co-author's personal experience with lake trout at this writing. We're looking forward to testing other productive laker waters discussed in this book. While the best gray trout fishing is found in Canada's far north, lakers have been successfully introduced in at least thirty of the fifty American states. Lake trout fishing is becoming more popular with easier angling accessibility and improved knowledge and techniques. The authors hope the information in this book will inspire more anglers to try forktailing, and make fishing for lakers more successful through new ideas and techniques. Ed and I wish you the best in what we like to refer to as "the lake trout experience." Please join us in this exciting adventure!

Notes

1. Since Sturgeon Lake (also known as Upper Kilburn) lies in a provincial park, an outfitter may not keep a boat there. Rob Rowe's only Zodiac inflatable boat holds two anglers, so when the authors fished Sturgeon in 1993, the other members of our party, Ron Tessada and Roger Cronin, gathered groceries for the Cleveland sojourn and fished Pakwash for the balance of the day.

Cronin, an admitted fishing neophyte, slow-trolled one of Tessada's saltwater lures, a mackerel finish Striker, near a rocky island and boated an eight-pound (3.6 kg) walleye. Boats are kept at fourteen other non-park fly-in lakes for which Rowe has commercial operating rights.

TWO

LESSONS LEARNED

On Poetry and Fishing

> The poet's craft . . . is akin to fishing.
> It involves luck, skill, dedication,
> patience, and disappointment. The poet
> throws the bait of his experience into the
> sea of language and waits and works for
> the right collection of words to attach
> themselves to it.
>
> —Seamus Heaney

Why this chapter? Lake trout, after all, receive little mention in the pages to follow. How can a series of personal stories about typical freshwater fishing be relevant to a book about lake trouting? It should be clear to the reader that we have a fire in our bellies for unsullied lake, river, or stream fishing in general, and forktail angling in particular. Before we became laker aficionados, we learned the lessons necessary to consistently catch small- and largemouth bass, walleye, northern pike, muskellunge, and various trouts. Somewhere along the line, we became particularly lured by the trout, a seduction that eventually led to a passion for lake trout fishing. This long-term instruction over a period of many years proved invaluable to our growth as gray trout fishermen.

The accounts of acquired knowledge covered in this chapter, and practical for lake trouting, spawn these inferences and comments:

- Like skillful batsmen, confident that they can hit any major league pitcher, we feel similarly assured in our quest to outfox an enigmatic fighter found throughout the water column of many of the continent's lakes. With all humility, this conviction is based on a determination to succeed and a wealth of varied fishing experiences.
- Family history underscores our enthusiasm for fishing in Canada. For instance, Ross Shickler's grandfather first plied Ontario's waters in the 1920s. The Canadian angling connection has continued with the zealous participation of other family members through the years.
- Appreciation for and familiarity with classic baits used for other freshwater fish, like the Jitterbug, Bass-Oreno, and Injured Minnow, are suitable inclinations for the successful use of legendary gray trout lures, such as the Dardevle, Len Thompson Spoon, and Flatfish.
- Certain general techniques, such as careful attention to lure action, are highly applicable to lake trout fishing.
- Admiration for virginal and vulnerable lake trout habitat, including dedication to the barbless hook and catch-and-release ethic, helps to maintain the forktail fishery.

- A respectful and savvy view of the great outdoors is indispensable to safe and successful laker angling.
- Generous sharing of angling know-how is returned to the giver many times over.
- Anglers can't hope to grow in fishing proficiency without making mistakes. We may make many, but can profit from them all.
- Modest receptiveness to assistance offered, rather than proud-hearted resistance, pays big dividends in fishing accomplishment.
- As might be expected, patience, resourcefulness, diligence, perseverance, optimism, discipline, teamwork, common sense, excellent equipment, careful planning, an adventurous spirit, and a sense of humor are essential elements in laker angling success.

The Shickler family returned to Commanda Lake in 1949 for the second time in two years. Commanda, a small, pretty, three-mile-long (4.8 km) lake 23 miles (37 km) southwest of North Bay, Ontario, was graphically pictured in Ross's youth with its west shore thickly treed with pine and birch, rolling farm pasture dotted with cattle to the east and south, and the smallish, quiet town of Restoule at its northernmost end. Although moderately fished for bass, northern, and walleye, Commanda produced the best fishing the young man had yet experienced.

During this much-anticipated visit to Orlan Jones's cabins among white birches on the southeastern shore, Henry Schrader and his wife, Charlotte, drove from Lakewood, New York, for a week's stay. Schrader, a junior high school principal in Jamestown, was highly regarded as a Chautauqua Lake muskie fisherman, regularly logging fish weighing from 20 to 30 pounds (9.1 to 13.6 kg), with some even larger. Shickler clearly recalls a giant muskellunge that Schrader landed, metal muskie license tag affixed through its gills, more than 50 inches (127 cm) long and weighing over 35 pounds (15.9 kg). With staring, mean-looking, golf ball-sized eyes, the leviathan curled in a huge washtub partially filled with water so as to loosen its scales prior to cleaning and dressing for the table. The huge muskie, displayed on the Schrader's lakeshore lawn, drew a large crowd of admirers on a summer Sunday afternoon in the late 1940s.

Shickler was thrilled to see this top-rated angler in camp. Both families resided in homes on or near the lake and knew each other. The young Shickler yearned to fish with the legendary muskie expert. He didn't have long to wait, as the elder angler asked if the two might go after some of Commanda's northerns. Schrader, taking over operation of the 3.5 horsepower Firestone outboard motor, steered the sturdy, wooden, round-bottomed boat to a shallow section abounding with weeds along the eastern shore. Shickler usually slow-trolled the edge of this cover every other day or so, hoping that a Dardevle or jointed Pikie-type plug would entice a couple of these toothy rascals to dart out of the weeds and open wide.

Schrader suggested that each of them clip a weedless Johnson spoon to the wire leader, and, to Shickler's surprise, headed straight for the center of the weedbed. With about 75 feet (22.9 m) of line reeled out, Schrader gunned the motor through tall, leafy cornstalks, lily pads, and floating weeds at what seemed like several times Shickler's normal trolling speed, the silver lures nearly breaking the surface. In about twenty minutes, the pair had boated half a dozen aggressively-striking northerns—considerably more than Shickler had been accustomed to catching along this same short stretch in a week. The young fisherman had learned from a skilled angler a never-to-be-forgotten lesson: Members of the pike family, at times, prefer a fast-moving bait, even in thick, weedy growth! This valuable learning experience later paid handsome dividends for him in terms of successful northern and muskie fishing.

Ed Eveland in 1955 taught at Woodrow Wilson High School in Long Beach, California. He and a fellow faculty member and fishing buddy Bill Raney had wanted to try Convict Lake, a small, idyllic mountain-shadowed body of water just east of the southern tip of Yosemite National Park in the Sierra Nevada range. In Convict's cool waters swam hefty brown and rainbow trout, and the two instructors yearned to learn the secrets of catching them.

The teachers were aware that members of a family residing in one of the school's attendance areas, Belmont Shore, had successfully fished Convict for years and looked for a way to talk to them about it. In the spring, a welcome opportunity unexpectedly presented itself. One of the family's sons enrolled in Eveland's junior English class, and, in danger of receiving a C in the course, approached his teacher to ask how he could raise the final grade to a B. Eveland told him that to obtain a B, the young man needed to earn an A on a major project, due near the end of the semester, in early June. When asked about a report topic, Eveland quickly suggested that a scholarly study, supported by research and personal experience, on the specifics of how and where to fish Convict Lake would be favorably received by his instructor.

The student's completed report included a detailed map of the lake and other pertinent information, such as trolling distance from shore (about 100 yards/91.4 m); fishing depth (30 to 35 feet/9.1 to 10.7 m); suitable terminal tackle (Luhr Jensen Dave Davis lake troll, a series of free-swinging, variable-sized attractor blades on a wire shaft and swivel to which six feet

[1.8 m] of monofilament leader and a U-20 Flatfish were attached); necessary weight (two ounces/57 grams); and the crucial throbbing action imparted to the rod tip by blade action and boat speed.

This story's happy ending produced smiles all around. The high schooler became the proud recipient of an A on his term paper and a final grade of B in English; the appreciative parents generously loaned the two teachers the family boat and motor, and even paid for a week's stay for the pair at a Convict cabin that summer; and Eveland and Raney became Convict Lake angling experts, catching a sizeable number of four- to six-pound (1.8 to 2.7 kg) browns and rainbows from the clear, deep waters over the next eight years.

Ross Shickler felt particularly blessed to participate in three fishing treks to Ontario in 1960. Two of the trips were absolutely top-notch, with varied species of fish pursued. The destination of the first visit, in late June, was Hollow Lake, in the Huntsville-Dorset area of southeastern Ontario. This was Shickler's first lake trouting adventure. A remote, cove-sheltered cabin, reached by inboard motorboat some 15 miles (24.1 km) from Russell Landing, served as headquarters over a three-day period while he and his three eager companions—Bret Everson, Louie Mangano, and Jim Concilla—trolled the deep water for lakers.

Each member of the group dragged lead-core line and an Abalone Killer, a small, thin spoon, no longer manufactured. The hard-working party caught a total of about ten three- to five-pound (1.4 to 2.3 kg) forktails, along with a few burly brookies on spinning tackle from a feeder stream. Everson and Mangano were the only anglers among the enthusiastic foursome who possessed practical knowledge of laker fishing and performed capably as mentors. Although the journey to Hollow thrilled Shickler about laker fishing possibilities, he and the others were driven to conclude that different approaches were needed to consistently boat this beautiful, enigmatic fighter.

In July, Fred and Mary Stoll took Shickler to ribbon-like Rice Lake, which slants northeast to southwest south of Peterborough, Ontario. It's an excellent fishing water for small- and largemouth bass, muskies, and walleyes. Fred, a machinist, and Shickler worked at the same plant in western New York that summer. Although the fishing itself was unremarkable, Shickler received instruction in the correct use of a favorite bait of the Stolls—the legendary South Bend Bass-Oreno, a wooden casting and trolling lure first manufactured in America about 1916.[1] The Stolls preferred the red head and white body finish in 5/8 ounce (17.7 g) size (no. 973).

Mrs. Stoll claimed, with a wink, that a feminine touch produced a delicate lure action superior to that exhibited by Mr. Stoll. The plug, she advised, should remain at rest for a few moments following an accurately placed cast to the edge of cover, permitting the splash rings to spread. The softest wrist action conveyed to the rod tip would cause the Bass-Oreno to dance enticingly on the surface. This teasing movement, depending upon the angler's patience, could be repeated several times with pauses between gentle tweaks.

At this juncture, the expectant angler is steeled for a water erupting, lily pad bursting, smashing strike from a maddened muskie or bass. Following the throw-and-hesitate routine, a varied retrieval—characteristically permitting the lure to weave over the top of submerged weeds and periodically bob to the surface—simulates an injured, struggling baitfish. The beauty of the Bass-Oreno is that it can serve as both a surface and an underwater lure, if caused to perform properly. Shickler vividly remembers Mrs. Stoll enthusiastically relating that, a few years earlier at Rice Lake, she had caught a big muskie and a hefty largemouth from the same weedpocket on successive casts with a Bass-Oreno. Needless to say, the Stolls were fervent about this highly effective lure!

The final expedition that year, to southeastern Ontario's Mud Turtle Lake, has endured in memory as a truly classic fishing trip. It was one of those "once in a lifetime" experiences played over and over again in the mind, repeatedly embracing the wonderful lessons of an all-time favorite film that take on new meaning with each viewing.

Ross Shickler first met Bret Everson when they became fellow faculty members in 1959. Everson had left a high school mathematics teaching job in West Virginia that year to accept a position as a junior high math instructor in western New York. At the time, Shickler was a second-year junior high science teacher on the same staff, and, with a common enthusiasm for fishing and teaching, the pair quickly developed a strong friendship. During the fall and winter of 1959–60, Shickler and Everson traded tackle and tales, but it was clearly evident to Ross that his new friend had better yarns to spin and was a superb outdoorsman to boot. Bret exhibited a sixth sense when it came to fishing and hunting.

While Shickler listened intently to Everson's accounts of fishing West Virginia's pristine Cheat and Greenbriar river networks for rainbows, browns, brookies, and smallmouths, and Hollow Lake for lake trout, the narratives dealing with Mud Turtle Lake really riveted his attention. Mud Turtle, probably named for reptilian inhabitants and through which the Crowe River flowed, was a superb smallmouth bass, walleye, and muskie fishery northeast of Peterborough, Ontario, in the Kawartha Lakes chain.

Night fishing, another portion of the Mud Turtle picture, intrigued Shickler. Lacking sufficient experience and knowledgeable companions, he, like most anglers, had been strictly a dawn-to-dusk fisherman. George Wilde, who owned a cottage on nearby Belmont Lake, had taught Everson the science of nightly angling, with both Belmont and Mud Turtle serving as outdoor laboratories. Everson told Shickler, who yearned to be similarly schooled, that he must learn by doing.

Surface lures required for nocturnal fishing at Mud Turtle included the Arbogast Jitterbug, Creek Chub Injured Minnow and Plunker, and Heddon Crazy Crawler. Baits to be used largely during daylight hours comprised the Creek Chub jointed and deep diving Pikie Minnow, Heddon Lucky 13, Tad Polly, River Runt, Vamp and jointed Vamp Spook, and the South Bend Bass-Oreno. An Everson favorite top-water tantalizer, the Heddon Chugger Spook, could be employed day or night.

While the information on artificial lures seemed sufficiently explicit, the expectations of what might be found in Mud Turtle's nighttime waters appeared to be more ambiguous. Tongue-in-cheek, Bret stated that "horses and cows" were hooked in the darkness; that an angler chosen by lot to fish the river outlet at night would be permitted only one cast; and that no one could be certain what would happen when throwing a lure into the big hole at the foot of the rapids from dusk onward!

Of the surface lures mentioned, the legendary Jitterbug, an all-time favorite introduced by Fred Arbogast in 1938, had been the top-water plug most familiar to Shickler at the time.[2] He recalled with a rush of memories his first experience with this classic. But first, some background may be in order.

At the time of World War II, the Shickler home fronted southwestern New York State's beautiful Chautauqua Lake. An ancient, wooden, flat-bottomed barge, about 50 feet (15.3 m) long and 20 feet (6.1 m) wide, faced the adjacent lakeside property on Maple Bay. The junked workboat had sunk perpendicularly to the shore, the exposed bow just a few feet (meters) from land and the stern barely submerged. Decking had long since disappeared, and waves washed unopposed into the tail section of the abandoned structure. No one seemed to know much about the disabled vessel's previous use, why it lay in this particular resting place, or how long it had been there. Some weathered timber pilings that protruded from the water on the windward side suggested the mooring of a ship in earlier days, possibly of the old barge itself.

The top of the wreck's windward side had largely deteriorated over the years because of continual wave action. The more protected leeward portion facing the Shickler residence, however, offered a largely uninterrupted flat surface along the ship's length about six inches (15.2 cm) wide, bridged to shore by a short, warped walking board. This narrow exterior, even though decayed in spots and sprouting rusty nails and bolts, offered a means by which an angler—especially a youngster with short feet—could carefully sidestep or crawl out to the end of the derelict to fish. Since the Shicklers' short dock didn't reach water deeper than four feet (1.2 m), negotiating the somewhat dangerous ledge to its end offered a satisfactory alternative to a fisherman deemed by his parents too young at the time to take a boat out alone.

While the dilapidated vessel probably constituted an eyesore to many adult neighbors, the wreck had become a haven for many kinds of fish and other freshwater life up and down the food chain. Depending upon the season, Shickler family members, employing long bamboo poles and bobbers with night crawlers, minnows, or crayfish for bait, caught crappie, pumpkinseeds, yellow perch, bullheads, and bass in and around the timeworn ship. Occasionally, a big muskie cruised inside the barge, hoping to waylay an unsuspecting baitfish that had sought refuge there. While Shickler can't recollect a muskellunge ever being taken in the immediate vicinity of the barge during the more than two years he lived at Maple Bay, there was one close call.

One summer evening, while his parents watched from lawn chairs, their son carefully worked his way out to the end of the barge's lee side, rod in hand. While the plan involved casting, like most kids—and we might add, like many adults—he hadn't thoroughly thought through the unexpected. What would he do if a heavy fish grabbed his lure while so precariously perched? Just as the lure swam to the surface, a good-sized muskie took a swirling, splashing swipe at the plug and fortunately disappeared empty-mouthed into deep water. The third grader, trembling and teetering following his first encounter with a rambunctious 'lunge, almost fell into the lake!

Now we're ready to relate that Jitterbug tale. In the summer of 1944, Howard Shickler arrived home from the office as usual for lunch. On a gray, overcast day that threatened showers, yet with little wind, he intended to get in a few casts near the barge while Mrs. Shickler prepared the midday meal. Picking up the family's only bait-casting rod at the time, a steel version about five feet (1.5 m) long with agate guides, he then unboxed a newly purchased, brightly colored, unfamiliar-looking lure. He told his son that the Jitterbug he held in his fingers was a wartime model, with its body manufactured of plastic rather than cedar. The double-lobed lip was produced from nylon, aluminum being unavailable during the war years. He tied the frog/yellow belly Jitterbug with its sunflower-hued lip to the tip of black braided nylon line and walked to the end of the shortish dock, as his young son watched expectantly from shore.

The elder Shickler's first cast slanted cornerwise beyond the barge's stern. The Jitterbug splashed down near the desired location and, after hesitating, he began a stop-and-go retrieval. As the bait plopped and spluttered past the barge's near corner, the surface erupted. A beefy largemouth bass clobbered the lure. Following a good fight and beaching of the bass, he again threw to the same spot. Wham! Another bigmouth blasted the 'bug. Eight-year-old Ross gazed wide-eyed with wonder. Two gorgeously green, three-pound (1.4 kg), supercharged largemouths on consecutive casts! He had not previously experienced the excitement of a smashing surface strike. Nor would he forget the lure that fooled both bass that day: the rhythmic, side-to-side popping bait with the unique water-disturbing lip—the famous Arbogast Jitterbug.[3]

Ross Shickler first accompanied Bret Everson and his brother Hobart to Mud Turtle Lake in late August 1960. Driving all night from western New York, the trio stopped early the next morning at the general merchant store in Cordova Mines, northeast of Peterborough, Ontario, to pick up groceries and gasoline for the outboard motor. From Cordova Mines, they motored the short distance to Carl McMillan's small farm on the edge of the Canadian bush. McMillan, equipped with a workhorse tractor and a four-by-eight-foot (1.2 by 2.4 m) two-wheeled wooden trailer, provided transportation for the party's gear over a rugged four-mile (6.4 km) trail into the lake. While the Eversons carefully packed the trailer, Shickler bait-boxed a batch of the numerous meadow-dwelling leopard frogs found leaping in the tall grass.

The bumpy trail, which cut through thick forest, spongy ground, and soggy streamlets, provided a prelude to the Crowe-Mud Turtle wilderness adventure. Upon emerging from the heavy tree growth about forty-five minutes later,

Shickler was thrilled to witness Mud Turtle's brilliant blue, reflecting a mid-morning cloudless sky. The forested shoreline mirrored glimmering greenness, like shimmering fingers dipping into the lake's becalmed borders. At first blush, Mud Turtle expressed stillness, purity, freshness—a primitive condition. It was a little jewel, lovely to behold.

In the days that followed, Shickler and his companions fished and explored the unique lake-river system. The small-scale lake, about one and a quarter miles long (2.0 km) and perhaps a third of a mile across (.53 km) at its widest point, appeared somewhat fish-shaped, with head pointing north, belly facing west, and dorsal fin forming Jitterbug Bay to the east. The Crowe River entered serenely from the north, flowed unobtrusively through the lake, and exited eastwards at the top of the fish's tail at Mud Turtle's south end. About a quarter mile (.40 km) west of the outlet, a small, heavily treed island, some 100 yards (91.4 m) in length, enhanced the scenic view. The log cabin, affectionately referred to by Bret Everson as "the old trapper shanty," perched on high ground amid tall conifers on the eastern shore.

The upper Crowe River was a gentle stream, its banks forested with pine, maple, birch, ironwood, and oak, edged with reeds and lily pads. Here was prime muskie and smallmouth territory. The Bass-Oreno proved an effective lure along this stretch. An outcropping of flattish rocks, roomy enough for two or three disembarked anglers to cast or use live bait for bass during the heat of the day, protruded just inside the river's mouth. A short distance beyond the outlet to the south, the Crowe suddenly changed character, descending precipitously 50 feet (15.2 m) in a quarter mile (.40 km). The torrent squirted as if fire-hosed through a narrow, deeply sculpted, granite-walled canyon forming the White Horse Rapids. Like a speeding truck slamming into a lake, the fast-moving stream slowed as it discharged into a broad pool at the base of the rapids. From this point, the river flowed smoothly eastward, its surface occasionally broken by lesser rapids, then abruptly turned southward about half a mile (.80 km) below White Horse. Linking the outlet with the lower river, a steep game trail rose to the top of a bluff overlooking White Horse, then dropped to the deep pool into which the rapids emptied.

To Shickler, the lower Crowe embodied a naturalist's paradise. The roar of the reckless rapids contrasted mightily with the serenity of the lush woods and quietly flowing river below White Horse. Imaged on the slackened surface of its yellowish-brown, denizen-dwelling current were quivering outlines of dense, verdant forest and underbrush; exposed, irregularly shaped tannish bedrock; polished, whitish logs piled on the riverbank at high water; and solitary, thick-bodied, long dead, gray tree trunks that, like silent sentinels, testified of former majesty. Huge timbers that had crashed into the river's edge pushed the current around them like giant, outstretched hands. The extraordinarily rugged beauty and peaceful surroundings were humbling.

A word or two should be inserted here about the atmospheric and lunar conditions encountered—factors highly significant to the overall success of the fishing trip. According to a record kept by Ross Shickler, the outing covered August 25 to September 1, 1960. Near-perfect, picture-postcard weather prevailed, with warm, clear, brightly sunlit days. No showers, storminess, or barometric swings of any kind developed. Lake-surface-hugging, patchy fog characterized the cool and deeply dark nights. Particularly important for nocturnal fishing, a new moon, its dark face toward the earth, and distant starlight ruled the blackness of largely foggy nights.

During the trip, the trio shared precious information on the proper techniques of fishing with two legendary lures—the South Bend Bass-Oreno (No. 973) and the Creek Chub Injured Minnow (No. 1500). Shickler, schooled by Fred and Mary Stoll earlier that summer on the virtues of the Bass-Oreno, imparted to the brothers his knowledge about the correct use of this floater-diver. In turn, the Eversons educated him on the most effective use of the Injured Minnow, a well-designed top-water teaser. For many years, Shickler had included the Injured Minnow in his tackle box but the bait hadn't yet clicked for him. This pattern of nonsuccess with the famous fish-catcher soon changed in dramatic fashion, particularly in dusk and dark angling.

The Injured Minnow No. 1500, introduced about 1924 by the Creek Club Bait Company of Garrett, Indiana, measured 3¾ inches (9.5 cm), and, like the Bass-Oreno No. 973, sported three treble hooks, with two mounted on one of its two flat sides, and the third attached just behind the tail propellor.[4] The cedar lure, its radiating blades affixed fore and aft, swam in a straight-line motion like a wounded prey-fish. The level parts of the plug body faced up and down, the hooks trailing underneath. Shickler preferred this tempting top minnow in a frog finish.

At the outset of a cast near a brushpile, for instance, the Injured Minnow, like the Bass-Oreno, would be allowed to remain motionless for a time, at least until the splash ripples dissipated. Intervals of rest and retrieve, accented by tantalizing twitches, were the recommended modes for returning the bewildering bait to boat or shore. The propellors could be induced to produce either more or less surface commotion by reeling rapidly or slowly. Shickler swiftly learned that a bass or walleye usually opted for a slower moving lure, with a muskie more likely to chase a fast fleeing one.[5]

The three friends delighted in describing the Injured Minnow's top-water antics, both seen and unseen. At twilight, the lure resembled a toy powerboat, its two-bladed twirling, pitched props creating spray and a wake as it hastened on its course. In darkness, when hearing dominated seeing, whirling spinners and swinging hooks scraped against plug hardware, producing a metallic ringing noise that reminded Bret Everson of "Marley's chain," a spooky reference to the clanking irons dragged by the ghost of Jacob Marley described by Charles Dickens in the holiday classic, *A Christmas Carol.*

Affectionately examining the same battered lure many years later, Shickler's faithful Injured Minnow appears physically to have been unceremoniously jettisoned from a high-flying aircraft into the bottom of Arizona's Grand Canyon. Its begrimed, lackluster frog-patterned body has suffered major paint loss, much chipping, toothy puncturing, and severely stressed props, trebles, and hook hangers. Yet he wouldn't part with the heavily used, 40-year-old plug. It bespeaks fishing nostalgia.

Shickler's first Mud Turtle fishing experience, a mid-afternoon float down the lower Crowe, is engraved in memory. After traversing the steep trail from the outlet to the base of the rapids, he and the Eversons climbed into the ancient, porous, flat-bottomed boat stowed in the brush at the big hole, and slowly drifted along the strikingly beautiful river. Downstream, Bret Everson pointed out a Bunyanesque, partially submerged log where a monster muskie had struck three years earlier. As the three passed by the spot, he recounted details of the classic battle, the great fish ultimately prevailing—a story compelling beyond the telling of it.

After enticing a few spirited smallmouths and chunky walleyes with plugs, the intrepid boaters entered a deeper part of the stream where the Crowe swung sharply to the south. The clear, tea-hued water revealed to a goose-pimpled Shickler a fascinating river bottom covered with huge, brownish boulders and heavy, dark timbers at a depth of 15 feet (4.6 m). This had to be a place frequented by colossal finny creatures!

Bret Everson, using a medium-action spinning rod and six-pound test (2.7 kg) monofilament line, tossed a deep-diving Pikie Minnow with silver flash finish toward the middle of the pool. After two or three cranks of the reel handle, the drag screamed, siren-like, and the rod snapped into a deep arc, signaling the sharp strike of a heavy fish. Moments later, as the line hissed through the water, a magnificent muskie, less than 20 feet (6.1 m) from the boat and parallel to it, arch-leaped into the air, its prominent green vertical barring and iridescent greenish-gold upper sides sparkling in the late afternoon sunlight. Like an Olympic high diver, the graceful jumper sliced into the surface with scarcely a splash. After a brief but brilliant struggle, Everson boated a beautiful, thick-bellied fish measuring 36 inches (91.4 cm) and scaling 12 pounds (5.4 kg). Shickler felt deeply impressed that so splendid a specimen could be so quickly caught on the first day of fishing, even in these untapped waters.

A few days later, the trio floated half a mile (.80 km) beyond this bend in the river, where the Crowe gradually shallowed, gently riffled, and formed clear pools. Smallmouth bass were plentiful along this seldom-bothered section and Shickler watched these feisty fighters aggressively attacking lures in the transparent water. Bass-tempting baits used included the Plunker, Lucky 13, Tad Polly, River Runt, Chugger Spook, and plastic worm. Occasionally, a bronze, basking muskie, startled by the boat, slowly glided away from the bow into deeper water, its menacing eyes flashing disdain rather than respect. While no one really kept count, the three anglers probably caught, among them that day, 150 one- to two-pound (.45 to .90 kg) spunky smallmouths. The fishermen hooked and lost many more of these aquatic acrobats. Except a few for the dinner table, all were released. At times, it was necessary to lay down the rod for a respite from the furious, non-stop action. River smallie fishing at its finest!

The first opportunity to fish the big hole at twilight, and outlet in darkness, presented itself a couple of days into the stay. After a customary early dinner, the group readied for fishing the broad pool at the tail of White Horse Rapids, and, after dark, the Crowe's outlet just above the head of the rapids. Since the Everson Rules Committee deemed that the sole outlet angler be determined in advance by chance, coins were ceremoniously flipped inside the cabin. Shickler was formally declared the winner.

Each fisherman packed light for the brief trip by footpath, carrying only rod, reel, and a cigar box containing a few choice lures. Allocated among the three were a flashlight, net, stringer, camera, insect repellent, and a packet of small tools for emergency repairs. The brothers told Shickler that the strict rules for transporting equipment in the forest after dark were necessary to traverse the path from the outlet to the big hole and back as simply, silently, and safely as possible. Actually, only a few surface or diving baits were needed anyway. An overloaded angler might accidentally bang a metal tackle box against a rock or trip over a tree root, creating fish-scaring noise, possibly damaging tackle, or, even worse, injuring himself. The boat, loaded with fishermen and equipment, motored the short distance from cabin to portage. Upon arrival, the three pulled up the craft on the rocky shore where the trail left the outlet.

The expanded pool at the bottom of White Horse proved an angler's dream. A fisherman had the option of casting into a slowing rapids at the pool's head; working a riffled current as the stream slackened and spread; fishing with plugs the shallow, rocky-bottomed water near the bank on the trail side; exploring deeper, fallen-timber-strewn flow on the opposite shore; or probing the depths of the river's midsection. Where trail met river, chunky, irregularly-shaped granite rocks projected from the water, providing a surefooted angler with multiple platforms from which to launch his lures farther into the pool.

Bank fisherman could be dispersed here, since big bass, walleyes, or particularly muskies could attack anywhere in the pool, even rising to the surface from the Crowe's depths to smash top-water plugs. The pool appeared to be about 200 feet (61 m) wide and the river's middle and opposite bank could be reached only by boat. We preferred to fish from shore near a point where the trail plunged to the pool. The thunderous rapids, charging like a wild, white stallion through the rock-ribbed canyon, magnified the exhilaration of this promising fishing spot.

Stories abounded about big ones caught, or hooked and lost, in the wide pool. The Eversons believed that lunkers moved into the pool at dusk to feed, while smaller fish, sensing a threat to their safety, sought more secure waters elsewhere. The previous summer, Hobart Everson had landed a powerful, vaulting 39-inch (99 cm), 15-pound (6.8 kg) muskie, following a furious fight.

This time, his brother, throwing an Injured Minnow into the rapids as it entered the pool, was jarred by a vicious strike. It sharply jerked his fiberglass bait-casting rod downward, and caused the oldie-but-goodie Pflueger Knobby reel handle to spin like an airplane prop, the whirling grips skinning knuckles on his right hand. "Probably a big, old muskie," Bret muttered. No fish was landed this time, but surely a challenge had been proclaimed by the king of the lower Crowe, *Esox masquinongy*, as to who reigned the broad pool's depths.

Other than the muskie near-miss just described, Shickler can't recall what else occurred while fishing the bottom of White Horse Rapids that evening. He was preoccupied thinking ahead to his lot-selected cast at the outlet as darkness fell. At any rate, what befell him later at the river's exit certainly overshadowed any big-hole angling experience that night.

Just before leaving the large pool, with aid of the flashlight, he knotted a ⅝ ounce (17.8 g) black Jitterbug to the end of six-pound (2.7 kg) monofilament line. With his 6½ foot (2 m), medium-action Garcia spinning rod and Mitchell 300 reel ready for action, the three climbed the steep trail above the rapids that descended to the outlet. The single flashlight with steady aim illumined the way, with special care taken to train the beam directly on the path to avoid startling any fish lurking in the watercourse below. As the river's exit approached, Hobart doused the light, and Shickler, with rod in hand, stepped noiselessly from the path onto the restricted rocky shoreline. The canyon walls and forest canopy seemed to close in, shutting out most of the starlight and deepening the blackness of a moonless night.

From daytime observations, he knew that the Crowe's stream here lay about 60 feet (18.3 m) wide and four feet (1.2 m) deep in the middle. The polished, rocky riverbed bore witness to 10,000 years of erosive flow. A smooth, gently rippled surface revealed a slow to moderate current. Practice tosses disclosed a need for precautionary measures. Tree branches drooped treacherously over the caster's head, and a rocky edge and more thick trees lined the steep side on the opposite bank. Although no fish, other than some minnows, had been observed here during daylight, it looked like an ideal spot for bass and walleyes to gather for feeding at dawn, dusk, or dark. Bret felt that during the day, fish, especially large ones, were to be found in deep water fronting the channel.

Even though he had heard stories for months about this favored spot, Shickler still wasn't quite sure what to expect. After all, the information provided by his friends sounded obscure, at best, with the angler chosen by lot, and only one cast permitted. The Eversons quietly withdrew a few steps up the trail and waited in the dark, chuckling. Last-minute advice from the brothers, mostly about what casting catastrophes could occur, further tensed the moment. Great drama!

Shickler had contemplated during the past couple of hours the tough cast about to be made. A black Jitterbug, perhaps better silhouetted against the night sky from a fish's-eye-view, appeared to be a good choice. However, the relatively short throw had to be near-perfect—just the right distance, arc, and splash. A lure tossed beyond the water's edge on the other side might become entangled in rocks or brush; those sagging overhead branches could easily snag a bait at the outset of the cast; and a Jitterbug's loud splash landing would possibly scare a bass lying in wait. Any unusual racket caused by trying to free a hung-up plug might spook a fish looking for an easy meal in this confined space. Fouling line and hooks could be avoided by slowing the cast just before impact, in effect, straightening the lure. The throw might be tricky, but certainly possible.

With sound, not sight, the overriding sense, Shickler exercised a few whips with his rod and let the plug go. He heard it strike the water lapping the opposite shore, just slightly upstream. The bail still open, he pulled off enough line to keep the bait bobbing along the bank, like a fidgety frog that had just fallen into the drink, simultaneously swinging his rod tip slowly in the direction of a drift that covered some 30 feet (9.1 m). A few seconds later, he closed the bail and began a steady, angled retrieval against the current, the telltale Jitterbug paddling noise clearly audible above the distant roar of the rapids and the encircling sounds of night.

It is difficult to find the words to describe what occurred next. The frog impersonator had been retrieved barely a foot (30.5 cm) when the surface exploded with the savage strike of a five-star smallmouth. It seemed as if Hercules himself had hurled a boulder into the river. With his rod tip high, Shickler hung on, as the battling bronzeback appeared to be everywhere at once in a sensational seesaw struggle. A continuous splash reverberated from the wooded canyon walls as the fish, apparently more often out of water than in it, tried desperately to throw the hooks with a nocturnal display of aerial acrobatics. In three or four minutes, the skirmish ended. Hobart flipped on the flashlight, and Bret netted a tuckered tiger that stretched 20 inches (50.8 cm) and weighed a robust five pounds (2.3 kg).

Inspired by the eye-popping, pulse-pounding episode, Shickler joined his companions in the boat and the group shoved off. The gist of the witty game that the brothers had played to the hilt—the hush-hush, coin flip, one-cast rule—was now abundantly clear. It would be long indeed before tranquility returned to the outlet's shallow, agitated waters that night! While outboarding the short distance back to the cabin for a nightly snack break, Bret reproved Ross for hogging the channel by unleashing such pandemonium. After all, he whimsically explained, each of the brothers also would have been able to throw a lure into the productive outlet if a less ruckus-making walleye had grabbed the Jitterbug.

Kidding aside, the heady, shaking experience had its thoughtful side, too. Shickler had brawled in the blackest of nights with a big smallmouth black bass, arguably the most exciting fighter, pound for pound, of any freshwater fish. For him, however, the nocturnal event has never been repeated—not at Mud Turtle nor anywhere else. It remains a top-ranking thrill, an extraordinary fishing encounter.

Since the focus of this trip remained night fishing, daytime activities—angling, exploring, cabin tending, frog catching, fish cleaning—were conducted in almost leisurely fashion. The really serious fishing occurred during the night shift, from early evening until after midnight. Because of the late-hour turn-in, the trio didn't roll out of sleeping bags until about nine o'clock the next morning. After a hearty breakfast, daytime angling usually didn't begin until just before noon, unless other recreation interfered.

An offshore rock pile, mentioned previously, broke the lake surface near the river mouth. This granite outcropping, to which the boat was secured, provided quick access to deep dropoff water on the eastern side of the protrusion. Mobs of midday smallies, gathered in the cooler depths, aggressively grabbed struggling leopard frogs hooked to six-pound (2.7 kg) monofilament line. Plastic worms provided great sport, too, tossed with light spinning tackle into the deep, dark water from this smallest of islets.

Another hot spot frequently visited day or night lay downriver. Just above where the Crowe turned abruptly southward—the place that yielded Bret Everson's muskie on the first day—the river branched around a small island. Slightly upriver from the island, a circular side-flow had carved a deep basin fronted by a sizeable, flattish granite rib.

With the boat moored in water intruding to the rear of the outcropping, the three fishermen could cast into the pool from the raised rock surface. Completing the picture of a complex flow configuration, a brook bubbled noisily into the Crowe behind anglers positioned on the rocky platform.

The pool edge to the left of a fisherman working this honey-hole contained fallen timber, bulrushes, pads, and weedgrowth. On occasion, a marauding muskie would assail a Bass-Oreno properly tossed into this enticing environment. The pool in general, however, produced heavyweight walleyes. In daylight, a Brooks Reefer, a sinking lure, or a weighted Flatfish dredged up fat walleyes to 30 inches (76.2 cm) in length. At night, top-water lures, such as a Crazy Crawler, proved equally efficient. Other than big walleye surface strikes, nightly surprises included a beaver tail's startling surface slap and the appearance of a black bear apparently hopeful of a tasty midnight snack of a stringer of walleyes. Enthusiastic shouts sent the unwelcome visitor scurrying into dense bush.

Preparation for nighttime fishing on the lake involved daytime detective work on the physical locale. This background task particulary appealed to Shickler, since he had not night-fished Mud Turtle prior to the visit. However, the Eversons were not indifferent to this preparation since it refreshed lessons previously learned. The brothers also were eager to share with Shickler their knowledge, experience, and boating wisdom about nocturnal angling. Ross found that time-tested skills were indispensable to successful and safe nightfall fishing.

Since they planned to cast near shore with top-water lures, during daylight hours the fishermen familiarized themselves with rocky reefs, shoals, shelf ledges, bouldered bars, sunken timber, weedbeds, and the lily pad periphery of Jitterbug Bay. While all these elements were clearly visible in mostly shallowish water under bright sunlit conditions, few, if any, fish could be observed. The Eversons told Shickler, however, that these shallows would be transformed by the presence of prowling, big fish populations at night. How to read a varied shoreline rather than a uniform water surface became a weighty part of nocturnal angling education.

The anglers also studied water-edge makeup, including possible nighttime plug overthrow hazards, such as shoreline rock and cobble and brush overhangs. In addition, they considered various landmarks, such as solitary trees or steep bluffs, that might be taken for granted in daylight, but the silhouettes of which would assist in identifying their location at night. The investigation of the surroundings, by the way, was not conducted in lieu of fishing, but in conjunction with it.

Following the usual late-afternoon dinner, the three fishermen outboarded either to the river mouth or to the trailhead leading to the deep pool for twilight plugging. At about nine o'clock each evening, shortly after sunset—earlier or later depending upon degree of eventide fishing success—the trio retreated to the cabin for a snack break of tea, coffee, or soft drinks, and crackers, Canadian sharp cheese, or cookies. Prior to leaving the old shanty for nocturnal action, one angler lighted the single-mantle Coleman lantern, suspended from a ceiling wire, to provide a beacon for the return later. With the exception of the honey-hole downriver, night fishing took place on the lake, normally in the general vicinity of the inlet at Mud Turtle's northern end.

At dusk, the fishermen outboarded at reduced speed to the desired spot, cut the motor, and rowed quietly into place near the shoreline. As darkness fell, the anglers' vision gradually adjusted to eventual pitch blackness. Treeline dips signalled locations of the river mouth and Jitterbug Bay, although most landform details were difficult to distinguish. If not already known, general direction in this latitude could be determined by finding the North Star, positioned in line with the "pointer stars" in the bowl of the Big Dipper. Facing the North Star (north), the stars, planets, and new moon appeared to rise in the east (to the viewer's right) and pass overhead toward the west, setting to the observer's left. Absent the interfering glow of city lights, the anglers, when fog lifted, were treated royally to a brilliant night sky featuring a vast luminous band of light—our dazzling Milky Way galaxy—and a multitude of sparkling, starry gems that seemed close enough to grasp. The beautiful nighttime scene could perhaps be best described as beyond spectacular.[6]

Former Mud Turtle fishing companion George Wilde had not only taught Bret Everson nocturnal angling know-how, but also the necessary discipline to support its success. To maintain an uncluttered boat and stealthy silence, all agreed to limit equipment for each angler to a single rod and reel, three or four lures (hooked to the inside of the boat), and a penlight to illuminate a small area in the bottom of the boat for changing plugs and solving tackle problems. Also available were a net, insect repellant, a small box of tools, and a wide-beam flashlight. Each angler wore a light jacket and hat for comfort in the cool, damp night air.

So as to become accustomed to each other's movements and to function best as a team, the trio assumed the same boat positions each night, with Hobart placed in the bow, Ross, stern-seated, and Bret, the oarsman, stationed in the middle. Ever the math teacher, Bret suggested that each fisherman confine his casting to no more than a third of an arc, or about 120 degrees. The three concurred that the boat's middleman, after first issuing timely warnings, be permitted to pitch lures to both port and starboard. While normal conversation produced no fish-spooking difficulties, accidental boat-bottom thumps were to be carefully avoided. In George Wilde's boat, Bret explained, a noisy nighttime thud would result in the craft's relocation to another lake spot without a word from Everson's nocturnal fishing mentor. So as not to interfere with retrieving lures and landing fish, oars were kept in the boat when not in use.

Self-control, good judgment, and etiquette produced solid night fishing payoffs. For instance, lines seldom crossed each other, precluding messy tangles. If one angler experienced a hookup, the other two fishermen promptly retrieved their baits to facilitate playing and netting the fish, while also preventing foulups (a workable ethic unless fish struck more than one plug simultaneously, a not-infrequent occurrence on this trip). And, fortunately, no one became impaled by the barbed treble hook of a carelessly thrown lure.

With sound paramount in nighttime fishing, the reverberation of routine conversation, splashing fish, and topwater lure racket helped provide a feeling for distance from shore. Under limited visual conditions, Shickler discovered improved casting accuracy if he looked just to the right of the selected lure impact point, instead of directly eyeing a specific target. Surface plugs tossed near shore scored heavily with eagerly striking fish, particularly big night walleyes. Shickler also discovered that lures, especially the durably constructed Injured Minnow, inadvertently tossed initially onto the rocky shoreline—the plug landing with a loud clank because of iron-bearing granite—were instantly siezed by fin-deep, night-roaming walleyes when jerked into the water. (Later on, he, in particular, purposely overcasted since the technique produced such banner results.) The surface strike of these aggressive yellows, with some heavyweights scaling as much as ten pounds (4.5 kg), produced a noisy, sucking sound as the fish inhaled the lure. The giants, invariably big females, were gently returned to the night-veiled lake to help maintain the walleye fishery.

The waters of Jitterbug Bay represented quintessential bronzeback domain. In the quiet of night, football-shaped smallmouths announced their presence with sudden, thunderous eruptions that rearranged lily pads and shuddered anglers. These spectacular performers were frequently lost when hooked because of their aerial antics. But the astonishing, atmospheric battles were more than worth it—fish or no fish.

Another nightly outing generated an additional angling surprise. At about one o'clock in the morning, midway through the retrieval, Shickler's Injured Minnow abruptly disappeared beneath the surface, as if the diminutive motorboat-like lure had been swallowed whole by some huge sea monster. The spinning rod bowed and pulsed, and the drag whined with the steady pressure of a good fish hooked on six-pound (2.7 kg) monofilament line. But what kind of fish had grabbed the plug? Unlike a frolicsome smallmouth, this Mud Turtle resident primarily stayed down, occasionally swirled the surface, and even pulled the boat in the direction of its struggle. A tough, strong fish, disinclined to give up, had been hooked. A weighty walleye? Perhaps.

After about ten suspenseful minutes, the battler postured alongside the boat. The flashlight beam revealed a golden, well-nourished muskie that glared at its tormentors with mean-looking eyes, the plug held crosswise in its jagged teeth. The 31-incher (78.7 cm) represented the first 'lunge ever caught at night by members of the fishing party. They had believed that muskies weren't nocturnal feeders, so the catch totally surprised them. Bret surmised that perhaps big night-ranging muskies, along with hefty bronzebacks and yellows, embodied the mystifying "horses and cows" that had won freedom in the blackness of night. As a result of this and other experiences, the three anglers revised their opinion on night muskies.

An observation reached near the end of the week is recalled with a chuckle. Mulling over a superb fishing trip on a still night, the anglers paused to listen to the peculiar dissonance springing from the concurrent retrieval of three legendary surface lures—a gurgling, wobbling Jitterbug; the creeping, moveable-winged Crazy Crawler; and "Marley's chain," an Injured Minnow. The resultant casting cacophony engendered a simultaneous burst of uncontrollable laughter. Although the mingling of discordant sounds provoked mirth, the three fishermen were reminded that these strange, classic top-water lures consistently surprised Mud Turtle's bronzebacks, walleyes, and muskies with deadly consequences.

For Shickler, the Mud Turtle experience set a splendid precedent. His fishing expectations were well exceeded, the weather was flawless, camaraderie exceptional, meals memorable, a wilderness strikingly beautiful, valuable outdoor information gained—virtually an unimprovable adventure. The outing proved to be one of those trips in which man, fish, and environment appeared, for a week at least, on the same page.

But Mud Turtle never again performed so splendidly as a fishery as it had done in 1960. Shickler accompanied the Everson brothers to the lake-river system twice more, in the summers of 1961 and 1962. (Jim Concilla joined the group during Shickler's final visit to Mud Turtle.) While absolutely delicious weather prevailed throughout the stay in 1960, changeable atmospheric conditions, including rainstorms and temperature swings, presented a very different meteorological picture in the next two outings. In addition, instead of a darkened new moon, a brilliant full-orbed satellite illuminated the land and waterscape all or most of the week during the later visits. Shickler's journal described Mud Turtle fishing as generally poor in 1961 and only average to good in 1962, although some notable fish were caught. Night angling for bass and walleyes, largely slow both years, produced better results before a full moon climbed over lingering storm clouds, usually around ten o'clock. Muskie fishing, good in 1961, proved better in 1962, day or night, while not equaling the excellent 'lunge angling of 1960.

Over the next several years, Bret Everson guided a number of parties into Mud Turtle. In the fall of 1964, the lake briefly flashed its former renown. Everson and a companion visited the watershed over the October weekend that marked the American Columbus Day and Canadian Thanksgiving. A north wind that carried a knife with it accented the leaves' cavalcade of color. With cooler weather and water, ravenous muskies were on the prowl—and how! The two anglers either lost or boated some 25 muskies, the best one day 'lunge fishing Everson—or maybe anyone else—has ever experienced. The length of one majestic muskellunge, lost at the boat, was estimated at over 40 inches (101.6 cm).

Accompanied by two fellow western New Yorkers, Everson last visited Mud Turtle in the early 1980s. Change was clearly evident. Fire had destroyed the old trapper shanty a few years earlier. The onetime natural condition exhibited evidence of growing human presence. Bret observed pensively that increased angling pressure had upset the fragile balance of a vulnerable ecosystem, resulting in the gradual deterioration of a once-proud fishery.

Today, Bret Everson lives in retirement with his wife, Betty, in Erie, Pennsylvania. The couple's longtime cottage on Kamaniskeg Lake, near the border of Algonquin Provincial Park in southeastern Ontario, remains their principal headquarters for serious fishing, especially during spring and fall when there are fewer vacationing powerboaters, jet skiers, and anglers. Everson eagerly pursues early season lakers and walleyes, and targets bronzebacks in mid-September. By outboarding the short distance from his Blackfish Bay cottage to the mouth of the York River on connecting Negeek Lake, he has hoodwinked cattle-sized spring walleyes with jigs in recent years, the fish ranging in size from nine to sixteen pounds (4 to 7.3 kg).[7]

When Ross Shickler relocated to California in the fall of 1960, he had the good fortune to gain access, through close friends, to a small, privately managed reservoir which contained largemouth bass. His first visit to the lake in January 1961 resulted in a catch of about a dozen lethargic, cool-water fish of unremarkable size on spinners, the lure recommended by locals. To a transplanted western New Yorker, however, catching fish in the dead of winter without chopping a hole through the ice proved a decidedly *remarkable* experience![8]

That spring, Shickler again journeyed to the reservoir, arriving early on a brilliantly sunlit Saturday morning. Patchy fog hugged a polished lake surface, encircled by round-shouldered hills carpeted with chaparral, sagebrush, cacti, and grasses greened by welcome winter rains. The colorful little artificial lake occupied a beautifully tranquil setting, particularly at this time of year. Shickler rowed the short distance to the southern shore where grayish, stick-like tops of submerged brush poked through the surface. Using spinners, small spoons, and a Heddon Sonic, he caught some 50 largemouth bass by ten o'clock. While this represented an amazing total, none of these bass exceeded two pounds (.9 kg), and most were much smaller.

Shickler had been told that lunker largemouths dwelled in the reservoir. However, for whatever reason, he had never caught a bragging-size bigmouth anywhere, despite devoting considerable time to the task. Many years earlier, his grandfather had boated a bodacious bass, an exciting event readily recalled.

In late summer 1944—a few weeks after Shickler's dad had bedeviled those two barge bass with a wartime Jitterbug—his grandfather, Edward "Ted" Rogers, visited the Shickler's Maple Bay home on western New York's Chautauqua Lake for a weekend of fishing with Ross and his father. A day of fruitless casting drew to a close as the sky darkened, with dramatic thunderheads framing the patchwork of forested and farmed hills that ringed the lake. A cool breeze from the northwest picked up, rippling a previously placid surface. Rogers asked if he could take one more cast before the three proceeded to outrace the impending storm to the dock. Using a plug borrowed from Howard Shickler's tackle box, a greenish-hued Paw Paw Midget—referred to fondly by Ross's dad as "little greenie"—Rogers fired a looping, reel-whirring cast that appeared to Ross's eight-year-old mind to head for Jamestown, a city at the lake's eastern end. Like a shotgunned bird, the lure dropped from the sky, landing about 100 feet (30.5 m) distant, above the tips of weedy cornstalks just below the surface. Suddenly, as the buoyant bait bobbed to the top, a terrific, roaring splash conveyed the aggressive strike of a ponderous fish. The steel rod throbbed sharply as the prewar black silk line knifed the surface in a thrilling battle etched in Ross's boyhood memory. In a few minutes, Howard Shickler netted a glorious gapemouth that scaled six pounds (2.7 kg). The big bass graced the family's dinner table that evening.[9]

Over the next two years, Ross Shickler occasionally plied the reservoir waters, enjoying the outings immensely, but bagging only ordinary-sized bass. To reach these alleged tackle-busters, a strategy emerged to fish with plugs at night. Since he didn't believe it wise to boat alone after dark, any nocturnal angling scheme meant convincing another fisherman to join him. Despite Ross's bubbling enthusiasm for night fishing, which included impassioned telling of Mud Turtle tales, it took a while before a suitable partner could be persuaded to try night-shift bassing. Evidently, nighttime angling wasn't everyone's cup of tea.

On a Saturday evening in May, Shickler and a friend shoved off from the dock and moved slowly up the northern shoreline. Using cranks and top-water lures in the gathering dusk, some bigger-than-usual bass provided pleasurable sport. With the onset of darkness on a moonless night, the lake surface came alive with splashing bait fish. Deep-voiced, broad-bellied bullfrogs called their resounding "jug-o-rums" from hiding places amid water-edge foliage. Similarities and differences marked the night settings at the reservoir and Mud Turtle. No smallmouths, walleyes, or muskies were on the prowl here. How would a bruising bigmouth react in the dark? This question would soon be answered with a vengeance.

Around ten o'clock, the halt-hasten retrieval of Shickler's black Jitterbug brought it near the boat following a throw near shore, some 50 feet (15.2 m) away. Concluding that the remaining short distance represented the least fruitful portion of the cast, he quickened the return, the plug popping noisily. All of a sudden, just before he lifted the bait from the surface, a tremendous boatside blast rocked the craft, drenching and stunning the fishermen.

His buddy excitedly asked, "Have you got him?" Ross, dazed by the watery explosion, paused a few moments before responding. Sensing only the lure at the end of the line, he mumbled, "No. No, I don't."

Illuminated by the flashlight, a seemingly terrified Jitterbug bobbed on a troubled black surface, the only waterside evidence of the outburst. The plug's gentle, up-and-down motion, however, appeared somehow odd. Upon examining the beleaguered bait, Ross was astonished to behold an aluminum-lipped plastic plug body missing both trebles and hook hangers and all four screws! An electrifying strike by a prodigious fish had ripped out all that lure hardware, and the angler hadn't felt a thing!

What actually occurred is probably anyone's guess. While contemplating this incident over the years, Shickler supposed that the big bass stealthily followed the baffling bait, and, perceiving the possible escape of an accelerating critter, attacked it at the boat. He may have barely moved the lure while preparing to lift it from the surface just prior to the undetected strike—forming some slack line in the process—and that slight motion may have caused the giant to misjudge the plug's position by a narrow margin. But that's conjectural. At any rate, a huge bass sideswiped the bogus bullfrog with great force and speed, and, instead of a tasty late-evening snack, wound up with a mouthful of metal. So much for *alleged* tackle-busting reservoir bigmouths!

Because of marriage, family, and California droughts that created havoc with reservoir water levels, Shickler didn't visit the lake again until 1978. Ed Eveland joined him as a reservoir angling pal in 1980 and the two have fished the lake once or twice a year ever since. In the early 1980s, a number of three-pounders (1.4 kg) were caught, but no exceptional fish were added to the stringer. However, a tortuous experience for Eveland in 1981 crystallized in our minds the skulking monsters that so far had avoided the net.

Sun-splashed hilltops with shadows beginning their retreat to the lake surface greeted the two of us on a picture-perfect early summer morning. Fishing the glassy waters opposite the dock, Eveland eyed a shaded pocket beneath a bushy Arroyo willow overhanging the shoreline. Carefully flipping a brown scale Jitterbug about 20 feet (61 m), the low-angle cast skidded the plug to a stop within inches (centimeters) of the bank, a perfect presentation of a frog-like bait. Without warning, like a Richter scale–busting earthquake, a bass of stupendous proportions pounced on the plug, the shocking eruption shaking the willow's slim branches, trembling the tree's dark, yellow-green leaves, and propelling a mini-tsunami that slapped the side of our 12-foot (3.7 m) aluminum johnboat.

Thoughts flashed to Ross Shickler, as he immediately reversed the electric motor to move the boat into deeper, less risky water, hoping to balance the battle in favor of his buddy. From where Ed had sidearmed his cast, the depth measured about eight feet (2.4 m), with the lake bottom in this spot covered with flooded brushwood. We had learned that these oversized largemouths, when hooked, did not jump as readily as smallmouths, but instead plunged to the depths, like harassed submarines attempting to elude a destroyer's depth-charges. An undersurface covered by tangle of roots provided a big advantage to a bottom-sulking behemoth hooked on light line.

But it was too late. "Old slope shoulders" had managed to loop the monofilament line around an underwater limb. Ed tried to maintain a tight line, but the hooks had worked free and the unencumbered Jitterbug floated to the surface. Although momentarily dejected over this latest setback, we knew it would be just a matter of time before a blimp-sized bass would be boated. Whatever technique needed to be mastered, we were determined to get the job done. But wow!—did these big largemouths ever produce an uproar when they slammed a lure on the surface, day or night!

Over the next three or four years, we experimented with various types of lures—small prop-baits, critter-baits, rattle-baits, spinner-baits, jerk-baits, soft-bodied twitch-baits, jigs, and, of course, cranks. While the Jitterbug remained a favorite, its use was limited to dawn, dusk, or night angling. From this period of trial and error emerged a handful of lures that began to entice more and bigger fish. Our progress toward achieving this goal could have been speeded by using live bait, such as night crawlers, minnows, or crayfish. But as artificial lure afficionados, we never seriously considered this option.

The steady producers included the Cordell Big-O, Rapala Fat Rap, Bagley's Bang-O-Lure, and Bill Lewis Big L and Rat-L-Trap. But one plug, a classic old-timer, outperformed them all and justifiably earned recognition as indispensable to successful reservoir fishing. The cherished bait: a Bomber, manufactured in Gainsville, Texas.

We might never have discovered the Bomber's effectiveness had Shickler not possessed a seldom-used example in his tackle box. It was a wooden, ¾-ounce (21.3 g), silver-and-white shad model purchased in 1962 after he read a *Popular Mechanics* magazine article on great fishing lures.[10] Actually shaped like a World War II bomb, the Bomber was a superlative floater-diver.

As a floating bait, the Bomber, after remaining at rest for a few seconds, could be made to dance alluringly by twitching the rod tip. As a diver, however, the plug had no equal. Caused to plunge deeply—as far as 12 feet (3.7 m)—the buoyant lure could then be compelled to cover much of the water by alternately slackening or tightening the cranking pressure. Retrieved as a deep-runner, the Bomber's diving bill might be induced to burrow along the bottom, kicking up mud clouds and debris, attracting bass attention in the process. The bait possessed an uncanny knack to avoid entanglement with underwater obstruction. Its bill protected the backward swimming bait's hooks from snags—a handy characteristic when fishing an obstacle-infested reservoir. The sharply diving plug even had the idiosyncrasy to be reeled from under the boat. While the Bomber's wildly erratic action almost defied description, a dramatic video portrayal of a frightened, springing, twisting gazelle chased by a ravenous, swiftly-moving cheetah on Tanzania's Serengeti Plain comes to mind.

Although the wooden Bomber, in particular, proved to be a super bait, it was in scarce supply. When a big bass stole Shickler's only such lure in a heavy boatside smash, we scrambled for wooden replacements. After exhaustive searches, a few wooden baits in dust-covered boxes were located in hidden corners of local tackle shops. New plastic Bombers, of course, were readily available, but we found these somewhat less effective than their cedar predecessors. In 1985, Ed Eveland encountered Rick Edmisten, a top lure historian, author, and collector, at a boat and tackle show in Long Beach, California. Through him, Ed arranged to buy a few secondhand wooden Bombers. These acquisitions have continued over the years, with other collectors and anglers assisting with our quest. When one can locate them, authentic wooden Bombers in very good to excellent condition command prices as high as fifteen dollars each. (Most of our Bombers probably grade from fair to good, but serve our casting purposes in excellent fashion.) We choose the used vintage Bomber in medium size, 5/8 ounce (17.7 g) and in dark colors. Frog finish is preferred.

Why do we continue to purchase these baits? First, both of us use the Bomber almost exclusively in this lake. Second—despite our best efforts to prevent it—Bombers become lost, sometimes on bottom brush, but more often when bass attack with great intensity at the boat. In these instances, a sudden, hard assault on short line—without rod-and-reel drag support—frequently exerts excessive knot pressure and the lure is gone before we know it. As far as we're concerned, the Bomber surpasses by a large margin any other lure in unexpected boatside blows by big bass.

Why would a timeworn, woody wobbler function better as a bass catcher than today's high-tech, plastic plug of the same model, size, and finish? We believe there may be a couple of explanations. The old wooden Bomber's bouncy flotation quality is perhaps one reason. Another consideration might be the natural chemistry that exists between a heavier cedar bait and the underwater brushwood with which the lure occasionally collides. Instead of the markedly irregular clicking sound produced by plastic crankbaits, wood plugs generate a more normal thump when bounced off flooded timber and other submerged objects.[11]

With our growth in crankbait knowledge, five- and six-pound (2.3 to 2.7 kg) bass were no longer uncommon. On an outing in January 1986, Shickler's wooden frog Bomber befuddled an eight-and-a-half-pound (3.9 kg) pot-bellied porker, a reservoir weight that would not be matched by us for another ten years.

A journey to the artificial lake's grayish-green waters in 1996 produced blue-ribbon results. Swinging around the picturesque reservoir's western shore, where a number of fish in the three-pound (1.4 kg) class were caught and released, a noontime breeze gently pushed our johnboat along the brushy southern bank. A glorious spring day smiled on us, and we thoroughly relished the beautiful setting and solid bass action. Eyeballing a familiar spot where a steep outcrop fell into deep water, Ed tossed a Bomber to the edge of the rocky face and began to retrieve it. In a flash, a hard strike slapped the spinning rod tip under the surface. As the lunker largemouth characteristically hunkered down, Ed yelled, "Get the net! It's a good one!"

Ross, seated in the stern, at once deposited his rod and quickly, yet carefully—sudden moves, especially in a small boat, can result in all sorts of difficulties, including injury—maneuvered toward the johnboat's bow. There the net, yet to be employed this day, was stowed against the metal hull behind the standing figure of Eveland. As he gripped the handle, Shickler discovered to his horror that the net was still in its stored position, with the front portion of the telescoping handle compressed across the hoop! It had been a year since last used, and he couldn't recall how to release the catch to elongate the sliding handle. Nor could he, under the circumstances, search for the release, since successful netting meant keeping an eye on the struggling fish. Shickler suddenly found himself in big trouble.

Ed, involved in fighting a powerful bass, nevertheless noticed the delay in net deployment as well as the oddball handle position and gave Ross a fleeting, gimlet-eyed glare. Shickler needed somehow to net a dandy largemouth with half a hoop opening! The future of a wonderful, thirty-year fishing partnership hung in the balance. As Ed brought the bass to boatside, Ross, with netting submerged, scooped the bruiser's large head and body into the restricted opening, the plug's hooks barely averting a rim hangup. While it turned out to be a narrow escape from disaster, a sag-bellied seven-pounder (3.2 kg) flopped in the boat bottom. Congratulating each other, we enthusiastically shook hands. What a relief!

A few minutes later, we drifted into a willow-edged cove. The backside of the small, sheltered inlet featured a field of bare brush tops that resembled inverted pitchforks, their handles driven into the soft, muddy bottom. Using a Shimano Bantam Chronarch bait-casting reel and a six-foot (1.8 m), medium-action Fenwick Crankshaft fiberglass/graphite composite rod, Shickler unsuccessfully probed the leading edge of the flooded brush. Then he threw the frog Bomber to the rear of the stick field, the barbless hooked bait splashing near the shoreline. As if fired from a skulking submarine, a torpedo-like black blur shot from the shade of a water-edge willow and blasted the crankbait. "I've got the biggest bass in the lake!" he shouted.

A crisis unfolded immediately. The force of the strike curved the ten-pound (4.5 kg) monofilament line around interposing brush, quickly dragging the slender branches underwater. Happily, the line slid undamaged over the smooth limbs, which then snapped back into vertical position. Since unobstructed water lay toward the middle of the cove, Shickler, holding his rod tip high, muscled the mighty bigmouth through the timber infestation into open water. So far, so good. With the heavy fish now in a shallow, obstacle-free section of the cove, the battle became ours to lose.

As the contest moved into close quarters, Ross, aided by polarized sunglasses, observed with amazement that the thick-bodied bass had company! Matching the darting movements of the struggling largemouth, another bass, somewhat smaller—but still huge—moved rapidly alongside and slightly below its hooked companion. Shickler reckoned the bass's buddy to be an anxious nest-minding male. Ed, who missed sighting the largemouth's partner, groused about a net properly readied for Ross's big fish, but not for his.

As the weary warrior reached netting distance, Eveland swept a beautiful ten-pound (4.5 kg) bucketmouth into the johnboat. Two toads in less than thirty minutes—our best big-bass job yet! Following the usual quick photos, both egg-laden females had been returned to the reservoir. As with our laker fishing, we liked to release the beefy bigmouth—but keep the memory!

While we conversed during this outing, the picture for our 1997 lake trouting venture snapped into sharp focus. In 1995, our visit to northwestern Ontario's Cleveland Lake had been purposely cut back to allow more opportunities for a one-day fly-in to Sturgeon Lake, a first-class forktail water. However, as things turned out, two precious days of bush flying were washed out by heavy storms. Fortunately, the rains ended the night before the final day of our short stay at the Pakwash Lake base camp, enabling Rob Rowe, our pilot, to squeeze in the 50-mile (80 km) flight to Sturgeon after all. Our decision to reduce the Cleveland stay to four days, accommodated by a canceled reservation, unfolded while at Pakwash. This time we hoped that any alternative plan would be determined prior to our arrival in Canada, precluding a host of uncertainties.

Two weeks earlier, Shickler had telephoned Snake Falls Airways, based at the northern end of Pakwash, and touching the mouth of the Chukuni River, to discuss trip ideas. Ross asked Rowe if the Cleveland visit could be scheduled for only three days this time, leaving the balance of Tuesday and all of Wednesday, Thursday, and Friday for possible fly-outs to a few proven gray trout lakes: Sturgeon; smallish Bunny Lake, a previously untried waterway just north of Sturgeon (or Upper Kilburn), also situated in Woodland Caribou Provincial Park on the Ontario-Manitoba border;[12] or any of the additional laker bodies of water in the Red Lake District that include fly-in camps operated by outfitters with whom arrangements could be made for boat rental and guide service—such as Trout, Sydney, Birch, Roderick, and Deer. Flying distance from the Pakwash base to lakes in the latter group, some of which, like Trout, Birch, and Deer, loom quite large on maps, ranged from Trout (24 miles/38.6 km) and Birch (72 miles/115.8 km), to Deer (136 miles/218.8 km). Walleye and northern pike also inhabit most lakes mentioned.

(For a discussion of how Woodland Caribou's geologic past affected gray trout distribution in park lakes, see chapter notes.)

Rowe, while heartily endorsing the stirring possibilities, volunteered to check with outfitters managing other outposts to determine if we could be accommodated for a one-day fly-in. He didn't see any problems in realizing this aspect of the plan. (It probably goes without saying that a wilderness dinner of freshly caught lake trout and walleye, following a great day of fly-out fishing, represents the pinnacle of culinary delight, a never-to-be-forgotten experience!)

The added expense for this ambitious plan was another consideration. The price of Cleveland's four- or seven-day package is based on a party of four, with an understandably higher rate charged per person if only two anglers are flown to the outpost. Also, fly-outs to Sturgeon, Bunny, Trout, Birch, or Deer would add significantly to overall trip costs. While the flight tab for one of the more distant lakes can amount to several hundred dollars each, we share this expenditure. Cost aside, it is difficult to properly describe the intense exhilaration felt during a one-day fly-in to an unspoiled lake, especially one seldom fished. As matters stand, too few anglers ever experience the wonders of Canadian bush flying. We can readily assure the reader that the cost is more than worth it. With these exciting trip arrangements agreed upon, we mailed a deposit for a late June reservation. (The venture turned out to be a huge success. We flew for the first time into three lake trout water bodies. The details of the 1997 visit are discussed in chapter 9.)

While co-writing this book, Ross Shickler began to accumulate a modest collection of the classic lures mentioned in this chapter. With the generous assistance of super-collector Dick Wilson of Kent, Ohio, a plastic-bodied frog Jitterbug with ripe lemon-colored nylon lip, manufactured between 1942 and 1945, became the initial purchase. Ross's dad, who bagged the pair of barge bigmouths with a similarly hued, all-plastic Jitterbug from Lake Chautauqua's waters on that cloudy day long ago, would be pleased with the acquisition.

Notes

1. Murphy and Edmisten, *Fishing Lure Collectibles*, 128.
2. *Fred Arbogast Company, Inc.,* "Backgrounder," 2.
3. After a motorcoach tour of Montreal, Quebec City, Ottawa, and Toronto in July 1996, Ross Shickler and his wife, Merrie Lyn, visited the Chautauqua Lake area of western New York State, where he had grown up. Gilbert "Gibby" Wells, a boyhood barge-fishing partner of his from 1943–45, whose family had lived across Fairmount Avenue from the Shicklers' Maple Bay home in Lakewood, informed the Shicklers during this visit of the aged structure's removal in the 1950s. Wells lives today in Jamestown, at the lake's eastern end.
4. Murphy and Edmisten, *Fishing Lure Collectibles*, 12.
5. Levy, *Man against Musky*, 12.
6. Johnson and Adler, *Discover the Stars*, 12, 13, 27, 67, 127.
7. Appreciation is expressed by the authors to Bret Everson for his generous assistance, through many telephone calls and considerable correspondence, in reconstructing the marvelous

Mud Turtle narrative. While co-author Ross Shickler drew upon his notes and color slides of their visits, Bret's sharp memories of persons, places, and pertinent details enabled the full story to be told about this exceptional lake-river system. Shickler and his wife, Merrie Lyn, visited with the Eversons in their home in Erie, Pennsylvania, during a trip to the eastern United States and Canada in the summer of 1996.

8. Because of respect for the reservoir's private management and a vulnerability due to the closeness of population centers, the authors chose not to identify the lake's precise location.

9. Murphy and Edmisten, *Fishing Lure Collectibles*, 74. The Paw Paw Midget, an extremely buoyant, river runt-type lure, measures 2½ inches (6.4 cm). Our thanks is extended to Rick Edmisten, co-author of the beautifully photographed book, *Fishing Lure Collectibles*, for his generous assistance with regard to the history and characteristics of antique wooden lures mentioned in this chapter.

10. Kirkpatrick, "Fishing's Deadly Dozen," page unknown.

11. Prorok, "Rick Clunn and Bill Murphy Talk Crankbaits," 68–73.

12. The southern boundary of Woodland Caribou, officially opened in 1983, lies about 70 miles (112 km) directly north of the famed Lake of the Woods. Its 1.2 million acres (462,000 hectares) of unspoiled wilderness constitute Ontario's fifth largest provincial park and are accessible primarily by aircraft. More than one-half degree of latitude separates Sturgeon Lake (or Upper Kilburn), positioned in the southeastern corner, and Bigshell Lake, near the park's northeastern limits. Woodland Caribou shares part of its western boundary with Manitoba's Atikaki Provincial Park. (*Woodland Caribou Provincial Park*, Ontario Ministry of Natural Resources; brochure and canoe route map.)

During our 1997 visit to the Pakwash base camp, we met octogenarian Walt Jones, a veteran of nearly fifty years of fishing and guiding experience in northwestern Ontario, and who had immediately preceded the Rowes as owner of the Snake Falls Camp and Flying Service. Jones believed that lake trout were more numerous in bodies of water where walleye were absent—in park lakes such as Bulging, Haggart, and Sturgeon. While this opinion was a revelation to us, we had experienced doubts about any walleye population in Sturgeon, having never caught one there in four trips. If his assertion was correct, which park bodies of water supported only lake trout and pike populations and why?

Upon returning to California, we telephoned an official at the Ministry of Natural Resources in Red Lake for further information on the intriguing topic. Claire Quewezence, Woodland Caribou's assistant superintendent, quickly verified the Jones claim and sent us the data we needed to answer a host of questions.

A ministry canoe route map revealed some 100 named and mostly small lakes, all or partially located within the park. (Overall, hundreds of park lakes had been surveyed.) Of this number, about a third held lake trout. Nineteen of the water bodies canvassed by the ministry included lakers and northerns only—no walleyes. Some of the lakes included in the latter category were Adventure, Blueberry, Bulging, Bunny, Dragon, Haggart, Hatchet, and Sturgeon/Upper Kilburn. Interestingly, the lake trout-pike-only lakes were grouped in the southern half of the sprawling park. (We also learned that muskies and northerns—but not forktails and walleyes—were found in Irregular Lake, spread-eagled in the park's southwestern portion. The muskellunge population in Irregular—the only park lake where muskies were located—represented one of the most northerly ranges of this fish in Ontario.)

According to ministry studies, the park's distribution of lake trout, northerns, and walleyes was tied to lake productivity, a phenomenon associated with Woodland Caribou's geologic past. Following the retreat of the Wisconsonian glacier 10,000 years ago, melting ice formed vast Lake Agassiz, the largest freshwater lake in North American history. In the park's northern zone, fertile silts and clays were deposited in the deep, quiet waters of the lake. In the southern half, wave action left large areas of bare bedrock.

Today, surface runoff washes dissolved nutrients from glacial overburden into northern sector lakes, increasing their productivity. In the park's southern portion, exposed bedrock and minimal surface deposits contribute to lower lake nutrient levels. Also, northern lakes are less deep than those in the south, providing shallow bays that support walleye habitat and expose a larger percentage of bottom areas to light penetration.

In the transition from north to south, establishment of fish communities reflect this pattern of nutrient availability combined with different water depths. Dominating in nutrient-rich northern lakes are walleye and pike groupings. Toward the south, where lake productivity begins to decrease, lake trout appear with pike and walleye. In the park's southern segment, walleye begin to disappear as lake nutrient levels and shallow areas further diminish. Deep, glacially gouged basins favor a trout environment, and walleyes are replaced by lake trout and northern pike populations. ("MNR Fish Community/Yield Report A," 1986, 97–106; Quewezence/Thiess, personal correspondence, 1997; *Woodland Caribou Provincial Park: Background Information,* Ontario Ministry of Natural Resources, 1986; "Woodland Caribou Provincial Park: Lakes and Fins," no date.)

THREE

LAKE TROUT: BIOLOGICAL, GEOLOGICAL, AND HISTORICAL PERSPECTIVES

To capture the fish is not all of the fishing.

—Zane Grey

Biological References

The lake trout, also called togue (eastern United States), Mackinaw (western United States), and gray trout (Canada), is a large char.

—C. C. Lindsey, "Lake Trout," *McClane's New Standard Fishing Encyclopedia* (1974)

"Trout," in reference to the laker, is really a misnomer, since the fish is actually a char (*Salvelinus)*, not a trout *(Salmo)*. The lake trout is also known as Mackinaw, lake char, salmon trout, gray trout, masamacush, togue, and taque. The French call it *touladi*, a name derived from Lake Touladi in Temiscouata County, Quebec. In its nomenclatural history, the lake trout was originally named by Walbaum in 1792, based on a specimen from the Hudson Bay area. *Salvelinus* is an old name for char and *namaycush* is derived from the language of the native peoples.[1]

The typically troutlike body of the lake trout, *Salvelinus namaycush*, is marked by a stout head, large mouth, a snout that usually protrudes beyond the lower jaw when the mouth is closed, well-developed teeth in both jaws, and a deeply forked caudal fin. The whole body, including head and fins, is covered with innumerable light-colored spots on a darker background that varies in color from light green or gray to dark green, brown, or almost black. In large lakes, body color is so silvery that the spots are difficult to see. The ventral surface may be dirty white to pale yellow.[2]

The natural North American range of the lake trout lies almost entirely within the limits of Pleistocene glaciation. In Canada, lakers occur in portions of Nova Scotia, New Brunswick, Labrador, Quebec, Ontario, Manitoba, Saskatchewan, Alberta, and British Columbia and are widely distributed in the Yukon and Northwest Territories. Gray trout also are established on several islands of the Arctic archipelago, including Baffin, Southampton, King William, Victoria, and Banks. In the United States, lake trout are found in New England, most states bordering the Great Lakes—New York, Pennsylvania, Michigan, Wisconsin, and Minnesota—and the western states of Montana, Idaho, and Alaska. The lake trout has been widely introduced outside its natural range in many areas of the United States as well as to places such as South America, Sweden and New Zealand.[3]

Spawning usually occurs in the fall, but actual dates vary considerably. Timing is affected by latitude, weather, and size and topography of lakes. Throughout most of Canada, spawning normally occurs in October, but sometimes as early as August or September in the north or as late as November in the south. At Lac la Ronge, in central Saskatchewan, lake trout spawn during the first two weeks of October. Spawning may be delayed until December in New York State lake trout waters.[4]

The spawning act, which occurs after dark, takes place over areas of boulders, rubble, or gravel along the lakeshore at depths usually less than 40 feet (12.2 m). Males arrive first, and often clear loose sand and mud from rocks with the body or tail fin or by rubbing them with the snout. More than one male may be associated with a spawning female, or a group of males and females may spawn together. Males approach the female, crowd against her sides, and begin to quiver. No redd or nest is built, and eggs and sperm are extruded over the rocky bottom. The fertilized eggs, measuring .20–.23 inch (5-6 mm), lodge in crevices in rubble on the lake bottom. The number of eggs deposited depends upon the size of the female. For example, a Great Lakes female 32 inches long (81.3 cm) may deposit up to 18,000 eggs. Mature females do not spawn every year. In Great Slave Lake, most females appear to spawn every other year, while they may spawn every third year in the more northern waters of Great Bear Lake.[5]

Some experienced lake trout anglers and fisheries biologists believe that, in their mating behavior, big lakers travel in pairs while smaller fish move about in groups. Bruce Ranta, Canadian biologist and fisherman, provides an authoritative opinion about this unusual bonding behavior:

> Over the past number of years there have been some sketchy observations by anglers and biologists on rather remarkable and complex mating behavior by lake trout. One school of thought is that at least some individual lake trout, in some populations, have exhibited pair bonding behavior.

> A number of instances I am aware of involves tagging studies done on lake trout on Lake of the Woods. On different occasions, fisheries biologists Val Macins and Tom Mosindy observed (caught) the same two ripe male and female trout together on spawning shoals in different years. They have encountered this phenomenon on a few occasions. In addition, on a couple of occasions, when one of these trout was subsequently captured by an angler, the "mate" was caught in almost the exact vicinity, also by anglers, within a day or so. . . .
>
> It is very obvious from such examples that lake trout have much more complex behavior patterns than generally reported in the literature. I believe some of this complexity is at least partly related to the extremely long life spans lake trout can exhibit.[6]

Other ichthyologists also have provided evidence in some lakes of homing, that is, returning to the same spawning beds year after year. Studies have shown that after spawning, lake trout disperse throughout the lake and may wander many miles away. The eggs require about four to five months in their rocky incubators before hatching. Hatching usually occurs in March or April, but is delayed until June in Great Bear Lake.[7]

Lakers inhabiting the cold waters of the far north grow slowly and indeed can experience lengthy life spans. A comparison of ten-year-old lake trout in different areas of their range is instructive. A fish that dwells in Great Bear Lake can be expected to weigh about two pounds (.91 kg) at the end of a decade, while a similarly-aged laker that swims in Utah's Fish Lake would tip the scales at just over 12 pounds (5.4 kg). The life expectancy of a really large gray trout living in Great Bear Lake would be many years.[8]

Ranta supplies background on determining the age of lake trout:

> Lake trout are one of the longer-living freshwater fish. Based on the interpretations from calcified structures called Otoliths (an "inner ear bone"), lake trout older than 20 years of age are quite common. By way of contrast, a 20-year-old Walleye is a rarity and a 20-year-old smallmouth bass is virtually unheard of. A 25-pound (11.3 kg) lake trout recently caught and killed near Ignace, Ontario, was estimated by a number of interpreters at 55 years of age. Lake trout from some of the more northern waters of North America quite likely have life expectancies between 60 and eighty years.
>
> Unlike scales, which essentially stop growing once the fish has reached maximum length (maximum lengths, and hence size, are usually based on a number of ecological factors like lake nutrient status, food webs, the length of the growing season, etc.), otoliths continue to lay down calcified deposits on an orderly, yearly basis as long as the fish lives. This has been shown to be true even on very old, very slow-growing fish. Unfortunately, the fish must be killed for the researcher to collect the otolith.[9]

Sexual maturity, usually attained by age six or seven, requires thirteen years in Great Bear Lake. Lake trout can reach weights of fifty pounds (22.7 kg) or more. One weighing 102 pounds (46.2 kg) was caught commercially in 1961 at Lake Athabasca, Saskatchewan. The current International Game Fish Association lake trout angling record—72 pounds (32.65 kg)—was established in 1995 at Great Bear Lake, Northwest Territories. The gray trout usually inhabits lakes and rivers that are clear and cold. Lake trout can be found in shallow water following ice-out in the spring, and in the fall when waters cool and the fish rise onto their spawning beds. In more southern areas, lakers move into deep water during the summer. Lake trout may remain near the surface throughout the summer in far northern lakes, including those in Canada's Northwest Territories.[10] The fish is highly sensitive to water temperature, with a preferred range of 48°–52°F (8.9°–11.1°C).[11]

Lake trout, however, can be found throughout the water column at any season. John Roush wrote that he had caught Mackinaw in Lake Tahoe from 15 to 400 feet (4.6–121.9 m) deep and that Jim Briscoe, a Tahoe guide, once pulled up a gray from a depth of 700 feet (213.4 m). Other zoologists have observed that a shrimp-feeding lake trout had been taken on the bottom of Great Bear Lake in 1,400 feet (426.7 m) of water.[12]

Both the lake trout and the cisco or lake herring (*Coregonus artedii*), the preferred natural food of the north country laker, are anatomically adapted for striking vertical movement in water. Both fish have a vented swim bladder, or physostomous, which permits them to move upward quickly with no apparent ill effects.[13]

Lake trout are the least tolerant of brackish water of all the chars, although their presence in Canadian coastal waters has been noted. Rivers emptying into the ocean and riding over denser sea water may have aided the crossing of gray trout to islands in the Canadian Arctic.[14]

The predaceous lake trout feeds upon a broad range of organisms, including freshwater sponges, crustaceans, aquatic and terrestrial insects, plankton, and fishes such as ciscoes, smelt, whitefish, perch, shiners, sculpins, sticklebacks, suckers, alewives, and smaller lakers. Biologists even have observed mice and shrews in the stomachs of opportunistic forktails in the Ungava Bay region of northern Quebec.[15]

The lake trout is highly prized both as a game fish and as a commercial species. It is an esteemed food with a flesh color—white, pink, orange, or orange-red—influenced in part by diet. Irrespective of flesh hue, the flavor is usually excellent. It is most often eaten fresh, but sometimes smoked. A small amount is canned.[16]

Geological Relationships

> Glaciation is probably responsible for the formation of more lake basins than any other single geologic process.
>
> —L. Don Leet and Sheldon Judson, *Physical Geology* (1958)

> The present natural range of lake trout lies almost entirely within the limits of Pleistocene glaciation.
>
> —C. C. Lindsey, "Lake Trout," *McClane's New Standard Fishing Encyclopedia* (1974)

Lake trout and the natural lakes that hold them have been around for a long time. For millions of years, geological forces have shaped North America, profoundly influencing both the distribution of gray trout and the human culture and industry of Canada, where most lakers are found, as well as portions of the United States.

During the Pleistocene epoch, or Ice Age, which began two to three million years ago, four major glaciations, covering about 97 percent of what is today Canada, spread southward across the Great Lakes region into the Mississippi Valley. These four glacial periods, each lasting approximately 100,000 years, were separated by three long warm ages during which ice melted away, forests developed over glaciated regions, and plants and animals migrated northward beyond their present limits. About 100,000 years ago, during the Wisconsonian, or most recent of the four Pleistocene glaciations, ice caps formed in several parts of Canada and, in time, coalesced to form the Laurentide Ice Sheet. The Wisconsonian advance gouged, stripped, and polished the underlying Precambrian bedrock of the vast Canadian Shield. Wisconsonian glacial recession was generally rapid, with ice withdrawn from the northern United States and most of Canada by 10,000 years ago. The scouring of the Shield by the repeated advance and retreat of Pleistocene glaciation left its surface strewn with a bewildering maze of rivers, lakes of irregular shape, and unique land forms.[17] Many visitors have been attracted by the Shield's "stark and rugged beauty [that] has become almost synonymous with Canada itself."[18]

All this melted ice has left behind a staggering amount of water. Surveys indicate that there may be two million lakes in Canada, including some 250,000 in the province of Ontario alone. Enough water is contained in these lakes and rivers to flood the entire country to a depth of more than six feet (1.8 m).[19] The Northwest Territories and Nunavut hold two-thirds of the world's supply of fresh water.[20] In the United States, Minnesota represents a glacier-carved land of more than 15,000 lakes.[21]

The countless glacial lakes and streams that exist today include some of the largest, deepest, and most beautiful on this planet. Today's trophy trout lakes—Athabasca, stretching across northeastern Alberta and northwestern Saskatchewan, and Great Bear and Great Slave in the Northwest Territories—are remnants of a single postglacial pool.[22] Similarly, Lake of the Woods, in southwest Ontario, is a remainder of former glacial Lake Agassiz, which once covered virtually all of Manitoba and portions of Saskatchewan, Ontario, North Dakota, South Dakota, and Minnesota.[23] In the distribution of lake trout, other important lakes that were glacially gouged, deepened, and ultimately filled by meltwater are the Great Lakes and the Finger Lakes of central New York State. Since Canadian Shield waters are surrounded by thin soils and rocks resistant to weathering, these lakes tend to be clear and relatively long-lived because of slower sedimentation—factors vital to sustaining strong, healthy lake trout populations.[24]

The existing native environment of the lake trout lies almost wholly within the bounds of Pleistocene glaciation. While these fish are found, for example, in some lakes in Minnesota and Wisconsin as part of their natural distribution, lakers have been successfully planted (to establish self-sustaining populations) in the waters of Canadian prairie provinces and in lakes and reservoirs of many American states.[25]

The only recorded fossil lake trout was found in Wisconsin, near the southern limit of glacial advance. Radiocarbon techniques have dated the surrounding beds, which also contained elephant, mastodon, and caribou remains, at about 12,500 to 16,000 years old, corresponding to the closing stages of Wisconsonian glaciation. Some experts believe, however, that lake trout probably survived throughout the Wisconsonian and perhaps also during earlier Pleistocene glacial periods.[26]

Historical Connections

We caught an amazing fine [lake] trout.

—George Back, British naval officer, descending the Coppermine River, Northwest Territories; journal entry for July 2, 1821.
—C. Stuart Houston, ed., in *Arctic Artist* [1995]

It is likely that the people to first enter the New World crossed from Siberia to Alaska some 18,000 years ago, traversing a Bering Strait land bridge exposed by late Pleistocene glacial recession. For thousands of years, small bands of these former immigrants probably separated from one another and filtered southward toward warmer regions, eventually reaching the Atlantic coast of North America and the tip of South America.[27]

Excited by the voyages of Columbus, professional explorers began a 400-year search for a western passage to the fabled riches of the Orient. John Cabot's discovery of the North American continent in 1497 was the first recorded landfall since the Norse voyages. His sighting of what Henry VII of England called "the newe founde lande" gave England the basis for a later claim to North America.[28]

During the first third of the sixteenth century, Francois I of France charged Giovanni da Verrazzano, an Italian, and Jacques Cartier to search for a route to India. Verrazzano in 1524 ranged along the eastern coastline of North America from what is now North Carolina to Newfoundland. Cartier discovered and charted the St. Lawrence River in 1535, which, along with its tributaries, enabled the French to explore and dominate much of the northeastern portion of the continent in the seventeenth century.[29]

Explorations by the English, in particular, beginning in the 1570s made repeated attempts along the icebound shores of the eastern Arctic to find a water access to the Pacific.[30] Martin Frobisher's three voyages in 1576, 1577, and 1578 found the way blocked by sprawling Baffin Island,[31] where, by the way, lake trout are established.[32] John Davis explored steep-sided Cumberland Sound in 1585–87 and located the entrance to Hudson Strait, south of Baffin Island.[33] Henry Hudson in 1610 navigated his tiny vessel through the ice and fog of the treacherous strait and then sailed southward into the immense bay now bearing his name. After desending into desolate James Bay, resentment among Hudson's crew broke into mutiny. The explorer's fate, after being set adrift in the open sea, has never been determined.[34]

Robert Bylot and William Baffin explored Baffin Bay in 1616, but mistakenly judged Lancaster and Jones Sounds to be closed bays. After these voyages, the North American coasts remained unexplored by Europeans for the next two centuries. Samuel Hearne (1771) and Alexander Mackenzie (1789) followed the Coppermine and Mackenzie Rivers, respectively, to their points of Arctic discharge, but did not explore the adjoining shorelines.[35]

Samuel de Champlain, the "Father of New France," founded the great fur trading center of Quebec in 1608. He discovered in 1609 Lake Champlain, a ribbon-like lake trout waterway with its northernmost tip in southern Quebec province. The major portion of the lake, bordering northeastern New York and northwestern Vermont, served as a convenient invasion route for participants in native conflicts—the French and Indian War (1754–63) and, later, the War of 1812. Champlain drafted a comprehensive map of eastern Canada, including the Great Lakes, which he explored in 1632.[36]

Other French groups explored new portage routes linking Lake Superior, Georgian Bay, Lake Ontario, the Niagara River, and Lake Erie. Jesuit missionaries, while also recording details of rivers, forests, severe winters, and brief, insect-ridden summers, contributed an accurate map of Lake Superior and northern Lake Michigan in 1672. The native peoples, as guides and helpers, were important to the French advance. In addition, Europeans imitated their methods of travel—the birchbark canoe in summer and the snowshoe in winter.[37]

French adventurers Mèdard Chourart des Groseliers and Pierre-Esprit Radisson first broached the idea of trading furs through Hudson Bay, bypassing French posts on the St. Lawrence River, to Prince Rupert, cousin of the English King Charles II, about 1665. The marketing of hundreds of thousands of New World beaver pelts in Europe appealed to Rupert, who persuaded the English monarch to back the venture. The royal charter granted to Rupert and associates by Charles II on May 2, 1670, included all land and exclusive trading rights within the vast drainage basin of Hudson Bay. The historic proclamation enabled the newborn Hudson's Bay Company to become the oldest and largest corporate landowner in the English-speaking world.[38]

The beaver, so familiar to today's northcountry adventurers, once colonized waterways from the Rio Grande to the Arctic Circle. Some ten million animals were believed to have lived in present-day Canada when the Hudson's Bay Company was founded in 1670.[39] The profound effect of the furry rodent on the development of Canada is described by Peter Newman, a Hudson's Bay Company historian:

> Seldom has an animal exercised such a profound influence on the history of a continent. From the early 1650s to the late 1850s the beaver became the breathing equivalent of gold. There was nothing genteel about the hunt. Men risked their lives and reputations, caught up in a feverish trade that transformed this pug-nosed rodent with its lustrous fur into a cause for war.
>
> The beaver is a nonmigratory animal that needs relatively large spaces to thrive, so that once a creek was "beavered out," the hunters had to move farther into the new land. Just as the stalking of elephants for their ivory tusks lured white hunters into the heart of Africa, so the beaver pelt drew traders from Hudson Bay and the St.

> Lawrence River toward the snowcapped Rocky Mountains and, eventually, to the shores of the jade green Pacific. Without anyone being particularly aware of it, the hunt for beaver became the quest for a nation.[40]

After a fierce fifty-year rivalry with the Montreal-based North West Company, the competitors merged in 1821 under the banner of the Hudson's Bay Company. Although the fashion in beaver hats had passed its peak by the mid-nineteenth century, the Hudson's Bay Company still managed to sell three million pelts from 1853 to 1877. In 1870, three years after Canadian confederation, the company transferred all but seven million acres (2,835,000 hectares) of its holdings to the new nation for £300,000. As part of a tough cost-cutting measure, the Hudson's Bay Company sold its London and Toronto auction houses and northern stores in the late 1980s. Now into its fourth century of operation, the company's financial resources are concentrated in what are today the core businesses of department store retailing and real estate.[41]

The fur trade rendered beavers almost extinct. Today, however, populations again abound in the United States and Canada. Indeed, the comeback has been impressive: some six to ten million of the rodents are found in Canada, and at least two million in the United States. Driving the increase in numbers is a decrease in consumer demand for pelts, now bringing only about $20 American dollars ($28 Canadian dollars) apiece. The thriving populations of the 1990s are a serious concern to farmers and landholders, since beaver tree cutting and dam building floods crops, blocks waterways, and backs up sewer systems. Interestingly, the name of central Saskatchewan's outstanding lake trout fishery, Lac la Ronge, is derived from the French verb *ronger,* "to gnaw," a reference to the local beaver population. The beaver is rightly Canada's national symbol.[42]

French exploration continued late into the seventeenth century. Jacques de Noyon is believed to have reached Lake of the Woods, an important laker habitat in southwestern Ontario, in 1688.[43]

British explorer and fur trader Samuel Hearne experienced a remarkable adventure in 1770–1775 as he sought a western passage to the Arctic Ocean across Canada's barren lands for the Hudson's Bay Company. In the late summer of 1770, he observed large numbers of Arctic terns diving at the surface of a sprawling island-dotted lake in the southeastern Northwest Territories. In recognition of the event, Hearne named the lake Snowbird. The explorer probably didn't realize that he was watching an important element of a lake trout feeding frenzy, a phenomenon evidently unique to Snowbird.[44]

During the winter of 1771, Hearne, with a band including the skillful caribou hunter and Chipewyan leader Matonabbee, was the first to cross massive Great Slave Lake in the south-central Northwest Territories. Great Slave, the fifth largest lake in North America and home to huge lakers, was named by Hearne after the Slavey Indians. Other trophy trout lakes discovered by Hearne were Dubawnt, a large body of water that borders the Northwest Territories and Nunavut (1770); Athabasca, Canada's eighth largest lake, extending from northeastern Alberta to northwestern Saskatchewan (1771); and Nueltin, straddling the boundary of Nunavut Territory and northwestern Manitoba (1770–72).[45]

Peter Pond, an American, learned of the general location and immensity of Great Bear Lake, source of record lake trout, in 1783-84, and a year later became the first to map what is today called the Mackenzie Basin. Alexander Mackenzie discovered in 1789 that the great river now bearing his name issues from the extreme western end of Great

Slave Lake. The fur trade came to the Great Bear Lake area around 1800.[46]

After the Napoleonic Wars, the British Admiralty renewed its search for the Northwest Passage. In 1818, John Ross rounded Baffin Bay, but as did William Baffin 200 years earlier, believed that Lancaster Sound was just another inlet—an error common to Arctic explorers. W. E. Parry in 1819–20, sailed 496 miles (800 km) along ice-choked Parry Channel (Lancaster Sound, Barrow Strait, Viscount Melville Sound) and penetrated to Melville Island, proving the narrow passageway to be the gateway to unknown western seas. Credit for actual discovery of the long-sought Northwest Passage, however, is reserved for John Franklin, arguably the greatest explorer of the British-American Arctic. Franklin's three expeditions (1819–22, 1825–27, 1845–47), earned him fame and knighthood for the charting of much of Canada's Arctic seaboard and subsequent determination of the fabled passage. They dominated Arctic exploration in the first half of the nineteenth century. But disaster struck the third expedition before Franklin could navigate the passage he had finally found. The fame associated with the mystery of the lost Franklin expedition has enhanced his legacy and legend.[47]

After a trying voyage from England, Franklin's first expedition landed at York Factory on the southwestern coast of Hudson Bay in 1819, and experienced a tough journey through prime lake trout country across central Manitoba and Saskatchewan, before reaching Lake Athabasca in the spring of 1820 and Great Slave Lake in July.[48]

Franklin's exploring party in 1821 descended the turbulent Coppermine River, a shallow watercourse heading in an excellent lake trout fishery, Lac de Gras, in the Northwest Territories, and flowing northward 524 miles (845 km) to its Arctic discharge in Coronation Gulf. The expedition of 20 men paddled eastward in two fragile overloaded birchbark canoes from the mouth of the Coppermine to Kent Peninsula, south of Victoria Island, dodging drift ice while encountering weather extremes and heavy seas. Including the search of Bathurst Inlet, Franklin's party explored some 600 miles (966 km) of Arctic coastline that Hearne and Mackenzie had only approached fifty years earlier.[49]

The triumph of extensive coastal charting, however, nearly turned to catastrophe during the expedition's return overland trek 320 miles (515 km) across the treeless plains known as the Barren Grounds in the fall of 1821. Only nine of twenty members of the party survived famine and bitter cold. It was a close call indeed for Franklin and the others—including John Richardson, a surgeon-naturalist, and George Back, topographer, artist, and sport fisherman. Without the compassionate intervention of the Coppermine Indians, they probably would have perished from starvation. The murder of a British officer, Robert Hood, the execution of a voyageur, and probable cannibalism marred the overall success of the arduous journey.[50]

References to lake trout often turn up in the Arctic exploration literature. The scholarly and fascinating journal of Richardson, Franklin's surgeon-naturalist on the first expedition, included a number of entries showing that, when food was sufficient, lake trout supplemented the men's diet of caribou, bear, musk ox, goose, duck, and partridge.[51] The pleasant taste of the fish when boiled or roasted was also noted by Richardson, who contributed greatly to Arctic knowledge in the areas of medicine, geology, meteorology, botany (including lichenology), ichthyology, ornithology, mammalogy, and geography.[52]

In the well-organized second expedition, Franklin, again teamed with naval officers Back and Richardson, approached the Arctic in seaworthy boats of mahogany and ash by way of the more navigable Mackenzie River in the summer of 1826. Franklin and Richardson parted near the mouth of the Mackenzie, with Franklin, hampered by fog, mapping 374 miles (602 km) of ocean shoreline to the west and Richardson charting 863 miles (1389 km) of new coastline eastward to the Coppermine. As prudently arranged by Franklin, Richardson's party made a quick, safe return overland after completing its assignment.[53]

Richardson further supported the work of his commander in 1825–26 by mapping 450 miles (725 km) of the northern shoreline of Great Bear Lake, the fourth largest lake in North America and today home of world-record lake trout, and the southern shoreline as far as Richardson Island, located in the bottom of McTavish Arm. The five arms of this giant lake were named after fur company men by Richardson during this period. He himself was knighted in 1846 for his achievements in the Canadian north.[54]

George Back, who accompanied Franklin on both overland expeditions, discovered and explored the treacherous Thlew-ee-chow, or "Great Fish River," later named for him, and reached its mouth in July 1834. The Back River, rising in Contwoyto Lake, north of Great Slave, is turbulent in its upper and lower reaches and expands into large lakes in midcourse. In its final leg, it plunges through a rocky section before falling into the sea at deep Chantrey Inlet, 604 miles (974 km) northeast of its source. Back's wonderful watercolor sketches of rapids, forest fires, campsites, rock formations, and native life along his exploration routes are preserved in the National Archives of Canada. He was knighted for his achievements in 1839. Back's discoveries associated with the Great Fish River figured prominently in the third Franklin expedition some fifteen years later.[55]

The "Great Fish River" was appropriately named by eminently knowledgeable native people. Today's intrepid anglers seek the big lakers and Arctic char found in its historic waters. (The Back River's outstanding laker and char fishing was described by Gerald Almy in a *Sports Afield* article in 1987.)[56]

The purpose of the third Franklin expedition was to join together discoveries of the narrow seaway along the continental shore with Parry Channel to the north, and thus to sail through the Northwest Passage. While attempting to thread the renowned and newly discovered passage, the last Franklin voyage ended in disaster. It cost the lives of all 128 beleaguered officers and sailors, its bold and resourceful commander, and the loss of both exploration vessels, HMS *Erebus* and *Terror*.[57]

Franklin's ships were last sighted in the ice pack of Davis Strait, heading for Lancaster Sound, in late July 1845. When public concern mounted over Franklin's unreported expedition, Britain and the United States undertook in 1848–54 the greatest search in the history of exploration. John Richardson commanded one of these rescue operations for his old chief in 1848–49, searching in vain the familiar coastline between the mouths of the Mackenzie and Coppermine rivers. John Rae, who had accompanied Richardson in his search five years earlier, concluded in 1854 on the basis of Inuit reports and remains of crew members that all had perished. Leopold McClintock, dispatched to the Arctic by an unconvinced Lady Franklin in 1857, explored King William Island and located additional relics and the only written record of the tragedy in a cairn at Victory Point.[58]

The one-page Victory Point record—two entries a year apart on a standard printed sheet—detailed the expedition's discoveries of 1845–46; the besetment of *Erebus* and *Terror* in the ice stream of Victoria Strait, west of King William Island, since September 1846; the death of Franklin in June 1847; abandonment of the ships by the remaining 105 men in April 1848; and a plan to start for Back's "Great Fish River." Faced with a lack of European witnesses before and after the abandonment, scanty physical evidence, absence of journals, and ambiguous native recollections, historians continue to debate the exact chain of tragic events.[59]

Historian David Woodman, in his enthralling book, *Unraveling the Franklin Mystery: Inuit Testimony,* bases his reconstruction of the puzzle primarily on native recollections. According to him, Captain F. R. M. Crozier, who took command after Franklin's death, chose to march the scurvy-ridden and, later, starving survivors southward along the bleak, cold, and foggy western coast of King William Island to the estuary of the Back or "Great Fish River," the nearest source of fresh food. Here it was hoped that abundant caribou, musk ox, wild fowl, Arctic char, and lake trout, as well as native assistance, could restore the health of the men. (Lakes dotting King William Island are inhabited by lake trout; but a dearth of game renders the island's desolate western coast unable to sustain human life more than briefly.)[60]

With severe cold, cannibalism, and death stalking the weakened crews, some followed eastbound the south coast of King William Island. Others may have crossed the narrow Simpson Strait to Adelaide Peninsula on the mainland. But few, if any, expedition members completed the trek to the mouth of the "Great Fish River." The mystery surrounding the most dramatic tragedy in the chronicles of Arctic exploration rivals any fictional tale, capturing widespread interest to this day. The final answers await further discoveries.[61]

The Northwest Passage was finally navigated by the Norwegian explorer Roald Amundsen between 1903 and 1906, when his 80-ton (72.6 metric tons) *Gjoa*, propelled by an internal combustion engine, punched its way through the ice pack from ocean to ocean, despite two icebound winters. In 1969, the voyage of the *Manhattan*, a United States tanker, revealed that the most nearly usable passage from the Atlantic to the Beaufort Sea lies by way of Parry Channel and Prince of Wales Strait.[62]

Pleistocene glaciation stripped from the eastern and southern portions of Canada one of the country's greatest resources—her soil—and spread it widely and deeply on the north-central United States. While Canada lost much of its rich topsoil, the unevenly scouring ice exposed the mighty Canadian Shield with its vast mineral wealth and thousands of basins now occupied by lakes drained by countless rivers and streams.[63]

Most of Canada's immense forested land—about fifty percent of total land area, excluding water—swings in an arc south from the Mackenzie River delta and Alaskan border on the Beaufort Sea to northeastern British Columbia and across optimum lake trout habitat in northern Alberta, Saskatchewan, Manitoba, Ontario, and Quebec, terminating in northern Newfoundland on the coast of the Labrador Sea. This forest cover supplies the timber industry, serves as home to many of Canada's native peoples, and provides a domain for fishing, camping, hunting, hiking, photography, and sightseeing.[64]

Canada possesses enormous mineral wealth, including deposits of copper, cobalt, iron, lead, nickel, platinum, zinc, coal, oil, and natural gas. Prospectors discovered gold in the Klondike, Yukon Territory, in 1896, and near Yellowknife Bay, Great Slave Lake, in 1934. Pitchblende, a radium-uranium ore, was found on the eastern shore of Great Bear

Lake in 1929. A major diamond discovery in 1991 at Lac de Gras, an excellent gray trout fishery, 180 miles (290 km) northeast of Yellowknife, the capital of the Northwest Territories, touched off the largest mineral rush in North American history.[65]

Bush flying, which began as aerial reconnaissance for spotting forest fires around 1920, transformed the Canadian north. Thanks to today's highly skilled bush pilots, the lake trout enthusiast can reach by float plane otherwise inaccessible lakes and rivers and enjoy the quintessential fishing experience of a unique and storied land.[66]

Notes

1. McPhail and Lindsey, *Freshwater Fishes of Northwestern Canada and Alaska,* 137, 141; Scott and Crossman, *Freshwater Fishes of Canada*, 221, 227.
2. McPhail and Lindsey, *Freshwater Fishes of Northwestern Canada and Alaska*, 137; Scott and Crossman, *Freshwater Fishes of Canada*, 220.
3. Lindsey, "Lake Trout," 530; McPhail and Lindsey, *Freshwater Fishes of Northwestern Canada and Alaska*, 138; Scott and Crossman, *Freshwater Fishes of Canada*, 221–222.
4. Scott and Crossman, *Freshwater Fishes of Canada,* 222.
5. McPhail and Lindsey, *Freshwater Fishes of Northwestern Canada and Alaska*, 140; Scott and Crossman, *Freshwater Fishes of Canada*, 222–223.
6. Ranta, personal correspondence, 1993, 1–2.
7. Scott and Crossman, *Freshwater Fishes of Canada*, 223.
8. *Sport Fishing Guide*, Northwest Territories, 8.
9. Ranta, personal correspondence, 1993, 1–2.
10. Scott and Crossman, *Freshwater Fishes of Canada*, 223, 225.

11. *Trophy Lake Trout Tactics*, 1990 (videocassette SLTO1, 39:24–31).

12. McPhail and Lindsey, *Freshwater Fishes of Northwestern Canada and Alaska,* 139; Roush, *Enjoying Fishing Lake Tahoe, the Truckee River, and Pyramid Lake*, 179.

13. *Trophy Lake Trout Tactics*, 1990 (videocassette SLTO1, 14:52–15:06).

14. Scott and Crossman, *Freshwater Fishes of Canada*, 223.

15. Ibid., 225.

16. Ibid., 226–227.

17. Dunbar, *Historical Geology*, 386–402; Marsh, "Shield," 1687-1688; Rutter, Glaciation," 742–744.

18. Marsh, "Shield," 1688.

19. Boyce, "Lake," 966.

20. Gierach, "Snowbird and the Kazan: Still Pumping Out Big Fish."

21. Boyer, "Minnesota, Where Water Is the Magic Word," 201.

22. Marsh, "Great Slave Lake," 771.

23. Dunbar, *Historical Geology*, 401; Marsh, "Lake of the Woods," 968.

24. Boyce, "Lake," 966.

25. Lindsey, "Lake Trout," 530.

26. Ibid.

27. Tindall and Shi, *America: A Narrative History*, 5–7.

28. Parsons, "Cabot, John," 253; Tindall and Shi, *America: A Narrative History*, 18–25.

29. Tindall and Shi, *America: A Narrative History*, 41; Williams, "Exploration," 602.

30. Williams, "Exploration," 602.

31. Neatby, "Arctic Exploration," 88.

32. Scott and Crossman, *Freshwater Fishes of Canada*, 221–222.

33. Neatby, "Arctic Exploration," 88.

34. Marsh, "Hudson, Henry," 842.

35. Neatby, "Arctic Exploration," 88.

36. Marsh, "Champlain, Lake," 315; Trudel, "Champlain, Samuel de," 315–316.

37. Williams, "Exploration," 602–603.

38. Newman, "Canada's Fur-Trading Empire," 208; Ray, "Hudson's Bay Company," 843–844.

39. Newman, "Canada's Fur-Trading Empire," 196.

40. Ibid., 205.

41. Ibid., 194, 196, 225.

42. Boonstra, "Beaver," 154; Francis, "Lac La Ronge," 963.

43. Williams, "Exploration," 603.

44. Marsh, "Hearne, Samuel," 802; "Snowbird Lake Lodge—Housekeeping in Style," in *North of Sixty News*, 3.

45. Boyce, "Lake," 967; Evans, "Nueltin Lake," 1302; Lee, "Matonabbee," 1100; Marsh, "Athabasca, Lake," 112; Marsh, "Great Slave Lake," 771; Marsh, "Hearne, Samuel," 802; Zoltai, "Dubawnt Lake," 520.

46. Graham, "Pond, Peter," 1449; Marsh, "Great Bear Lake," 769; Marsh, "Great Slave Lake," 771.

47. Houston, *Arctic Artist*, xiv; Houston, *Arctic Ordeal*, xxii; Neatby, "Arctic Exploration," 88; Neatby, "Franklin, Sir John," 690.

48. Houston, *Arctic Ordeal,* xxiv–xxv.

49. Ibid., 207–208; Marsh, "Coppermine River," 423.

50. Houston, *Arctic Ordeal*, 209–219.

51. Ibid., 12, 38, 120, 144, 165.

52. Ibid., 257.

53. Ibid., 219; Neatby, "Franklin, Sir John," 690.

54. Houston, *Arctic Ordeal*, 219, 222.

55. Marsh, "Back, Sir George," 124; Marsh, "Back River," 124; Woodman, *Unravelling the Franklin Mystery*, 18.

56. Almy, "Back River Char and Lakers," 55–57, 91, 92.

57. Neatby, "Franklin, Sir John," 690; Woodman, *Unravelling the Franklin Mystery*, 3.

58. Kupsch, "Richardson, Sir John," 1582; Marsh, "Franklin Search," 690; Woodman, *Unravelling the Franklin Mystery*, 3.

59. Woodman, *Unravelling the Franklin Mystery*, 5–6, 30–31, 79, 98–100.

60. Scott and Crossman, *Freshwater Fishes of Canada*, 221–222; Woodman, *Unravelling the Franklin Mystery*, 98–109.

61. Woodman, *Unravelling the Franklin Mystery*, 150, 157–158, 161, 166, 168, 177, 192, 246–247, 316.

62. Bockstoce, "Changing Images of the Northwest Passage," 13, 20–21; Francis, "Amundsen, Roald," 54; Neatby, "Arctic Exploration," 89.

63. Dunbar, *Historical Geology*, 396–397.

64. Stanton, "Forest Regions," 670–671; Stanton, "Forestry," 671.

65. Drolet, "Mineral Resources," 1138–1139; Marsh, "Great Bear Lake," 770; Marsh, "Great Slave Lake," 771; Walsh, "The Great Canadian Diamond Rush," D1, D10.

66. Marsh, "Bush Flying," 244.

FOUR

LAKE TROUT LIVE IN GREAT PLACES

> The lake burst upon us a noble sheet of blue water lifted six thousand three hundred feet above the level of the sea, and walled in by a rim of snow-clad mountain peaks. . . . I thought it must surely be the fairest picture the whole earth affords.
>
> —Samuel Clemens (not yet Mark Twain), beholding breathtaking Lake Tahoe in 1861

The pursuit of lake trout is only part of the story. Factors relating to the laker's dwelling places appeal to us also. We think of unspoiled beauty, pure waters, spectacular views . . . fascinating geologic and human history, a dizzying diversity of animal and plant life, and, in many cases, a remote, untouched wilderness experience.

We have selected, for consideration, eight bodies of water and one lake region that exemplify these attractions. Our list is incomplete; other lakes could be included. Some lakes are more familiar to us. All were chosen by reputation. Four water bodies have produced record fish. Several lakes are located in the United States, but most are found in

Canada. The lakes and regions, for no compelling reason, are presented in alphabetical order. We believe that our research on these lakes will either enhance the next trip to one of them, or prompt the angler to study a lake trout waterway of his or her choice in similar fashion. Here is our list.

- Fish Lake, Utah
- Flaming Gorge Reservoir, Utah/Wyoming
- Great Bear Lake, Northwest Territories
- Jackson Lake, Wyoming
- Nejanilini Lake, Manitoba
- Nueltin Lake, Manitoba/Nunavut Territory
- Lake Placid, New York
- Snowbird, Obre, Wholdaia, Flett and Dubawnt Lakes, Northwest Territories/Nunavut
- Lake Tahoe, California/Nevada

Do lake trout live in great places? We think the reader will agree that the answer is a resounding "yes!"

Fish Lake, Utah

Fish Lake, a beautiful natural body of water in south-central Utah just northwest of the northern tip of Capitol Reef National Park, has been around for a long time. The lake was formed when parallel fault lines at the base of Mytoge Mountain on the south and Fish Lake Hightop to the north dropped over millions of years to form a trough, or graben. Water trapped on the surface of the graben created the lake.[1]

Set between aspen and spruce-covered slopes at an elevation of 8,700 feet (2,652 m), the six-mile-long (9.6 km), one-mile-wide (1.6 km) lake has a maximum depth of over

120 feet (36.6 m). The Utah Division of Wildlife began stocking lakers there in 1906. A fair number of 20-pound (9.1 kg) fish are caught each year in this lake, designated by the State of Utah as a trophy fishery. The lake record stands at 38 pounds (17.2 kg).[2]

Flaming Gorge Reservoir, Utah/Wyoming

> The Green River enters the Uinta Mountains by a flaring, brilliant, vermilion gorge, a conspicuous and well-known locality, to which, several years ago, I gave the name Flaming Gorge.[3]

So wrote explorer, geologist, and scholar John Wesley Powell in 1876. Today, a dam, completed in 1964, has tamed the river and created an outstanding lake trout fishery extending 91 miles (145.6 km) northward to Green River, Wyoming, in the southwestern portion of that state. When full, the high-water line of the reservoir reaches 6,040 feet (1,841 m) above sea level. The dam, rising 502 feet (153 m) above bedrock, is situated near Dutch John, in northeastern Utah. It is estimated that the Green River supplies nearly half of the Colorado River's water volume when the two streams merge in southeastern Utah.[4]

Outdoor enthusiasts appreciate the area's impressive geology and absorbing human history. Rising in the wondrous Wind River mountain range in west-central Wyoming, the Green surges southward across the desert until it runs into the northern and eastern Uinta Mountains at Flaming Gorge, Utah. The river traverses Brown's Park, legendary hideout of the outlaw Butch Cassidy and his notorious "Wild Bunch" who terrorized southern Wyoming, eastern Utah and western Colorado in the 1890s. It then slices spectacularly through the mountains at Ledore Canyon in Dinosaur National Monument.

The great canyon systems formed by the Green River have been sources of awe and wonder since the days of early man, some 10,000 years ago; the Shoshone and Ute Native Americans about 1500 A.D.; and the mountain men of the early nineteenth century, such as Jim Bridger and Kit Carson.[5]

Massive geologic processes shaped this beautiful land. The Uinta Range, the only major mountain system in the United States running in an east-west direction, has a long, complex and dynamic geologic history. A spur of the Rockies, the Uintas were built on a Precambrian mountain range eroded to its roots more than two billion years ago. The emergence of the Uintas was marked by flooding of ancient seas and lakes, large-scale faulting, crustal warping, and frequent falls of volcanic ash. The area is renowned for its extraordinary fossil deposits—brachiopods, trilobites, dinosaur bones, fish, insects, and mammals.[6]

How did the Green River manage to cut its way through the Uintas? It is theorized that during the last ten million years the entire western half of the continent began to rise, steepening stream gradients of the Green, Bighorn, Wind, Snake, and Colorado Rivers. Thus these great rivers were superimposed across mountain ranges and plateaus, carving most of the American West's scenic canyons.[7]

Flaming Gorge, carved into Jurassic and Triassic rock, takes its name from the riot of reds, golds, and oranges in the shaley Triassic beds. Lake trout drifted into the reservoir in the late 1960s from a cluster of small lakes (known locally as the Finger Lakes) that hugs the western edge of the Bridger-Teton National Wilderness Area in Wyoming's upper Green River area. Six of these lakes—New Fork, Willow, Fremont, Halfmoon and both of the Green River Lakes—were stocked with lakers in the early 1930s. Lower Green River Lake, through which the Green flows after heading in the nearby

Wind River range was the most likely source of reservoir lakers initially. But other Finger Lakes contributed to the laker drift through tributaries into the New Fork River, which flows into the Green farther southward.[8]

The depth of the reservoir, nearly 400 feet (122 m) at the dam, has enhanced the development of a top lake trout fishery. A fish weighing 51.5 pounds (23.4 kg), a Utah record and one of the largest lakers ever caught in the United States, was boated in 1988 near Antelope Flat. Gray trout have been stocked in Flaming Gorge reservoir since 1979.[9]

Great Bear Lake, Northwest Territories

Fabulous Great Bear Lake needs no introduction. One of the last frontiers. Isolated, breathtaking back country. Spectacular summer weather. Unpolluted Arctic serenity. Pristine blue waters. Icebound for eight months of the year. Home of trophy lake trout and another world record in 1995.[10]

Situated in the northwestern Northwest Territories, this massive lake of some 12,000 square miles (31,080 square km) and a maximum depth of 1,355 feet (413 m) is the eighth largest in the world and fourth largest in North America. The distinctive shape of Great Bear has been described as resembling a giant amoeba with five great arms which meet at a common center. The southern and western arms extend into the tundra, and the eastern shore laps the hard eroded crags of the Canadian Shield. Dease Arm, above the Arctic Circle and reaching northeastward, is named for explorer and fur trader Peter Dease, who spent the winter of 1837–38 at Fort Confidence at the northern tip of Great Bear. The name of the lake, adopted in 1902, probably refers both to the bears in the area and to the lake's huge size.[11]

Great Bear's cold, crystal-clear waters are the most productive anywhere for lunker lake trout. Fish in the 30- to 40-pound class (13.6 to 18.1 kg) are common and a number of specimens in the 50- to 60-pound range (22.7 to 27.2 kg)—and even larger—have been recorded. Another all-tackle world record was established in 1991 when a 66.5-pounder (30.16 kg) was caught by veteran Great Bear angler Rodney Harback of Harriman, Tennessee, while trolling the sand flats of Mackintosh Bay on Smith Arm.[12]

In 1995, another seasoned Great Bear fisherman, New York's Lloyd Bull, released a 72-pound (32.65 kg) leviathan that was recognized by both the National Fresh Water Fishing Hall of Fame (in Hayward, Wisconsin) and the Canadian National Fish Registry (in Waterdown, Ontario) as a new, all-tackle world record for lake trout. Because the length of Bull's monofilament leader exceeded its specifications, the International Game Fish Association (headquartered in Pompano Beach, Florida) did not acknowledge the catch as surpassing the Harback world record at the time.[13] However, in 1997, after thoroughly reviewing the tested strength of line sections, the IGFA belatedly approved the Bull catch as a new lake trout world record for both all-tackle and the 30-pound (13.6 kg) line class.[14]

Current records aside, it is evident that in recent years some enormous lake trout have been hauled from Great Bear's pure, productive waters.

Jackson Lake, Wyoming

Jackson Lake, at an elevation of 6,770 feet (2063.5 m), lies at the base of the spectacular Teton Range in Grand Teton National Park, just south of the Yellowstone National Park boundary, in northwestern Wyoming. While geologic processes beginning more than two billion years ago, marked by ancient oceans, volcanism, and faulting were important to uplift of the Teton Range, glaciation over the past 150,000 years—particularly the Yellowstone ice mass some 20,000 years ago—scooped out the depression occupied today by Jackson Lake. Glacial ice melted to fill the lake basin. The scenic Snake River, with headwaters in Yellowstone park, flows through Jackson Lake, winds across southern Idaho, cuts through Hells Canyon (the deepest river-carved chasm in North America), and joins the Pacific-bound Columbia River in south-central Washington.[15]

A log dam, constructed at the outlet of Jackson Lake in 1906–07, quickly washed out and was replaced by the U.S. Bureau of Reclamation with a concrete barrier in 1916. The dam increased the size of the lake by a third, provided a maximum depth of 400 feet (122 m) and enhanced the growth of the lake trout fishery.[16]

The story of the development of the Mackinaw fishery in Jackson Lake is reminiscent of sagas about the old West. In the summer of 1890, a large container was unloaded from a boxcar at a railroad depot in Cinibar, Montana, just north of the Yellowstone park boundary. The container, which held lake trout fry brought by train from the Northville federal hatchery in Michigan, was unloaded onto an army wagon driven by Sergeant John Shive, a veteran of Indian skirmishes, and a scout named Wilson. The pair drove south into the park some 60 miles (96.5 km) to the Old Faithful geyser area where the fish were transferred to oblong cans. The vessels were then loaded onto pack horses and mules for the 18-mile (29 km) trip over the Sheridan Trail to Shoshone and Lewis Lakes, just west of Yellowstone Lake, where the fish were planted. The laker fry quickly drifted from the outlet of Lewis Lake through the Lewis and Snake Rivers to Jackson Lake, a distance of about 16 river miles (25.7 km).[17]

The fish thrived in their new habitat. In 1906, men on barges shuttling logs for the dam construction at the lake's outlet caught grays weighing up to 15 pounds (6.8 kg) while trolling. Shive, for his contribution to laker lore, has been called the "grandfather of the Jackson Hole Mackinaw." His involvement in the venture evolved from the U.S. Army's administration of Yellowstone Park before organization of the National Park Service in 1916. Fingerling lake trout were first stocked in 1937. Jackson Lake has become one of Wyoming's foremost Mackinaw fisheries, with a 50-pounder (22.7 kg) caught there in 1983.[18]

Nejanilini Lake, Manitoba

Translated from the Chipewyan, *Nejanilini* means "the water that makes people sing." Located in north-central Manitoba near the border of Nunavut Territory, Nejanilini is 710 miles (1142 km) north of Winnipeg in Canada's unspoiled tundra land. The unevenly shaped lake is 39 miles (58 km) long and 12 miles (19.3 km) wide, with approximately 140 miles (225 km) of shoreline. It has bays, islands, reefs, feeder creeks, and rushing rivers.[19]

In 1985, sportfishing was introduced into Nejanilini on a regular basis and the lake became strictly catch and release. During the previous thirty years or so Nejanilini had experienced negligible fly-in angling pressure but had gained a reputation for its abundance of large lake trout. Nejanilini Lake management reported that a fish weighing 46.5 pounds (21 kg), the current lake record, was caught (and released) in 1989.[20]

Fishing isn't the only pastime at Nejanilini that makes people sing. Photographers can capture on film some of the thousands of barren land caribou that migrate through the area annually in late August. Artifacts from ancient Inuit and Chipewyan encampments still can be found. The tundra flora and fauna and rolling sand eskers are a naturalist's paradise.[21]

Nueltin Lake, Manitoba/Nunavut Territory

Nueltin Lake, 120 miles (193 kg) long and irregularly shaped, straddles the border of Nunavut Territory and northwestern Manitoba. Its shoreline is heavily indented and the lake is peppered with small and large islands. Nueltin, two-thirds of which lies in Nunavut Territory, is drained northeastward into Hudson Bay by the Thlewiaza River. The lake's name is from the Chipewyan, Nu-thel-tin-tu-ch, meaning "sleeping island lake." A large bay is named after Britisher Samuel Hearne, who explored the huge lake in the early 1770s. Nueltin still lies in primitive wilderness. It is home to world-class lake trout fishing and is Canada's original catch-and-release lake. The lake's biggest fish to date is 56 pounds (25.4 kg), although larger lakers have been hooked and lost at the boat.[22]

Lake Placid, New York

The boundary of Adirondack Park encircles most of northern New York State between Albany and the Canadian border. The six-million-acre (2,430,000 hectares) preserve, largest in the United States outside of Alaska, encompasses an area as large as Vermont—or the size of Glacier, Yellowstone,

Great Smoky Mountains, Yosemite, and Grand Canyon National Parks combined.[23]

In the north-central portion of Adirondack Park lies jewel-like Lake Placid, a small, mountain-ringed body of water with a big reputation. The lake stretches just northeastward of the village of Lake Placid, host of the Olympic Winter Games twice in the twentieth century. In 1932, the world was captivated by Sonja Henie, a blonde, dimpled 15-year-old Norwegian girl who won the gold medal in figure skating and popularized that sport for generations to come. The individual star of the 1980 games, Eric Heiden, a 21-year-old United States speed skater, captured five gold metals. But the heart-capturing highlight of these games, for Americans, proved to be the stunning gold-medal-winning performance by an unheralded United States ice hockey team that bested both a heavily favored Soviet Union squad in an emotional semifinal contest and powerful Finland in the final.[24]

Lake Placid, figure-eight shaped and only five miles (8 km) long, is also a superb lake trout fishery. Its waters yielded a 32-pounder (14.5 kg) in 1986, a New York State record until 1994. The lake is known for its high water quality and abundant, wild, naturally reproducing lake trout population. A maximum depth of 150 feet (45.7 m) supports laker development and attests to glacial gouging during the last ice age.[25]

Snowbird, Obre, Wholdaia, Flett and Dubawnt Lakes, Northwest Territories/Nunavut

The surface covered by these lakes and their associated river systems, about 10,000 square miles (25,900 square km) of unsullied beauty, is located in the southeastern Northwest

Territories and western Nunavut at the tree line and 800 miles (1287 km) north of Winnipeg, Manitoba. This immense area is drained by three north-flowing river systems, well known for their outstanding lake trout fisheries—the Dubawnt, Kazan, and Kamilukuak. Snowbird Lake, noted for its unique laker feeding frenzies, and Obre and Atzinging lakes form the headwaters of the famous Kazan.[26]

Wholdaia, Flett, and Anaunethad Lakes feed the spectacular Dubawnt River. Both the Dubawnt and Kamilukuak flow into Dubawnt Lake, situated at the region's northern end. The waters of all three rivers ultimately empty into Hudson Bay at Chesterfield Inlet. Treeless Dubawnt, icebound most of the summer, was discovered by Samuel Hearne in 1770 but remained virtually unknown until explored by Joseph Tyrrell, a Canadian geologist and historian, in 1893.[27]

The length of the fishing season reflects the vastness of this region—twelve weeks for Obre Lake in the southern portion and seven weeks for more northerly Dubawnt Lake. Daylight lasts 24 hours during the first few weeks of the season. Flett holds the official record for lakers in this area, yielding a 57-pound (25.9 kg) lake trout in 1990. However, a laker believed to be in excess of 60 pounds (27.2 kg) was caught and released in Snowbird's waters after a quick photograph in 1988.[28]

Lake Tahoe, California/Nevada

Lake Tahoe, for many, would head our list for its beauty alone. Gilbert Bailey, author and professor of geology at the University of Southern California, has referred to Tahoe as "the gem of the Sierras."[29] Tahoe trouter John Roush has described it as "the clearest large lake in the world, and the most unique lake in North America."[30] Soldier and explorer John C. Fremont wrote of spotting Lake Tahoe from Carson Pass in 1844: "We had a beautiful view of a mountain lake at our feet, about fifteen miles in length, and so entirely surrounded by mountains that we could not discover an outlet."[31]

The largest mountain lake in North America, Tahoe lies 6,226 feet (1898 km) above sea level, measures about 22 miles by 12 miles (35.4 by 19.3 km), is fed by 63 tributaries, and has a maximum depth of 1,645 feet (501.4 m), making it the continent's third deepest lake. A oligotrophic (low nutrient) lake, of composite volcanic and glacial origin, it was formed before the Pleistocene Epoch which began more than two million years ago. Tahoe's name is likely of Washoe Indian derivation and means "big water." Two thirds of the lake lies in California and the remainder in Nevada. Lakers, first introduced from the Great Lakes in 1889, were well established by 1920 and have become the dominant species in Tahoe.[32] Tahoe yielded a record laker for California and Nevada waters in 1974, a 37-pound, 6-ounce fish (16.9 km).[33] It is believed that the lake contains considerably larger Mackinaw, probably in excess of 50 pounds (22.7 kg). Tahoe, arguably the most picturesque of American lakes, today enjoys a reputation as one of the world's most delightful vacation spots.

It is evident from a review of the literature that the lake trout and its attractive surroundings have been long studied. As early as 1908, E. A. Preble wrote admiringly:

> Athabasca Lake, the eastern and northern arms of Great Slave Lake, and Great Bear Lake abound especially in these fine trout, and as the water is there beautifully clear the traveler frequently sees them pursuing their prey in

the depths, or lying motionless near the bottom. In the swift streams which enter these lakes, and in some which fall into the Arctic Sea, the pools at the foot of rapids are always tenanted by these voracious fish.[34]

Yes, lake trout really do live in great places!

Notes

1. *Geology of the Fish Lake Area*, 1979; *Information about History, Recreation, Trails, and Management of the Fish Lake Basin,* 1989.

2. Hepworth, personal telephone conference, 1992; *Information about History, Recreation, Trails, and Management of the Fish Lake Basin,* 1989; Thomas, "Fish Lake Lakers," 1992.

3. Hansen, *The Geologic Story of the Uinta Mountains*, 39.

4. Williams, *Flaming Gorge*, 29–30, 37.

5. Hansen, *The Geologic Story of the Uinta Mountains*, 29, 40; Williams, *Flaming Gorge*, 27, 34–35.

6. Hansen, *The Geologic Story of the Uinta Mountains*, 14–66, 77–105; Williams, *Flaming Gorge*, 17–26.

7. Williams, *Flaming Gorge*, 27.

8. Balford, personal telephone conference, 1993; Hansen, *The Geologic Story of the Uinta Mountains*, 40; Schneidervin, personal telephone conference, 1992.

9. Schneidervin, personal telephone conference, 1993; Wharton, "Angler Glows After Record Catch."

10. Leech, correspondence to Bull, 1997.

11. Francis, "Dease, Peter Warren," 477; Marsh, "Great Bear Lake," 769–770.

12. O'Brien, "Northwest Territories," 698; *World Record Game Fishes*, International Game Fish Association, 1997 ed., 229.

13. Brown, correspondence to Bull, 1996; Bull, Correspondence to Leech, 1997, 1–2; "Canadian National Fish Registry," 56; *Official World and U.S.A State Fresh Water Angling Records*, National Fresh Water Fishing Hall of Fame, 1999 ed., 36.

14. Leech, correspondence to Bull, 1997.

15. *Journey through the Past: A Geologic Tour*, 1992; Rennicke, "America's Deepest Canyon," 111–121.

16. Kiefling, *Jackson Lake Completion Report*, 1; Rollefson and Erickson, "Jackson Lake's Big 'Macks,' " 22–23.

17. Kiefling, *Jackson Lake Completion Report*, 1; Rollefson and Erickson, "Jackson Lake's Big 'Macks,' " 20–21.

18. Kiefling, *Jackson Lake Completion Report,* 1–2; *Official World and U.S.A State Fresh Water Angling Records*, National Fresh Water Fishing Hall of Fame, 1999 Edition, 76; Rollefson and Erickson, "Jackson Lake's Big 'Macks,' " 21.

19. *Nejalini Lodge—In Canada's Tundra Land*, no date; Malz, "Manitoba's Nejalini Lake," 57.

20. Malz, "Manitoba's Nejalini Lake," 56; *Nejalini Lodge—In Canada's Tundra Land*, 1993.

21. *Nejalini Lodge—In Canada's Tundra Land*, no date.

22. Evans, "Nueltin Lake," 1302; *Nueltin Lake*, Nueltin Fly-In Lodges, no date.

23. Beamish, "An Embattled Wilderness," 36; Mouat, "N.Y.'s Adirondack Park Celebrates 100 Years," 10–11.

24. *Final Report: XIII Olympic Winter Games*, 17–18, 43, 54.

25. *Fishing Lake Placid and Surrounding Waters*, no date; *Official World and U.S.A. State Fresh Water Angling Records*, National Fresh Water Fishing Hall of Fame, 1995 Edition, 59; Preall, personal telephone conference, 1993.

26. "Far Northern Outpost Camps," 4; "Obre Lake—The Main Lodge," 3.

27. Frederickson, personal telephone conference, 1992; Marsh, "Dubawnt River," 520; McNicholl, "Tyrrell, Joseph Burr," 1861; Zoltai, "Dubawnt Lake," 520.

28. "Cover Story: Lake Trout Release," 7; Frederickson, "For The Record . . . ," 9; "Record-Breaking Lake Trout Released!" 1.

29. Bailey, *California: A Geologic Wonderland*, 82.

30. Roush, *Enjoying Fishing Lake Tahoe, the Truckee River, and Pyramid Lake*, 1.

31. Fergurson, "Lake Tahoe—Playing for High Stakes," 115.

32. Bailey, *California: A Geologic Wonderland*, 82–88; Fergurson, "Lake Tahoe—Playing for High Stakes," 117–118; Roush, *Enjoying Fishing Lake Tahoe, the Truckee River, and Pyramid Lake*, 1–5.

33. *Official World and U.S.A State Fresh Water Angling Records*, National Fresh Water Fishing Hall of Fame, 1999 ed., 62, 69.

34. McPhail and Lindsey, *Freshwater Fishes of Northwestern Canada and Alaska,* 140–141.

FIVE

BIG FISH

> Lord, suffer me to catch a fish so large that even I in talking of it afterward shall have no need to lie.
>
> —Anonymous

Lake trout, we know, can reach impressive size. The magnitude of these big fish can be expressed in various ways, such as by photograph, videotape, measurement, observation, narrative, or listings in record books. We use all these means to describe the greatness of a fish with lengthy life span.

Historical Observations

It is fascinating to study the juxtaposition of Arctic history and early lake trout observations. A journal entry of John Richardson, surgeon and naturalist during the first expedition of British explorer John Franklin in 1819–22, noted the huge size attained by lake trout:[1]

> We frequently observed trout weighing forty pounds, and were informed by the residents that fish of sixty pounds

> were not very uncommon in particular lakes. In Manito, or God's Lake, between Hill and Severn Rivers, they are reported to attain the enormous size of ninety pounds.[2]

Biologist Kenneth Carlander has questioned an 1836 record of a 120-pound (54.4 kg) fish netted in the Straits of Mackinac, connecting lakes Huron and Michigan, but has accepted an 1864 Lake Michigan netting mark of 88 pounds (39.9 kg).[3] However, C. W. Greene, a New York biologist, has placed the upper limit for lake trout at 125 pounds (56.7 kg).[4]

The largest known lake trout in North American waters was caught by gillnetter Orton Flett in Lake Athabasca, Saskatchewan, on August 8, 1961. The giant, barrel-shaped fish weighed 102 pounds (46.3 kg) and measured 49.5 inches (126 cm) in length. This was a relatively young fish, 20 to 25 years old, with its rapid growth probably related to the fact that the big laker never had become sexually mature. Other specimens in excess of 80 pounds (36.3 kg) were netted in Lake Athabasca about 1961.[5]

Big Laker Narratives

Anglers revel in stories of big fish catches. These vicarious experiences are the next best thing to being there. A memorable, head-to-head meeting with a great Mackinaw in 1981 was related by Lake Tahoe angler Ed Berry of Minden, Nevada:

> In May, just north of Sand Harbor, I caught something on my lure, so I stopped trolling and pulled in my line. When the lure was still some distance from the boat I could see it [the lure] had indeed caught something, a twig about eight inches long, just as I thought. Then, to my surprise,

I saw the Mack that was following it up. My first thought was that it was a submarine it was, in a word, *huge*! It followed the lure almost to the boat, giving me a long, good look. I have caught a number of Macs over fifteen pounds, but I'd never seen one like that. There is no doubt in my mind that there are fifty pounders in Tahoe, for that one I would guess was well over forty pounds.[6]

John Gierach described a dogged fight with a big lake trout hooked while jigging at Snowbird Lake in the Northwest Territories:

It was four or five days into the trip, after drifting off a shelf, when eight-year-old Kelly hooked what would have been the largest fish of the party. At first we thought he'd snagged bottom, but when the line started moving slowly towards the middle of the lake, we all started shouting instructions at the same time. It was a heavy fish and we knew we were in for a siege. Kelly fought that fish with the patience of an old hand, and two hours later and several miles down the lake, the fish came in sight in the clear water. Guy La Blank, our guide, guessed it at 40 pounds or better and his voice had gone up an octave. When your guide gets excited, you know you're playing in the big leagues. It was shortly thereafter that the line parted and the rod went straight. The fish had been fought well, but the strain was just too much for the light line. Kelly didn't cry, but I think he wanted to. For that matter, we all wanted to.[7]

A possible all-tackle world-record lake trout was caught in 1988 by Ted Alsobrook of Woodbridge, Illinois, at Snowbird Lake in the Northwest Territories. We say a "possible" world record because the giant fish, never weighed, was released, after a quick photograph. A photo of Alsobrook's trophy catch appeared on the cover of a 1989 issue of *The Splash*, a quarterly publication of the National Fresh Water Fishing Hall of Fame. It reported the event as follows:

> This past fall, Ted Alsobrook from Illinois boated a fish estimated to be well into the 60-pound class. Maybe a new record, but we'll never know. A quick photo was taken. He chose to release the fish. The following was submitted by North of Sixty Lodge management:
>
> DATELINE: SNOWBIRD LAKE, N.W.T.: September 2, 1988, will never be forgotten by those who were present and those of us who weren't. A giant trout was allowed to live that day, but how big was it? We will never know. It immediately buried the 50-pound scale—the only one available in the boat. All world-record fish, for all line classes, are required to be kept for verification and official weighing. What a shame. Ted Alsobrook of Woodridge, Illinois, caught and released this monster lake trout one windy afternoon in the heaving waters of Snowbird Lake, N.W.T. It was nearly time for the lake trout spawn and she was heavily laden with eggs. It is fantastic to know a fish of this age is still able to reproduce! It takes a special kind of sportsman to recognize the value of such a fish, and be able to release it with pride.[8]

Dave and Ron Frederickson, owners of North of Sixty Lodges Ltd., believed that the freeing of this huge fish "is still, and may always be, the most outstanding achievement of our catch-and-release program."[9]

During the 1990s, elated fisherman have enticed some mighty big fish from the chilly, transparent waters of northern Canada's Great Bear Lake. In 1996, angler Bill Dodson and guide Pat Alexander collaborated to boat a laker estimated at 70 pounds (31.8 kg), an unofficial record at the time for this world champion of trout lakes. However, because of serious gill damage inflicted by the spoon's hooks, the anglers were unable to revive the monster for release purposes. Furthermore, the scale used was not certified.[10]

Current International Game Fish Association regulations for certification of record catches do not require that all fish be kept. While boat-weighing is not acceptable, it is certainly possible to quickly and gently transport most fish to land. Fish and net may be left in the water. Then the specimen may be measured, weighed, photographed, and released.[11]

Regarding scale certification, the IGFA permits the use of certified portable scales. IGFA regulations state that:

> In extremely remote areas where no weighing scales are available, it will be permissible for the angler to use his own scales providing that they are of a quality type and have been properly certified both before and after returning from the fishing trip. . . . IGFA now offers a scale testing service for members only.[12]

Accounts of Record Catches

Only a few pounds or kilograms have been added to world hook-and-line records in the last 50 years, demonstrating the challenge facing an angler hoping to capture lake trout of trophy size. On May 25, 1952, Hubert Hammers of Duluth, Minnesota, boated a 63 pound, 2 ounce (28.6 kg) trout in Lake Superior's Canadian waters. This mark stood unsurpassed until August 8, 1970, when Larry Daunis, a Detroit, Michigan, butcher, netted a 65-pound (29.5 kg) fish from the cool, clear depths of Great Bear Lake in Canada's Northwest Territories. On July 19, 1991, veteran Great Bear angler Rodney Harback who runs a family-owned auto body shop in Harriman, Tennessee, bettered the Daunis catch with a

66.5-pound (30.16 kg) trophy, establishing a new record at the time.

The current world mark recognized by the International Game Fish Association, Canadian National Fish Registry, and National Fresh Water Fishing Hall of Fame belongs to Great Bear expert Lloyd Bull, a petroleum industry retiree from Glenfield, New York. Bull's record-breaking laker, caught and released August 19, 1995, weighed 72 pounds (32.65 kg), measured 59 inches (149.86 cm) in length and 32 inches (81.28 cm) in girth.[13] (Bull and others who witnessed weighing of the giant laker state that the certified scale read 72 pounds, 4 ounces. However, since the scale didn't include quarter-pound markings, the IGFA recognized a world record and all-tackle weight of an even 72 pounds. The Registry and Hall of Fame accepted a record of 72.25 pounds (32.77 kg). To avoid confusion, we report the IGFA-recorded weight of an even 72 pounds (32.65 kg)—although the fish evidently weighed slightly more.)

State angling records compiled by the National Fresh Water Fishing Hall of Fame show the largest lake trout ever taken in the United States, a 61.5-pounder (27.9 kg), to have been caught in Lake Superior's Michigan waters by Lucas Lanczy in 1997.[14]

The record for America's third largest laker, boated at Utah's Flaming Gorge Reservoir in 1988 and weighing 51.5 pounds (23.4 kg), belongs to Curt Bilbey.[15] Bilbey provided an exciting account of the record-breaking catch:

> My record laker was boated June 4, 1988, at about five o'-clock in the evening. That morning, my son, Chuck, and I tried to fish the reservoir, but strong winds pushed us back to camp. By late afternoon, the wind settled down and my wife, Cathy, and I motored to Antelope Flat. The screen of the X15 Lowrance sonar showed big fish

in about 80 feet of water as we released 600 feet of 140-pound-test steel lines over the run. I was trolling with a seven-foot, medium-action, Sabre Grafast rod, Penn 49L reel, and K16 frog Kwikfish. Our lures hit bottom and we had trolled approximately 100 yards when I turned and saw that my holdered rod was raising cain. I grabbed the rod, set the hooks, and shut off the motor as Cathy retrieved her line. It took me around 40 minutes to get the fish near the boat, as it put up a heck of a fight.

While I battled the trout, all my wife could say was, "Oh, my heavens!" I exclaimed that the odds of landing this fish were slim to none, as I had tied into big lakers like this before but never boated them. The huge Mack came up on the port side, flipped its broomlike tail, then swam out so we could really see it. A few moments later, I handed Cathy the rod, gaffed the fish, and somehow threw the heavy laker into the boat. I sat exhausted and my wife yelled, "Let's get to the dock." As soon as we docked, Herb Cummings, marina manager, looked at the fish and declared, "You've beaten the record by a long ways!" The trout, weighed on someone's heavy scale, straightened the hook. Finally, the Manila postmaster certified the laker's weight at 51.5 pounds, a new Utah record. The catch was my greatest fishing thrill to date.[16]

The boating of a record fish was no isolated occurrence for Curt Bilbey. He has caught and released many trophy lake trout in more than two decades of angling at Flaming Gorge.

An account of a world record-setting catch is appealing to any angler. One such account features Rodney Harback, a highly experienced lake trout fisherman. Having plied Great Bear Lake annually since 1977 (except in 1994, when he fished in Alaska), Harback was one of the first to employ a temperature probe in that lake, regularly used muskie-style tackle to handle heavy fish, and had caught many big lakers there. In 1978, Eddie Harback, Rodney's father, landed a 52-pound (23.6 kg) laker at Great Bear on 20-pound-test (9 kg) line—an IGFA line-class record at the time.[17]

Rodney Harback and his fishing partner, Toronto dentist Art Ross, were slow-trolling the shallow sand flats of Smith Arm's Mackintosh Bay on July 19, 1991. Harback's equipment included a six-foot (1.8 m), heavy-action muskie rod, 7000 Ambassadeur reel, 30-pound (13.6 kg) Trilene XT line, and metallic silver/blue scale T-60 Flatfish. Fishing conditions were excellent. The bay's water temperature on this calm, bright, sunny Arctic day was about 50°F (10°C). Fish of 30 pounds (13.6 kg) or more were seen gliding past the boat in three to five feet (.9 to 1.5 m) of water. Harback had predicted some years earlier that the next record lake trout would come from Mackintosh Bay. Prophecy was about to be fulfilled.[18]

Harback had about 150 feet (45.7 m) of line out, his Flatfish digging into the sand and fine pebble bottom, when the huge fish hit shortly after noon, producing a tremendous swirl. Line was repeatedly lost and gained during the tough, 20-minute battle. When guide Noel Sinclair expertly netted the great fish, he shouted, "That's a whale!" The scale bottomed out at 50 pounds (22.7 kg) as Harback and Sinclair struggled to weigh the husky laker in the boat. Scales on shore pushed the weight past 60 pounds (27.2 kg). Later in the day, the balance beam at Trophy Lodge certified a weight of 66.5 pounds (30.16 kg)—a new IGFA all-tackle world record at the time.[19]

Another event of special interest occurred on the same remarkable outing. Shortly after measuring, weighing, and photographing the big fish on shore, Harback returned to the same spot where he had caught his trophy and hooked what he thought to be an even larger forktail. After fighting the heavy gray for about five minutes, his line suddenly went limp. While the lunker was gone, something—a dead weight—was still on the line. Harback's Flatfish, when reeled in, had caught the tail of the headless remains of a partially digested lake trout—evidently pulled from the giant's mouth—with live length and weight estimated at 26 to 29 inches (66 to 73.7 cm) and 10 to 12 pounds (4.5 to 5.4 kg), respectively. The fish that Harback had hooked was huge indeed, and may have been a mate to the record-setter. In Harback's expert judgment, only a laker approximating 60 pounds (27.2 kg) could have swallowed, head first, a fish of that size. And this giant fish, having nailed a T-60 Flatfish, obviously was still hungry![20]

United States, Canadian, and World Lake Trout Records

Current records of the National Fresh Water Fishing Hall of Fame reveal the presence of lake trout in the waters of 30 states. Table 5.1 includes state angling records for lake trout exceeding 20 pounds (9.07 kg). Since a national registry for Canadian provinces and territories does not currently exist, comparable angling records are available through natural resources departments of provincial and territorial governments. Table 5.2 compiles lake trout records in Canadian territories and selected provinces. Table 5.3 presents International Game Fish Association freshwater line-class world records for lake trout. Laker waters dominating these data are Great Bear Lake in the Northwest Territories and Flaming Gorge Reservoir in Utah. IGFA freshwater fly rod world records are shown in table 5.4.

Table 5.1. U.S. State Angling Records for Lake Trout over Twenty Pounds (9.07 kg)[21]

State	*Pounds/ Ounces*	*Kilograms*	*Angler*	*Where Caught*	*Date*
Alaska	47-0	21.3	Daniel Thorsness	Clarence Lake	1970
California	37-6	16.9	Robert Aronsen	Lake Tahoe	1974
Colorado	38-10	17.5	Jerome Vinet	Blue Mesa Reservoir	1998
Connecticut	29-13	13.5	Dr. Thompson	Wononscopomuc Lake	1918
Idaho	57-8	26.1	Lyle McClure	Priest Lake	1971
Illinois	37-8	17.0	Alan Burchfield	Lake Michigan	1995
Indiana	29-4	13.3	Harold Rodriguez	Lake Michigan	1993
Maine	31-8	14.3	Hollis Grindle	Beech Hill Pond	1958
Massachusetts	22-10	10.3	Anthony Wieczorek	Quabbin Reservoir	1988
Michigan	61-8	27.9	Lucas Lanczy	Lake Superior	1997
Minnesota	43-8	19.7	G. H. Nelson	Lake Superior	1955
Montana	42-0	19.0	Dave Larson	Flathead Lake	1979
Nevada	37-6	16.9	Robert Aronsen	Lake Tahoe	1974
New Hampshire	28-8	12.9	Albert Staples	Newfound Lake	1958
New Jersey	24-14	11.3	Carl Bird	Round Valley Reservoir	1994
New Mexico	25-9	11.6	Diana Rios	Heron Lake	1996
NewYork	39-8	17.9	John Mamrak, Jr.	Lake Ontario	1994
Oregon	40-8	18.4	H. V. Hannon	Odell Lake	1984
Pennsylvania	27-13	12.6	Tom Illar, Jr.	Lake Erie	1996
South Dakota	20-10	9.3	Keith Van Buren	Pactola Reservoir	1998
Tennessee	20-13	9.4	Eddy Southerland	Watauga Reservoir	1994
Utah	51-8	23.4	Curt Bilbey	Flaming Gorge Reservoir	1988
Vermont	34-0	15.4	John Staples	Lake Willoughby	1981
Washington	30-4	13.7	Ken Janke	Loon Lake	1966
Wisconsin	47-0	21.3	Waino Roose	Lake Superior	1946
Wyoming	50-0	22.7	Doris Budge	Jackson Lake	1983
Wyoming	50-0	22.7	Randy Calkins	Flaming Gorge Reservoir	1995

Table 5.2. Canadian Lake Trout Angling Records for Selected Territories and Provinces[22]

Province/Territory	*Pounds/Ounces*	*Kilograms*	*Angler*	*Where Caught*	*Date*
Alberta	52-12	23.93	Mrs. Erickson	Cold Lake	1929
Manitoba	62-15	28.55	Mrs. Grayson	Athapapuskow Lake	1930
Northwest Territories	72-0	32.65	Lloyd Bull	Great Bear Lake	1995
Ontario	63-2	28.63	Hubert Hammers	Lake Superior	1952
Saskatchewan	51-10	23.41	Unknown	Kingsmere Lake	1958
Yukon Territory	55-0	24.94	Charles Bennett	Wellesley Lake	1992

Table 5.3. International Game Fish Association Freshwater Line Class World Records for Lake Trout[23]

Line Class	*Weight*	*Place*	*Date*	*Angler*
1 kg (2 lb)	12.84 kg (28 lb 5 oz)	Flaming Gorge Reservoir, Utah	31 Oct 84	Ray Johnson
2 kg (4 lb)	14.28 kg (31 lb 8 oz)	Flaming Gorge Reservoir, Utah	5 Nov 84	Ray Johnson
3 kg (6 lb)	12.08 kg (26 lb 8 oz)	Lac la Martre, N.W.T.	2 Jul 98	Gerald Ches n
4 kg (8 lb)	22.22 kg (49 lb)	Great Bear Lake, N.W.T.	5 Jul 87	Robert Vallee
6 kg (12 lb)	22.90 kg (50 lb 8 oz)	Great Bear Lake, N.W.T.	22 Aug 84	Marco Zonn
8 kg (16 lb)	24.15 kg (53 lb 4 oz)	Great Bear Lake, N.W.T.	19 Jul 86	Richard Simourd
10 kg (20 lb)	28.83 kg (63 lb 9 oz)	Great Bear Lake, N.W.T.	31 Jul 86	Mike Kroening
15 kg (30 lb)	32.65 kg (72 lb)	Great Bear Lake, N.W.T.	19 Aug 95	Lloyd Bull
24 kg (50 lb)	24.94 kg (55 lb)	Great Bear Lake, N.W.T.	9 Jul 89	Massey Lombardi
37 kg (80 lb)	16.78 kg (37 lb)	Great Bear Lake, N.W.T.	30 Jul 98	Marlin Coulombe

Table 5.4. International Game Fish Association Freshwater Fly Rod World Records for Lake Trout[24]

*Tippet**	*Weight*	*Place*	*Date*	*Angler*
1 kg (2 lb)	6.12 kg (13 lb 8 oz)	Wellesley Lake, Yukon Territory	12 Aug 86	T. J. Beeler
2 kg (4 lb)	12.02 kg (26 lb 8 oz)	Great Bear Lake, N.W.T.	11 Aug 92	Roy McGraw
3 kg (6 lb)	8.39 kg (18 lb 8 oz)	Nueltin Lake, Manitoba/Nunavut	20 Jun 96	James Boyer
4 kg (8 lb)	12.02 kg (26 lb 8 oz)	Great Bear Lake, N.W.T.	11 Aug 92	Roy McGraw
6 kg (12 lb)	11.05 kg (24 lb 6 oz)	Nueltin Lake, Manitoba/Nunavut	23 Jun 95	James Boyer
8 kg (16 lb)	11.90 kg (26 lb 4 oz)	Whale River, Quebec	5 Jul 97	Stephen Carta
10 kg (20 lb)	12.47 kg (27 lb 8 oz)	Nueltin Lake, Manitoba/Nunavut	24 Jun 94	James Boyer

*Fly rod world records are maintained according to tippet strength. The tippet is the fine end of the leader to which the fly is tied.

On occasion, a game fish record is recognized by one or more respected angling associations, but not similarly acknowledged at the same time—or perhaps not at all—by another highly regarded fishing fraternity. Such disagreements usually stem from differing angling regulations of organizations involved. A case in point was the enormous laker caught and released by Lloyd Bull at Great Bear Lake in 1995. The 72-pound (32.65 kg) fish was acknowledged as an all-tackle record by both the Canadian National Fish Registry and the National Fresh Water Fishing Hall of Fame, but not by the International Game Fish Association until two years later.[25]

This remarkable catch included equally remarkable angling sidelights. Despite a terrific battle that lasted nearly an hour, Bull—like other lake trout record-setters before him, such as Hubert Hammers, Larry Daunis, and Rodney Harback—demonstrated considerable ability in boating the monster fish in the first place. Furthermore, the veteran Great Bear angler held on to the humongous trout with only a single barbless hook attached to a Huskie Devle spoon. With Goliath finally aboard, Bull swiftly motored the flopping fish to nearby Plummer's Neiland Bay lodge for a certified weigh-in. After quick measuring, weighing, and photographing, the giant—astoundingly, still alive—was successfully returned by the sportsman-angler to its watery environment to fight again.[26] Bull recounted the dramatic event in 1999:

> The events of the evening fishing on August 19, 1995, are such that they should be recorded. I will relate them, and include some information on my many years of fishing that will substantiate the fact that we do not just get lucky and catch a big fish. Our group doesn't fish for anything but big fish. That's why we travel to Great Bear Lake.

On the last evening of our trip my friend Eddie House had not landed a trout over 30 pounds, so I took him out to do just that. There were twelve of us in camp, and no one else wanted to go out. We headed to one of my favorite reefs where the water was 25 feet deep and dropped off sharply to 100 feet. I worked on and off the edge of the shelf in a zig-zag pattern, speeding up as I made the turn on the edge and slowing down as the lure came off over deep water. Most fish hit on the turn at the edge.

Our group throughout the years has located many reefs in the lake proper, and no one else fished them. The shoal we worked that evening is large and we had a couple of miles of reef edge to fish. Initially Ed caught six fish of 18 to 25 pounds. Then he took one of 33 pounds and wanted to quit. It was a beautiful evening and only ten o'clock. The Arctic sun hadn't set yet, and I convinced him to stay out longer.

During the next hour, Ed landed seven more trout in the 22 to 29 pound range. His last fish, at about 11:15 p.m., was a 36-pounder, and Ed was elated and ready to go in. But I convinced him that we only had a short way to go to the end of the reef where I had caught my previous 56½ pound all-tackle world record. I had not taken a fish there all week, even though I tried it every day. Ed agreed we should troll to the end and call it a night.

While Ed was catching fish, you must understand that I was also catching lakers. Several times we had doubles, and I had taken one of 38 pounds and a couple in the low thirties. We had been fishing about three and a half hours and had hooked more than 30 fish, all over 18 pounds. As we cut across the end of the reef with only a couple of hundred yards to go before calling it quits and ending a fabulous week, I had a tremendous strike. That fish took off in the opposite direction like a freight train. My three hundred yards of line screamed off the reel at record speed, and at this rate would soon be gone. I yelled to Ed, "Get your line in fast," turned the boat, and fol lowed at full speed.

I troll with a fairly loose drag,, as I know that big fish, given the opportunity, will snap the line on a tighter drag. I never put my thumb on the spool. I knew this was a big fish, and told Ed I thought we had a new world record. That fish made the longest run I have ever encountered. It never stopped, and we traveled over a mile from where I hooked it before I could even begin to get any line back. The next 45 minutes were spent carefully playing the fish, hoping to at least get a look at it. I use a Huskie Devle with a single 10/0 hook and barb filed off, so I pay plenty of attention to keeping a tight line with no slack. Eventually, after several strong, deep runs, I saw bubbles coming up and told Ed it would not be long before we would see what we had.

When the laker first surfaced, there was no longer any question of whether it was a new record. It was huge. Big fish do not come to the boat readily. Some fifteen minutes later, I felt we could try to net the giant. I cautioned Ed that the trout would not fit straight in and that once started into the net, he would have to curl it in or it wouldn't fit. I brought the fish in, and Ed tried to lift the trout into the net. There was a struggle and the fish began sliding out. I expected the hook to catch in the net and all would be lost, but it didn't happen. The fish slid out and swam strongly away.

Another ten minutes went by before I was able to bring that fish up to the boat again. This time Ed, well instructed on the netting process, curled the fish in nicely. I dropped the rod and together we lifted the net and laid that monster across the bottom of the boat—the laker stretching from gunnel to gunnel. Wanting to weigh the fish with witnesses, we immediately headed for camp, now only a few minutes away. Not only did I want to officially record this fish but, if possible, desired to return it to the lake. When we reached the dock, I immediately put the fish and net back in the water and watched its gills work. Ed ran to camp to get the crew down to the dock, but only three disbelieving, sleepy anglers piled out of bed.

We certified the weight, measured the laker, and quickly took pictures with four cameras. Holding the fish by the tail, I worked it back and forth for several minutes to force water through its gills. We took more pictures as I released it, and the big trout swam slowly around the dock and back out to the lake. When the pictures were developed, I would have the new all-tackle record.

Little did I know that it was not going to be that easy. In the excitement, all four photographers experienced difficulty, from improper film insertion, non-removal of a lens cover, an extended telephoto lens that cut me and the fish in half, to a lanyard that partly obscured the picture but not the laker (a problem corrected by a photo shop).[27]

Because Bull's 30-pound (13.6 kg) monofilament leader, affixed to 27-pound (12.2 kg) lead-core line, exceeded by two feet (.61 m) the length specified for freshwater angling, the International Game Fish Association did not recognize the catch as a new lake trout world record at the time.[28] But after a complete review of Bull's file in December, 1997, IGFA officials reconsidered, acknowledging an all-tackle record on the basis of tested line strength within 30 pounds (13.6 kg), even though the line consisted of three different sections (leader, line, and backing).[29]

The biggest fish he ever caught was the one that got away.

—Eugene Field (1889)

During our fishing lives, many of us either have seen a big fish in its native element, experienced a sudden, startling near-miss of a lure, or hooked and lost a piscatorial monster after a brief or protracted battle. Even if we have also been privileged to catch a giant fish, it is the behemoth that has eluded our grasp that forms the fondest memories. Like a famed sports team that inspires our continual recalling of its exploits—possibly exaggerated—a huge fish that got away grows in our remembrance. Its length and weight are embellished in the impassioned retelling. In the words of laker record-breaker Lloyd Bull: "A big lake trout hooked and lost can work on the mind and haunt us. This is the stimulus that encourages us to return year after year in hopes of hooking the mighty fish again."[30]

Lloyd and Carol Bull have encountered a number of enormous trout during many joint visits to Great Bear Lake. While fishing together in 1983, Lloyd watched a mammoth lake trout follow a hooked laker to their craft. He recalls:

> While trolling, I hooked a trout and we stopped the boat to land it. As I stood up I saw a huge laker following the hooked fish to the boat. This fish was five feet long and thick. I have several times seen immense lake trout follow a hooked fish right up to the boat—fish far bigger than any we had caught, so I knew they were out here.[31]

Two years later, Carol Bull hooked a larger-than-life laker while trolling with her husband. Distinctly remembering the incident, Lloyd Bull later wrote:

> In 1985 Carol made her third trip with me. On the last day of fishing she had caught several lakers and had just taken fish of 31 and 33 pounds. I changed the frayed leader and she started fishing again. She immediately

> hooked what I consider to be the largest lake trout ever hooked in Great Bear Lake. We were trolling right on the edge of a steep ledge. At first she thought she was hooked on bottom, but the boat was still moving and she wasn't losing any line. I knew at once that she had tied into a big fish. Then in a great burst of speed, that fish went up on the shallow shelf, around the boat, and headed for deep water. I could clearly see the outline of this huge trout 30 feet away before it went over the edge and headed down deep. Carol had the rod braced over the gunnel because she could hardly hold on to it. I was sure the rod would break. The rod held, the reel screamed as line tore off—and then it was over. The 30-pound leader broke right in the middle. That one memory will last us a lifetime.[32]

We agree wholeheartedly with seasoned big-trout anglers Lloyd Bull, Rodney Harback, and the late A. J. McClane: The next all-tackle, world record lake trout will come from the prolific waters of Great Bear Lake in Canada's Northwest Territories!

Notes

1. Houston, *Arctic Ordeal*, xxii.
2. Houston, *Arctic Ordeal*, 257.
3. Carlander, *Handbook of Freshwater Fishery Biology*, 272.
4. Greene, "Lake Trout," D-11.
5. Scott and Crossman, *Freshwater Fishes of Canada*, 223.
6. Roush, *Enjoying Fishing Lake Tahoe, the Truckee River, and Pyramid Lake*, 188–189.
7. Gierach, "Snowbird and the Kazan: Still Pumping Out Big Fish."

8. "Cover Story: Lake Trout Release," 7.

9. Frederickson, "For the Record . . . ," 9.

10. "Potential New IGFA All-Tackle Record," 4.

11. Brown, personal telephone conference, 1993.

12. *World Record Game Fishes*, International Game Fish Association, 1999 ed., 142.

13. Henderson, "Anglers Hook Two World Records . . . ," 3D.

14. *Official World and U.S.A State Fresh Water Angling Records*, National Fresh Water Fishing Hall of Fame, 1999 ed., 66.

15. Ibid., 71.

16. Bilbey, personal correspondence, 1992.

17. Harback, "Reflections on Trips to Great Bear Lake in the Northwest Territories," 1992 (audiocassette recording).

18. Ibid.

19. Harback, "Reflections on Trips to Great Bear Lake in the Northwest Territories," 1992 (audiocassette recording); Harback, "Trophy Lodge: 901 Lbs. of Fish in One Day and a New World Record," 1991 (videocassette recording).

20. Ibid.

21. *Official World and U.S.A State Fresh Water Angling Records*, National Fresh Water Fishing Hall of Fame, 1999 ed., 60–76.

22. For Alberta: *Alberta Guide to Sportfishing*, 1993 ed., 50; for Manitoba: *Manitoba Fishing and Hunting Adventures*, 1993 ed., 19; for Northwest Territories: "Canadian National Fish Registry," 56; for Ontario: *Ontario Record Fish Registry*, 1992; for Saskatchewan: *Saskatchewan Angler's Guide*, 1993–94 ed., 18; for Yukon Territory: Thompson, personal correspondence, 1993.

23. *World Record Game Fishes*, International Game Fish Association, 1999 ed., 158–159.

24. Ibid., 191.

25. Brown, correspondence to Bull, 1996; "Canadian National Fish Registry," 56; *Official World and U.S.A. State Fresh Water Angling Records*, National Fresh Water Fishing Hall of Fame, 1999 ed., 36; Leech, correspondence to Bull, 1997.

26. Bull, personal telephone conference, 1997.

27. Bull, "Catching the 72¼ Pound Current World Record Lake Trout," 1–3.

28. Brown, correspondence to Bull, 1996; Bull, personal telephone conference, 1997; *World Record Game Fishes*, International Game Fish Association, 1998 ed., 134.

29. Leech, correspondence to Bull, 1997.

30. Bull, personal correspondence, 1997.

31. Bull, "Those Giant Fish of the Arctic," 6.

32. Ibid.

SIX

HELPING HANDS

> Treat your fishing guide exactly the way you'd want to be treated. Believe me, it pays off every time.
>
> —Carl Malz
> Managing Editor
> *Fishing Facts*

For a host of reasons, most anglers who dwell in the Northern Hemisphere do their fishing in the summer. Summertime is the usual vacation period and the season when optimal weather conditions prevail. Lake trout do their traveling in summer also, especially those that inhabit waters south of about 55 degrees north latitude. These cold-water fish can find their comfort zone in the shallows during fall, winter, and spring, but must retreat to deep water in summer for their desired water temperature. While trout dwelling in the frigid lakes and rivers of Canada's Northwest, Nunavut, and Yukon Territories may be located near the surface in midsummer and are therefore easier to catch, moderate-climate forktails, because of their penchant for a summer holiday in the depths, can present a serious angling challenge. Unless one is an expert, to consistently fool them, help may be needed—possibly in the form of a professional guide.

Of course, guides can be utilized by anglers visiting northern Canada, too, even though lake trout are plentiful. For a large lake, such as island-peppered Nueltin, unescorted trout-seekers unfamiliar with this 120-mile-long (193 km) waterway could experience difficulty in finding fish at times, at least in significant numbers and size. Practiced guides can place them in the most productive trophy localities.

A fundamental element for satisfying summer lake trouting is teamwork. Like an athletic team that is more effective working together to benefit the group—rather than pursuing selfish interests as individuals—an expert guide's intimate fishing and boating knowledge imparted to a pair of appreciative anglers makes for a successful combination. A competent laker guide does the following:

- Prepares thoroughly for the outing;
- Handles the boat and motor efficiently;
- Designates laker hot spots;
- Watches the electronic fish-finder screen;
- Suggests techniques, including methods and lures;
- Nets and weighs fish, removes hooks, and returns forktails to the water;
- Does not fish unless requested to do so by the paying angler;
- Leads the way through unfamiliar waters, such as fast-flowing, obstacle-infested rivers;
- Demonstrates a history of the area;
- Supports angler photography;
- Facilitates side trips;
- Provides a shore lunch, if desired;
- Keeps all boaters safe and aware of their location;

- Practices appropriate first aid and lifesaving measures;
- Accommodates angler idiosyncrasies (and vice versa!);
- Knows who is providing the employment and includes the client in fishing decisions (especially so with experienced anglers);
- Enables vacationing fishers to concentrate solely on the sport of catching gray trout, maximizing quality time on the water.

Guided, world-class laker fishing is available to anglers transported by chartered turboprop aircraft to isolated lodges in northern Canada offering full accommodations. Experienced, unguided lake trouters also may visit remote outpost camps reached by float plane from complete-service fly-in resorts at large wilderness lakes, such as Nueltin, Nejanilini in northern Manitoba, and Obre in the Northwest Territories.

The services of a professional guide are recommended for most first-time visitors to laker haunts like these, especially those inexperienced in the ways of the trout. The advantages of a luxury resort lodge in Canada's far north may include more than the amenities of home:

- Private modern cabins, each with lavatory and shower;
- Comfortable, roomy boats with high-powered outboards and fish locators;
- Home-cooked meals served in cozy, full-service dining room;
- A professional staff that includes lodge management, guides, chefs, maids, and maintenance personnel;
- A fully-stocked tackle shop and store;
- A classic Canadian shore lunch;

- Fly-out services to area lakes;
- Short walking or tractor portages to various bodies of water;
- A toll-free or satellite telephone line;
- Experienced native guide services;
- A relaxed and informal atmosphere.

Looks tempting, doesn't it? It should! After all, a complete personal service package such as this provides the angler with first-rate lake trouting—the adventure of a lifetime. All the visitor need bring is fishing tackle, clothing, and individualized items, such as a camera, film, and sunglasses. Everything else is provided by the lodge.

However, there is certainly something to be said for out-camp laker fishing where, because of the seclusion, experienced guides are not normally included as part of the outfitter's scaled-down package. While the outpost angler may lack the benefits of a deluxe resort lodge, he or she can savor exploration of virgin waters at less cost; relish the freedom to choose fishing hours; embrace unspoiled, spectacular scenery; and delight in seeing not another soul all day. For the intrepid lake trout enthusiast, the advantages of prime outposts include:

- Fewer anglers in camp, and therefore less fishing pressure (often, indeed, only one out-camp per lake);
- One or more plain, comfortable cabins (with a central shower and well-equipped kitchen, if more than one cabin);
- Availability of a full line of fresh foodstuffs;
- Radio communication with main lodge or base camp;
- Short portage, river, or float plane access to nearby lakes;

- Small cabins at more remote locations on the principal lake or nearby waters for overnight stays there;
- Camping equipment for further exploration;
- Presence of a camp manager to service boats and motors, supply basic tackle, cut wood, prepare meals (sometimes at extra cost), direct anglers to most fruitful trout areas, and otherwise assist vacationing out-campers.

Recently, the authors seriously considered a trip to Treeline Lodge, the principal resort, or to an outpost at huge, island-sprinkled Nueltin Lake, which stretches spread-eagled from northwestern Manitoba into Nunavut Territory. The lake, shaped somewhat like a giant, partially melted hourglass, includes two out-camps along its 120-mile (193 km) reach. One camp, situated at Nueltin Narrows, the cinched waist between the upper and lower hourglass chambers, lies about 36 air miles (58 km) north of Treeline. The second outpost, Windy River, is positioned in the upper cavity, some 63 miles (101 km) by air from the main lodge. While both of these outposts accessed an enormous amount of seldom-fished water, the more isolated Windy River camp appealed to our adventurousness. However, we decided that it was probably better to first visit Treeline Lodge, where veteran guides were available to teach anglers Nueltin's particular trout tactics. This prior instruction should enhance the success of unguided fishing later at Windy River.

The Windy River outpost, a comfortable, well-equipped complex constructed at the mouth of the river of the same name, accommodated only ten anglers per week during the short, ten-week season. Most out-campers were content to fish nearby Smith Bay, a huge chunk of water about 17 miles

(27.3 km) long and 6 miles (9.6 km) wide at one point, into which the snaking Windy River empties from the west. Venturesome anglers plied the main Nueltin Lake each year, with a few ranging as far north as Fox Narrows (named for seventeenth century Arctic explorer Luke Fox), Hammerhead Bay to the east, and the vicinity of Esker Island to the south. Even fewer each summer navigated the 20-mile (32.2 km) stretch of river to Windy Lake, a spidery-configured body of water extending northward some 35 miles (56.3 km), reached only by boat, float plane, or lengthy portage from Nueltin. Lake trout, Arctic grayling, and northern pike abounded in all these cold, pristine waters, with most trophy trout found in Nueltin.[1]

However, for personal reasons, the reservation for our much-anticipated stay at Nueltin had to be postponed for the time being. We look forward eagerly to visiting Nueltin and other productive lakes in northern Canada, the mother lode of lake trouting.

Our out-camp or lodge strategy is to find out as much as possible about the fly-in lake or lakes to be visited before we get there. With a government topographic map and notepad in hand, we have penned numerous letters and logged dozens of long distance and satellite phone calls over the years to outfitters, lodge owners, and other anglers to obtain precise information about prime habitat, seasonal methods, and lures designed to grab the gray trout.

For northwestern Ontario, we not only carefully study topographic maps of trout lakes for which guides are not available, such as Cleveland, Sturgeon, Dragon, and Cherrington, but also familiarize ourselves with the entire surrounding region, in this case the Red Lake district. This vast area includes hundreds of lakes, many holding trout. According to local sources, excellent forktail fisheries reached only by float plane comprise North Spirit, Donald, McInnes, Deer, Roderick, Trout, Birch, and Sydney Lakes. Some of these wild waters embrace solitary outposts with boat rentals and guide services provided by different outfitters. All may be reached easily from bush pilot Rob Rowe's Pakwash base near Red Lake. One-way flying distances to these trout lakes range from 24 miles (38.6 km) to 136 miles (218.8 km). We employed the services of a guide with blue ribbon results while visiting the Trout Lake Lodge island outpost for the first time on a one-day fly-in in 1997.

Other than advance preparation for a fly-in to a remote lake without a guide, invaluable assistance may be provided by a professional outfitter or bush pilot, whose task it is to be familiar with waters fished by his or her clientele. Rob Rowe, who has ably filled both roles for us for a number of years, has supplied us with a particular courtesy—help that is inestimable, especially when visiting waters for the first time. When approaching the lake to be visited by float plane, it is Rowe's practice to explore the body of water from an altitude of about 500 feet (152.4 m), pointing out productive fishing spots, dangerously shallow reefs, portages to walk-in lakes, and other points of interest.

When our bush flight aboard his Cessna 206 reached Meandrine Lake on our first visit several years ago, Rowe first probed by air the lake's river-like, labyrinthine pattern. This tour accomplished, our pilot then flew over Cherrington, a cold, walk-in trout lake reached by a short portage. Rowe identified the water edge of a steep cliff that sank into deep water along Cherrington's southwestern shore as a promising place for forktail trolling. A few days later, we outboarded to the location indicated earlier by our pilot. Within five minutes of beginning to troll parallel to the precipice, not more than 50 feet (15.2 m) from shore, Shickler caught a ten-pound (4.5 kg) gray on a bait eagerly recommended by Rowe, a small Thompson Spoon.

On our initial fly-in to Sturgeon (Upper Kilburn) Lake, in Ontario's Woodland Caribou Provincial Park on the Manitoba border, Rowe indicated from the pilot's seat a prime laker trolling spot between a small island and the southern shoreline. The area pointed out by our bush pilot turned out to be swarming with full-bodied, frisky forktails, and we later boated dozens of them. During one-day visits in subsequent years, we determined that trout could be caught virtually anywhere in the lake.[2]

By the time Rowe flew us to the new Cleveland Lake outcamp in 1991, we had figured out a way to pack a portable fish-finder along with all our gear and groceries. Rowe showed us from the air some deep water that stretched about a mile (1.6 km) from the island cabin to Cleveland's northeastern shore, as good territory for laker trolling. While this advice turned out to be sound—our biggest forktails usually have been hooked in this section of the lake—the sonar equipment located large concentrations of fish in troughs elsewhere previously unknown to the outfitter.

A few years ago we visited Cleveland Lake in the fall. According to our outfitter, the rocky shoals bordering a small island off the northern shore had proven in the past to be a spot where spawning trout congregated. Using a casting lure enthusiastically recommended by Rowe, a flashing Doctor Spoon, we caught many of these feisty fall forktails in the chilly shallows, their brilliant autumnal hues harmonizing with Cleveland's boreal palette of color.

Teamwork, as previously noted, is the secret of success when hunting lake trout. Since we have fished and worked together over thirty years, individual habits are well known, and we function smoothly as angling teammates. To facilitate

Sheep Creek Bay, Flaming Gorge Reservoir, Utah/Wyoming. While the reservoir is renowned as a lake trout fishery, the Flaming Gorge area is famous for its spectacular scenery, impressive geology, and absorbing human history. *Courtesy of Larry Friedman, Wilderness Concepts*

Jackson Lake, located in Grand Teton National Park, Wyoming. Lake trout fry, transplanted from Michigan to nearby Yellowstone Park lakes in 1890, drifted via the Lewis and Snake Rivers to Jackson Lake, where the fish are now established.

South-central Utah's Fish Lake, where lake trout were first stocked in 1906, owes its existence to geological forces deep within the Earth. *Courtesy of Kreig Rasmussen, wildlife biologist, Fishlake National Forest*

A summer sunrise at transboundary Nueltin Lake. Nueltin, home to world class lake trout fishing, is Canada's original catch-and-release lake. A large bay is named for British explorer and fur trader Samuel Hearne who discovered the huge body of water in 1770–72 while searching for a western passage.

View of northern New York's Lake Placid from the summit of Whiteface Mountain. Placid is known for its high water quality and abundant wild lake trout population. A maximum depth of 150 feet (45.7 m) supports trophy laker development. *Courtesy of Peter Finger, Lake Placid, Essex County Visitors Bureau*

Veteran Great Bear Lake angler Lloyd Bull hoists a replica mount of his 72 pound (32.65 kg) record-breaking lake trout, caught at Great Bear Lake, Northwest Territories, in 1995. The giant fish, following photographing, measuring, and certified weighing, was successfully revived. *Courtesy of Lloyd Bull*

A late-September forktail enticed by an Arbogast Doctor spoon.

A feisty laker taken on an Eppinger Huskie Devle spoon. Quality, outboard motor-powered inflatable boats are particularly adapted to fishing smaller fly-in lakes like this one in northwestern Ontario's Woodland Caribou Park. Regulations may not permit outfitters to store boats at many lakes in national, provincial, or state parks.

Northwestern Ontario's fly-in Cleveland Lake, home of lake trout, walleye, and northern pike, extends some seven miles (11.3 km) in length. The deepest water is found in the basin at the right fronting the narrow channel stretching toward the horizon.

Trolling with lead-core line for forktails at Cleveland Lake in northwestern Ontario. Excellent for intermediate-depth trolling, this versatile line can access water from shallow to quite deep simply by controlling the amount of lead-core dragged behind the boat. Weight may be added as needed.

A downrigger trailed by a Huskie Devle spoon delivered this 25-pound (11.3 kg) lake trout from the depths of northern Canada's Nueltin Lake. Nueltin achieved catch-and-release status in 1979.

Charger Spoon, made by Lake Products Company Manufacturing, Imlay City, Michigan. *Courtesy of Dean Lester Photography, Long Beach, California*

Huskie Devle, made by Eppinger Manufacturing Company, Dearborn, Michigan. *Courtesy of Dean Lester Photography, Long Beach, California*

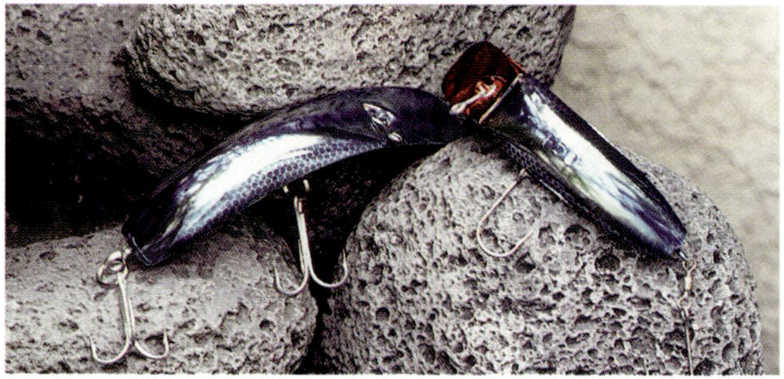

Flatfish, made by Worden's Lures/Yakima Bait Company, Granger, Washington. *Courtesy of Dean Lester Photography, Long Beach, California*

Kwikfish, made by Luhr Jensen & Sons, Hood River, Oregon. *Courtesy of Dean Lester Photography, Long Beach, California*

Rapala Lures, distributed by Normark Corporation, Minnetonka, Minnesota. *Courtesy of Dean Lester Photography, Long Beach, California*

Red Eye Wiggler, made by Eppinger Manufacturing Company, Dearborn, Michigan. *Courtesy of Dean Lester Photography, Long Beach, California*

Thompson Spoon, made by Thompson-Pallister Bait Company, Ltd., Lacombe, Alberta. *Courtesy of Dean Lester Photography, Long Beach, California*

Williams Spoons, made by Breck's International, Sherbrooke, Quebec. *Courtesy of Dean Lester Photography, Long Beach, California*

a fine-tuned collaboration, we maintain an uncluttered boat, with four or five rods each for trolling, casting, or jigging placed neatly in the bow and stern. A long-handled, deep, wide-mouthed net is stowed in the bow end of the port side. Both of our large tackle boxes rest in closed position while we fish. Wires or strings stretched along both sides of the boat hold one or two examples of our most frequently used lures. The chart-plotter/fish-finder normally rests on the middle seat where either one of us has access to it. Shickler, seated in the stern, operates the motor and trolls the port side. Eveland, positioned in the bow, fishes the starboard position. Thus situated, we're prepared to spring into action in the event of a strike.

When a lake trout slams a trolled lure, especially one with a barbless hook or hooks, it is essential that a tight line be sustained. To facilitate doing so, Eveland suggested continuing to operate the motor at a slow speed with a gray on the line. The moment one of us hooks a fish, the other angler, after retrieving his lure, reaches for the net. These procedures usually work out well, even when other factors may intervene to complicate matters while fighting a fleshy forktail.

While terms such as cooperation, collaboration, association, and combination serve to define teamwork as a blending of qualities to promote a common interest, another element can be added to our definition. Successful teamwork also includes a mental bond or connection between individuals. We can turn to athletics for examples of what we mean, and relate these instances to fishing.

In baseball or softball, a defensive player, alert to the particular game situation, knows precisely what to do with the ball should it be hit to him or her. Such basic game strategy can move to a higher level of teamwork. Like the second baseman and shortstop who spontaneously and gracefully link together on a scintillating double play, or the football quarterback and receiver who instinctively and artistically join to perfectly execute a difficult pass maneuver, two experienced anglers may intuitively and expertly team up in the sport of fishing.

This tie-up is illustrated in Howard Levy's enjoyable book, *Man against Musky*. Levy provides a fascinating account of a crucial decision reached when both he and a fishing guest, Gil McPherson, simultaneously battled big muskies while trolling western New York's Chautauqua Lake.[3] Because of impending twilight, strong gusts of wind buffeting the boat's prow, the danger of crossed lines, and line rapidly disappearing from his own reel, Levy decided upon a course of action that he had carefully planned previously while considering the possibility of comparable situations. Grabbing a yellow boat cushion–life preserver, he looped it around the big reel and through the butt of the handle of his 12-foot (3.7 m) Calcutta cane rod, and, with a prodigious heave, threw the rod, reel, and cushion into the lake.

As the yellow cushion sped away from the boat, Levy then gave his full attention to helping McPherson capture his massive muskie. But the generous gesture didn't succeed. The guest's fish eventually escaped by draping the line around the water-soaked branches of a huge sunken tree. Early the next morning, Levy found his seat cushion, rod, reel, line, and deep-diving jointed Pikie Minnow—sans muskie—floating peacefully among thick lily pads and water weeds deep in a pocket of Whitney Bay back of Prendergast Point. His equipment's resting place turned out to be about half a mile (.80 km) from where it had been jettisoned the previous evening.

We have discussed at length applications such as these over the years, giving rise to particular strategies that might be useful under certain angling conditions.

In the Levy illustration above, the concurrent battles for a brace of bruising muskies presented a dilemma for the two anglers. Both fish unfortunately had vanished by the time the encounter reached a conclusion. Had a guide been present on Levy's cruiser, might the story have had a different ending? Maybe. Rodney Harback, who set an IGFA all-tackle mark for the colossus of lake trouting, a 66.5-pounder (30.16 kg) boated at Great Bear Lake in 1991, has experienced double forktail hookups numerous times over the years at that lake. He has shared with us videotaped episodes in which a pair of fishermen simultaneously fought trout weighing 25 to 30 pounds (11.3 to 13.6 kg). A bothered and bewildered guide was shown attempting to determine which brawling fish to net first, or whether both mighty scrappers could fit at the same time into a net wholly inadequate in size. On several occasions, at least one gray has broken free. Because of Harback's thorough familiarity with Great Bear's waters, his guide serves more as facilitator than trout finder. The guide's boat-keeping duties are limited to operating the craft and motor; netting, unhooking, weighing, and releasing fish; and assisting with photography. Record-breaker Lloyd Bull, with 29 years of Great Bear lake trouting experience, indeed no longer employs a guide when fishing those waters.

On a cool, blustery, gray summer morning several years ago, the authors deep-trolled the eastern portion of northwestern Ontario's Cleveland Lake. The aluminum craft heaved and rolled as we pushed into a crisp northwest wind that whipped up whitecaps. Despite the strong breeze and threatening skies, our expectations were high; this particular track had produced good fish on previous trolls. Suddenly, a terrific strike nearly jerked the rod from Shickler's grip, yanking his left shoulder forcibly against the motor shroud. A hefty laker, seizing the large Thompson Spoon, felt the sting of the barbless hooks and the tension of the rod, and fought gamely.

While Eveland retrieved his lure and eyed the net, Shickler battled the big trout while endeavoring to maneuver the bouncing boat in the rough water. Several minutes passed with reel cranking barely gaining on drag braking. As waves splashed over the bow, footing on the wet deck became treacherous. An exchange of glances communicated a need for teamwork based on associated experience and a previously pondered course of action. Like the athletic and angling instances related earlier, our next move followed a premeditated strategy. Realizing that his double duty might cost him the trout—or worse, possibly precipitate a boating mishap—Shickler spontaneously handed his throbbing Shimano rod to his anticipative partner so that Eveland could fight the fish, freeing him to concentrate on handling the craft and motor. Following a 15-minute battle, Eveland played the fat forktail alongside the boat and Shickler netted a dandy dark-bodied lake trout. After a quick photograph, Eveland released the respected combatant by gently propelling the fish into the water at a sharp angle to facilitate a rapid return to the comfort of Cleveland's depths.

Additional authoritative advice on whether or not to obtain the services of a professional guide may be in order. A valuable insight comes from John Herrmann, a Nueltin veteran who visited that lake three times in the 1990s, twice sojourning at Treeline, the lavish lodge at the lake's southern end, and once staying at the remote Windy River out-camp.

Concerning the experience at Treeline, where guiding is included in the package, Herrmann says he learned much from highly regarded native guides—highly skilled as anglers and boatmen—and is convinced that more and larger lake trout are caught with professional help, even at an outstanding fishery like Nueltin. He finds the principal difference between Treeline and Windy River, other than the obvious disparity between wilderness resort luxury and out-camp basics, to be the manner in which the day's activities are scheduled. At the principal lodge, major meals are provided at fixed times, leaving opportunities on the water usually limited to the interval between breakfast and dinner. Subtracting the time needed for a boat ride to and from fruitful fishing areas—as much as an hour each way—along with a midday break for shore lunch, quality trouting hours are relatively few.

However, this "drawback" (depending upon one's point of view) can be circumvented by coupling angler imagination with lodge adaptation. For fishermen who desire more time on the lake, resort staff can prepare a delicious box lunch and dinner. An additional charge is levied for Chipewyan or Cree guiding services after the supper hour. Convenient light-tackle fishing for lakers, grayling, or northern pike following the evening meal, or at other times, may be found at the rapids where the Thlewiaza River tumbles into Nueltin's foot, about a mile (1.6 km) southwest of the lodge. The Thlewiaza flows northward through Nueltin's length, then surges east nearly 200 miles (441 km) before discharging into Hudson Bay. It is worth remembering that there are 24 hours of daylight nearly all of July at this latitude, with Nueltin's northern extremity only 380 miles (611.4 km) below the Arctic Circle. Although most Treeline visitors are probably satisfied with the lodge timetable—the resort experiences a high level of repeat clientele—anglers wishing more fishing hours certainly have ample opportunities and time to fulfill this desire, especially during the first few weeks of the season.

In contrast to Treeline Lodge, the remote Nueltin Narrows and Windy River outposts offer freedom of choice.

Experienced anglers have the option to fish on their own, whenever or wherever they prefer. Small, competent staffs prepare breakfast, dinner, and box lunches daily as part of the fly-in package. Camp managers will point out the most productive fishing spots, and can provide personal guiding for an added fee. Lake trouting advice is also readily available from other guests, many of whom are out-camp returnees.

Herrmann and his buddy, Marty Hamar, enjoyed the flexibility offered at Windy River to choose unguided angling times; cook/pack (or skip) meals; observe at close range the incredible variety of Arctic fauna and flora; sleep late, if desired; explore unspoiled tundra, geological formations, and unchartered islands; pilot their own boat; and fish untouched waters. In short, the out-camp scene enables guests to slow the pace in a setting of breathtaking scenery undisturbed by human activity.

So, should you obtain expert assistance in the quest for lake trout, or fish without professional help? Perhaps some final questions can lead us to answers.

Does the angler's experience, particularly in lake trouting, affect trip planning?

If the visitor's practical knowledge of freshwater fishing is somewhat limited, specifically in terms of forktail angling, an experienced guide can lead him or her to productive fishing locations, helping to ensure a safe and successful trip. Even if skilled as a laker angler, it might be wise either to employ a seasoned guide for a trip to unfamiliar waters or to fish with a colleague well acquainted with the lake or river in question. If the visit extends beyond a day or two, professional aid may not be needed to successfully fish a particular waterway for the balance of the stay. However, even if the angler is sophisticated concerning lake trouting ways, using a capable guide can provide a more enjoyable, trouble-free fishing experience. In any case, first-time visitors to a lake should be aware that watery environments differ to some extent and expert guidance can significantly increase lake trouting success.

The advantages of obtaining the services of a guide for one-day fly-ins to new waters were never more evident to us than in recent years. In June 1997, outfitter Rob Rowe flew us to Trout Lake, a large water body for northwestern Ontario, and the second of three lakes visited by float plane during a week's stay. Rowe had arranged our guide, Jason Green, through the management of Trout Lake Lodge, a full-service island outpost in the north-central area of the clear, cold lake. While familiar with the method for taking forktails here—spoon-trolling—the choice fishing spots were unknown to us. Our guide pointed out the best trolling runs, especially the western side of a rocky, wooded, somewhat egg-shaped island about a mile (1.6 km) from the lodge. The parallel troll proved a terrific producer, and we could have boated 50 or more stout lakers had we chosen to remain in that location.

However, we wanted to learn as much about the lake as possible during our brief visit and encouraged Green to try Trout's more northerly reaches. Our guide not only motored us to additional excellent trout spots, but probably kept us from losing our way. Had we been on our own, we might have become disoriented by variable weather that brought view-obscuring scattered showers and thunderstorms, and by unfamiliar waters characterized by more than 200 miles of shoreline, nearly 400 islands, and numerous look-alike bays.

How about cost of a fishing vacation?

If the angler wants or needs a guide, wishes to be pampered in the wild, and finds that price of the trip is not a particular problem, the luxury resort approach to lake trouting is one answer. Even if not booked at one of northern Canada's well-known, full-service resorts, a stay at a top-rated, less famous location that provides guide services should be fully satisfactory in terms of trip cost and trouting productivity. Because outpost visits are usually unguided and anglers—normally gray trout veterans—may prepare their own meals and generally rough it, expenses for a trip of this type are considerably less than for a stay at a facility with complete accommodations. As we have seen, a wilderness out-camp offers scenic remoteness, reduced fishing pressure, and freedom from time constraints—wilderness advantages difficult to assign a dollar value.

What are the lake trouter's trip options?

The giants of northern Canada's resort industry offer both luxury lodges and excellent outpost facilities for the discriminating lake trout angler. Fly-outs to superb walleye and northern pike fishing grounds are available from Great Slave Lake Lodge in the Northwest Territories. North of Great Slave, Great Bear's Trophy Lodge packages day or overnight trips to outposts at Neiland Bay, situated between McTavish and McVicar arms, and to the Coppermine and Tree Rivers for Arctic char. Great Slave and Great Bear, of course, both are outstanding lake trout fisheries.

Manitoba's Nejalini Lodge (on Nejanilini Lake) provides out-camps at Baralzon, Brownstone, McLeod, and Monroe Lakes for additional lake trout, grayling, and northern pike fishing. North of Sixty Fishing Lodges, Ltd., in the Northwest Territories offers outposts at Anaunethad, Wholdaia, and Flett Lakes to supplement angling for trout, grayling, and pike found at Obre Lake, where the main resort is positioned. Nueltin's Treeline Lodge, in northern Manitoba, includes two out-camps in Nunavut Territory, where the major portion of the lake rests. The lodges and outposts associated with Nejanilini, Obre (which connects with famed Snowbird Lake), and Nueltin feature barbless hook, catch-and-release fishing.

All of luxury trout fishing vacations at these lodges include direct transportation by chartered jet from Edmonton, Winnipeg, or Saskatoon, to private airstrips at the resorts. For those seeking other alternatives, hundreds—perhaps thousands—of outfitters in the United States and Canada offer a variety of attractive arrangements for guided and unguided lake trout trips, with camps and resorts reached by automobile, float plane, or turboprop aircraft. These helpful entrepreneurs may be located through advertisements in various periodicals, Internet Websites, angling articles in newspapers and magazines, state, provincial, and territorial fishing publications, local sport shows, and word of mouth. Many camp and resort managers adhere either to a voluntary or a mandatory barbless hook, catch-and-release policy, with only small fish kept for any shore lunches.

The guiding issue is many-sided, and whether or not to obtain professional assistance ultimately becomes a matter of personal preference. We hope that this background may help to clarify the subject as it relates to the angler's hunt for the freshwater prince of predators, *Salvelinus namaycush*.

Notes

1. Nueltin information was obtained through numerous conversations with Treeline Lodge administrators generous with their time, Garry and Lois Gurke, owners, and Shawn Gurke, operations manager, in 1995–99; lake trout angler John Herrmann in 1991–97; and various resort brochures and newsletters (*Nueltin News*), in 1991–99. Acquired in similar fashion in 1991–97 is material appearing elsewhere in this chapter on Great Bear, Great

Slave, and Nueltin Lakes. Information supplied by the management of the North of Sixty lake system, Nejanilini, and waters in northwestern Ontario covers the years 1987–93, 1990–94, and 1986-98, respectively.

2. No longer permitted to keep a boat at a lake in the provincial park, Rowe now transports by air—on each visit to Sturgeon (or Upper Kilburn) along with two anglers, tackle, an outboard motor, and other equipment—a roll-away inflatable boat. The roomy, comfortable, stable, rigid-floored Zodiac inflatable goes from storage bag to water in a matter of minutes.

3. Levy, *Man against Musky*, 203-211. A veteran muskie fisherman, whose varied repertoire includes a healthy dose of patience in the pursuit of these elusive and wary denizens, readily grasps that such an occurrence—two mighty muskies hooked at the same time by two anglers in the same boat—is indeed a rare experience.

SEVEN

AN OUTPOST FLY-IN: PREPARATIONS AND EXPECTATIONS

Plan ahead, nail it down, and get the whole ball of wax.

—Anonymous

Next to fishing, the preparation for a trip, particularly a one-week fly-in to a remote Canadian gray trout lake, is the most important aspect. Once at the outpost, the angler may be there for a week—virtually alone, with no source of supplies, no telephone, no fax machine, no television set, no pantry loaded with goodies, no clothing or tackle stores, no maid service. The fisher has only primitive beauty, boats and boating equipment, a place to sleep and prepare food, a refuge from rain, snow, bears, mosquitoes, and the like. Most of what is needed for an outpost stay must be brought with the visitor.

The authors usually begin preparing for a trip shortly after returning from one. Although a year away, the anticipation is heightened both by talking about the next trip and by planning it. The following discussion and anecdotes are not meant in any way to discourage the reader. Although there are a myriad of details and careful organization to complete, the preparation is fun. Moreover, the more fun—preparation—experienced, the more successful the fly-in fishing trip will be. We can offer the reader one assurance: A smooth, trouble-free week of successful angling for forktails on a breathtakingly beautiful northern lake will provide much satisfaction for a year—for some, even a lifetime.

For purposes of clarity and familiarity, the one-week fly-in we shall use as an example is a trip to Cleveland Lake in northwestern Ontario, to which the authors have traveled five times. The island outpost cabin, built in 1991, represents the very latest in this kind of facility. It contains most of the creature comforts one could ask for: propane cooking, food cooling; hot water heating for sink and shower; a roomy, well-organized kitchen; two big bedrooms; a modern, wood-burning firebox; and satellite telephone. A roof-mounted solar unit generates power to pump lake water to the sink and heating tank. Completing the out-camp are a cozy out-house and small storage shack containing extra motors, gasoline containers, propane cylinders, landing nets, some tackle, spark plugs, boat seats, cushions, and various tools. Obviously, this is a place for gentleman and gentlewoman living! Any woman known to us, who enjoys fishing, would be more than comfortable at the Cleveland out-camp. Although most outpost cabins for fly-in fishing trips are not this "luxurious," the preparations for staying there are the same as for most outcamps.

First, let's discuss bedding and related needs. Cabins normally will have beds and mattresses, but in most cases no blankets, sheets, or pillows. Bring whatever is needed to assure satisfactory sleeping. The choice depends, to a great extent, upon the time of year. If the visit comes just after ice-out or at spawning time, the weather can become quite cold. Anglers may experience snow, even blizzard conditions. The midsummer months can be variously hot or cold, dry or wet, calm or windy. At times, sheets alone would be comfortable; at other times, a heavy sleeping bag or several blankets would be necessary. The angler should be prepared for the best and worst of weather. We recommend the present-day sleeping bags—lightweight but well insulated, ones that compress into a stuff sack or small roll, occupying as little baggage space as possible.

Sheets and pillows are the visitor's choices. Cotton sheets work best in the summer, and flannel ones in May, June, late August, and September. One pillow should be sufficient; those preferring more elevation can use clothing or even empty canvas bags under the pillow. Again, less baggage space is taken.

Sleeping attire will, of course, depend on whether women have joined the fly-in party or if some anglers, for instance, want to impress male fishing buddies by donning colorful silk pajamas. Select whatever best promotes sleeping. Be sure to bring sandals, slippers, or go-aheads. A night trip to the outhouse doesn't lend itself to barefooting. Another important item is a "thunderbucket." A cabin pail for relieving oneself is a handy and easy substitute for a trek through the woods in the dark to the privy, especially if bears have been observed in the vicinity of camp. (Don't worry; bears want to avoid anglers as much as we want to avoid them.) Night venturing can also result in injury.

Next, let's consider clothing. If the fly-in is to last a week, even if the angler likes to really rough it, seven days is a very long time to wear a single outfit. While the traveler may be a tough, macho type, the anglers are sharing living quarters and a boat. Their likes and dislikes may differ greatly from one another. Furthermore, variations in weather conditions make it unlikely that garments will remain dry for the entire week.

Shorts and a T-shirt may be appropriate, even comfortable, at times. At other times, long johns, long pants, heavy socks, boots, and sheepskin or down-filled coats may be necessary. Be prepared, both in variety and number, for all possible conditions. Fortunately, except for boots and heavy jackets, clothes will usually consume little baggage space.

Good rain gear is indispensable. Waterproof and windproof Gore-Tex tops and bottoms—those that draw tight around the ankles and neck, with hoods—are excellent. These comfortable rain suits, easy to put on and take off, are lightweight, breathable, and assure maximum freedom and ease of movement—a must for fishing in the rain. A word of caution, though: Move quickly off the water at any sign of thunder or lightning. Fishing rods, the boat (usually aluminum), and the body make all-too-attractive electrical conductors, especially in the middle of a spacious lake. Rainwear should routinely be stored in the boat when fishing, as thunderstorms in northern Canada can develop quickly. Usually there isn't enough time to hustle back to the cabin to don rain gear, leaving the angler soaked by the time shore is reached. So another outfit of clothes will be needed, like it or not.

Thunderstorms of great power are legendary in northern Canada. British naval officer George Back, who joined John Franklin for two Arctic land expeditions during the 1820s, provided a colorful journal description of an intense thunder and lightning storm while he was encamped along the Slave River, north of Lake Athabasca, on July 18, 1820:

> At 6^{h} 40^{m} PM in consequence of an approaching storm, we were obliged to put up in a low marshy ground abounding in small willow and pine. . . . The men were scarcely sheltered under the canoes and our tents erected, than a thunder storm (unequalled by any I had yet seen) broke over us and discharged itself in torrents—

> the swamp was soon overflowed and we had the pleasure of enjoying our savoury meal . . . ankle deep in mud—In the mean time the lightening was more vivid and the peals of thunder more constant—a pale blue flash shewed us at one instant our situation and the next left us in gloomy darkness to meditate on it—(had we been so inclined).[1]

Depending upon how far we must travel from the cabin to fish, we usually carry our lightweight Gore-Tex rain jackets and pants with us in the boat, stuffed into small, waterproof, drawstring bags along with other clothing items. Since Shickler operates the motor and usually has his feet in any water that has collected in the stern, he wears Sperry Top-Sider mid-shin rubber sailing boots with non-skid soles over one or two pairs of wool socks, rain or shine. With the pant bottoms tucked into the boot tops, fish odors, blood, and boat stains are confined to the exterior of the boots, which are easily cleaned. The rugged, durable boots also are handy when stepping on slick rocks to climb in and out of the boat. Eveland is usually content wearing Sperry slip-ons, also with non-skid soles, with silk socks inside wool socks to keep his feet comfortable and dry. If his slip-ons become wet, the cotton canvas uppers dry quickly on the breezy porch when we return to the cabin. Quality waterproof and packable rain suits constructed of material other than Gore-Tex fabric are, of course, available in various weights and construction to help brave the elements.

Because our rain suits normally are kept in the boat, storms seldom, if ever, catch us without proper cover. Rain pants pulled over rubber boots, and hooded jackets with drawstring bottoms, leave only face and hands exposed to a downpour. Even the face is shielded if a baseball-type cap is worn under the hood. Neoprene gloves keep hands warm and water-free. These gloves also can guard hands and fingers from annoying and often painful cuts and scratches inflicted by honed hook tips and attempts to grab a slippery, flopping lake trout equipped with a large mouth and razor-sharp teeth, spiny, skin-puncturing fins, and unblunted gill rakers.

When fishing in Canada, we have experienced all sorts of rainstorms. Once, a heavy thunderstorm enveloped us, despite our efforts to accelerate the Mercury outboard and outrun the downpour. The torrent nearly took one's breath away, and the volume of rain pelting on us, the aluminum boat, metal tackle boxes, and lake surface produced a cacophony that all but drowned out any verbal communication. Then, as suddenly as it had come, the storm passed, the sun reappeared, and we resumed trolling. In this instance, there hadn't been sufficient time to reach our distant outpost cabin. A nearby island would have afforded refuge, but the storm moved on before we could motor there. Forceful rains of this type should be viewed as a normal aspect of the area's climatic pattern, although they are relatively infrequent. With proper rain suit protection, the experience may be enthusiastically recounted later as an element of a memorable fishing vacation.

A few years ago, we spent four or five hours in a constant downpour at Cherrington Lake, reached by a short portage from Meandrine Lake where our outpost cabin was located. Although the wet screen of our portable fish/depth finder displayed big, bottom-dwelling forktails at about 70 feet (21.3 m), vertical jigging and deep trolling failed to entice any of these finicky lakers into striking. The trek back to Meandrine took us through spongy bogs, deep mud, trail streams, and drooping water-soaked pine branches that unloaded on us as we negotiated the soggy path. Our rain suits and rubber boots served us well that day.

On another occasion—a week's fly-in to Cleveland Lake in late September to pursue spawning lakers a few years ago—we had brought along heavy clothing, but weren't prepared mentally for an abrupt change in weather which we encountered. Fair skies and typically cool fall days and nights prevailed early in the trip. Then, at mid-week, a frontal band of thick, gray clouds moved into northwestern Ontario, bringing increasing winds and decreasing temperatures. We were battling big, rolling waves around noon, as we trolled with lead-core line in 60 feet (18.3 m) of water in front of our island cabin. Although dressed for it, the windchill shivered us. It was becoming difficult to maneuver the boat into the forceful wind, and the pronounced wave crests and troughs caused the outboard's spinning prop to lift out of the water. Our boat seemed to make little headway as it plunged and pounded through the sullen swells. The issue was quickly settled when slack lines told us that our large spoons were resting on the lake bottom! With lines retrieved, we quickly headed for the cabin, as a light cold rain sprayed us. Gray smoke billowing from the chimney told us that our companions, Roger Cronin and Ron Tessada, having earlier sought refuge from the approaching storm, had built a crackling fire in the wood stove to warm the cabin. We spent the rest of the afternoon playing cards or resting on our bunks in the cozy, well-built structure, as the weather continued to deteriorate.

Later in the afternoon, the view of the lake to the south revealed that the chilling blast from the northwest was driving rain at a low angle—almost parallel it seemed—to the heaving surface. By dinner time, the temperature had dropped to the freezing point and light snow swirled against the cabin's picture windows. Fortunately for us, Rob Rowe, the outfitter, had made sure that plenty of pine and birch logs were on hand to feed the efficient wood-burning firebox. We went to bed early, and Cronin dutifully kept the fire burning during the night by adding a couple of hefty logs every two hours or so. Before drifting off to sleep, the four of us spoke of our great respect for winter storms that could be quite severe in Canada. We recalled Thomas James's rich narrative of a harsh winter spent in 1631–32 at the southern end of the bay that bears his name, and which discouraged further British attempts to seek the fabled Northwest Passage for 100 years.[2] This time, however, the temperature inside the cabin was maintained at a comfortable 70° F (21° C), while we slept peacefully.

A four-inch (10.2 cm) snowfall from the departed storm, rivaling an idyllic winter postcard scene, greeted us when we awakened at about five o'clock the next morning. The outdoor thermometer affixed to the trunk of a snow-dusted pine near the porch read a chilling 25° F (–4° C). Following a hearty breakfast of bacon, crispy hash brown potatoes, eggs cooked to order, and steaming hot coffee prepared by Eveland, the camp chef, we piled on clothing for the day's fishing. What Shickler wore that frigid morning is vividly recollected: long underwear, top and bottom; two pairs of jeans, one of which was flannel-lined; two long-sleeved shirts, one fully lined, overlaid with a roomy sweatshirt; three pairs of heavy cotton/wool socks; hunting boots with leather tops and waterpoof rubber soles; a wool watch cap pulled down over the ears; hooded goose-down parka with a Gore-Tex shell; and wool gloves. We might have looked bloated, and moved about like penguins, but we were warm!

To reach the boats pulled up on the shore, we stepped gingerly over the glaciated granite that sloped toward the lake. Slippery after a summer rain, the hard, smooth rock was downright treacherous when iced at this time of the year.

After sweeping the powdery snow out of the two boats, we launched them and dipped our reels and rod guides into the lake to melt their icy coatings. With the Mercury outboard starting on the first pull, we hustled across the lake to a small island topped with contrasting verdant pine and white-trunked birch in orange and yellow fall plumage. (Our companions motored to Cleveland's western end to test the action there.) Through previous visits during the week, we had learned that spawning grays were moving in and out of the island's rocky shallows throughout the day, especially early in the morning. Casting Doctor spoons with medium-light action rods and ten-pound (4.5 kg) monofilament line toward shore, we quickly boated and released several struggling forktails displaying the brilliant colors of spawning brook trout.

Observing the fall/winter morning scene at seven-thirty, we remarked that it already had been a memorable day: an unexpected snowfall deposited by a fast-moving storm the previous night; Southern California anglers properly dressed for northwestern Ontario's climatic surprises; a great night's sleep in a warm, comfortable, and spacious cabin; and spawning lakers hungrily grabbing our barbless hook lures in the cool surface waters the next morning. With rising temperatures, nearly all of the season's first fall of snow had melted by mid-day, and we were able to remove most of the cumbersome clothing. Fair weather returned for the balance of what turned out to be a most unique and enjoyable lake trout fishing trip.

A hat or baseball-type cap that provides shade from the summer sun's rays is a must, along with a good sunscreen. The hazards of being on the water during a clear, sunny day are well known. In the summer months, as previously noted, the high temperature can be downright unbearable, even on a cold lake in northern Canada. Even an angler who tolerates the sun well shouldn't take chances. And it's a good idea to include a tube of Lanacane in the toilet kit, just in case. In addition, high quality, polarized sunglasses are an absolute must for the serious angler.

Having mentioned remedies such as sunscreen and Lanacane, we wish to stress the importance of preparing well in the event of sickness or mishaps—colds, flu, cuts, and bruises. If prescription drugs are taken, be sure to bring not only a week's supply but also enough for the trip to the lake and the return home. Containers now available for a long period of pill-taking away from home are ideal, especially if more than one medicine is taken or swallowed more than once during the day.

We also always bring the following items: Tylenol codeine (in the event of serious pain from injury), antibiotics, a good first-aid kit (sometimes supplied by the outfitter, but don't count on it), a sling, bandages for closing cuts or wounds, and aspirin (or whatever everyday pain depressant may be used). Some of these items may necessitate a call or visit to the doctor to either prescribe or provide them. Usually all that is needed to get the physician's cooperation is to explain that one is taking a trip to an isolated locale.

What advice can we offer on repulsing Canada's notorious flying and biting insects, such as bloodsucking mosquitoes, flesh-tearing black flies, rapacious horse flies, and vampirish no-see-ums? In the bush, we're partial to repellents containing DEET (diethyl toluamide) such as Deep Woods OFF, Muskol, and—our favorite—maximum strength Ben's 100. While DEET is extremely effective in warding off ravenous insects, the product unfortunately damages plastic and some fishing lines, although we have experienced no problems in this regard.[3]

Inside the cabin, a smoldering coil which contains pyrethrum or a substance derived from powdered chrysanthemums has proven exceptionally efficient as an insecticide. Lighting one of these coils on a nightly basis, we have seldom, if ever, been bothered by a blood bandit while sleeping in the Canadian north. Headaches may result if they are burned in a confined area, however.[4]

These voracious pests probably have ruined more fishing trips than inclement weather, forest fires, and angler incompatibility combined. Canada's early travelers, similarly harassed, applied sturgeon oil, bear grease, and pine tar to prevent insect attacks.[5] Another early remedy employed smoke from embers to drive troublesome mosquitoes from tents—with unfortunate results on a least one occasion. While camping on the northern shore of Great Slave Lake in July 1820, the tent of Commander John Franklin, the great British explorer of the Canadian Arctic, was accidentally destroyed by fire in an unsuccessful attempt by a well-meaning seaman to remove mosquitoes by means of smoldering ashes.[6] While none of these prototypical repellents produced the desired result, lake trout anglers can be grateful for today's products that do provide effective relief. The rich history of these annoying flying insects can be found in nineteenth-century Canadian literature.[7]

Let's turn now to baggage. The term encompasses all the gear needed to transport clothing, footwear, sleeping bags, tackle boxes, rods, reels, fish-finder, and various personal items such as a toilet kit, flashlight, and photographic equipment—everything but groceries. Lake trouters seem particularly prone to loading difficulties with tackle, especially those fishing moderate climate waters. Heavy-duty rods, large-capacity reels spooled with lead-core and wire lines, fish-finders and fresh lantern batteries, a supply of sinkers, and a diverse collection of hefty spoons add considerable extra poundage for the fly-in party, compared to tackle needed for other types of freshwater angling. But years of experience have taught us ways to lighten loads without undermining fishing success or comfort. For instance, our number of duplicate rods, reels, and lures has been reduced, and unnecessary clothing is no longer packed. A single fish-finder suffices for the group, and one change of clothing has proven adequate for a week's fishing.

While a large commercial jet may be able to handle any lake trouter's luggage, sometimes weight restrictions are in force, particularly for small aircraft such as a float plane. Flying to Winnipeg, Manitoba, and then by chartered turboprop to a luxury lake trout resort in the Northwest Territories may pose no problem. But we utilize three airplanes of greatly differing size when traveling from Los Angeles, California, to an outpost cabin in northwestern Ontario. In other words, loading the gear on an Airbus 320 for the flight from Los Angeles to Winnipeg normally will not present problems. However, progressively limited space and weight are available on a fourteen-passenger Beechcraft connecting Winnipeg and Red Lake, Ontario, and a six-passenger de Havilland Beaver flying from the Pakwash base camp to the Cleveland outpost. Heaviness problems are minimized when visiting cold lakes and rivers in the Northwest Territories. In this northern region, lake trout remain close to the surface in the summer months, usually precluding the need for weighty lines and downriggers. Visitors to a full-service resort need not pack food, bedding, and fish-finders, which are provided. Total luggage for trips to luxury laker lodges should not exceed 50 pounds (22.7 kg) for each angler.

To clarify matters further for our out-camp trip, let's assume that four anglers are traveling together. Unless careful preparations have been made, crunch time arrives when loading the float plane on the evening prior to the early morning fly-out. Equipment, supplies, and anglers are weighed. Then gear, groceries, a filled propane tank or two for the cabin, and jugs containing outboard motor fuel are carefully stored and secured behind the plane's rear seats and in the pontoons by a safety-conscious pilot. For obvious reasons, a responsible outfitter and pilot will not fly an overloaded aircraft. Any weight difficulties must be resolved at this time. While we have been fortunate over the years, occasionally some gear and groceries have had to be left behind. If a consensus between pilot and angler can't be reached on specific load lightening, excess poundage—including some anglers—can be transported to the outpost on a second flight at additional cost. So far, we have managed to avoid the latter option, considering it a waste of money and valuable fishing time. The reader should be aware, however, that flight weight problems seem to increase geometrically with the number of anglers! Unfortunately, some of us just can't say "no" to packing additional gear. A helpful approach may be to think backward in terms of weight. In other words, project only in accordance with the gear and groceries absolutely essential for a week of out-camp laker fishing. By visualizing what the float plane can carry, disciplined planning and packing prior to trip departure should naturally follow.

On our first trip to northwestern Ontario in 1987, Shickler suffered an angling near-catastrophe when his rods were severely damaged during the flight from Los Angeles to Winnipeg. While transferring his baggage from the float plane to the cabin, he detected some ominous rattling sounds from within the tube holding his rods. Fearing the worst, he uncapped the end of the tube and the pieces of what remained of four of his best rods tumbled out. Fortunately, he was able to purchase at reasonable cost two rods from a sympathetic angler whose party had completed their week's stay and was flying back to the base camp. Evidently, heavy luggage piled on top of the thin-walled tube in the plane's baggage compartment had crimped it, breaking the rods inside. Upon our return home, one of our first tasks was to obtain PVC pipe of appropriate length and diameter, and build sturdy rod containers for both of us. We've had no such problem since. The airline, by the way, proved very apologetic and later graciously paid to replace the broken rods.

> A man seldom thinks with more earnestness of anything than he does of his dinner.
>
> —Samuel Johnson

Next, we turn to meal planning and the purchase of ingredients. There is much more to it than meets the eye. First, if a member of the party is a good cook who enjoys the task (*good* cooks usually do), he or she is the right one to plan menus, make a list of groceries, meats, fruit, milk, and other items to be purchased. To do so, the chef needs to confer with each traveler as to likes, dislikes, "can't eat," and "druthers." While this may sound a difficult assignment, it's surprising how easy it becomes to satisfy a group of people when all share the same goal—a successful fishing trip.

In the event that one member of the group either can't, or won't, perform all of the cooking chores, then meals will have to be assigned according to the talents and wishes of each. In any case, the following process will need to be undertaken:

- Planning the menus—seven days—twenty-one meals—seven breakfasts, seven lunches, seven dinners.

- Deciding where to purchase everything.
- Actual buying of the items needed. Twenty-one meals for four hungry anglers is a considerable load of provisions.

Co-author Ed Eveland, a gourmet chef, has written his own cookbook, *Real Men Cook on Sundays*. Here is his complete list of menus for a typical one-week fly-in (the reader will observe that we eat well!):

	Breakfast	Lunch*	Dinner
Saturday	Bacon Eggs (to order) Hash brown potatoes Toast Coffee	Sandwiches (everyone makes own) (*Lunch is the same each day)	Steaks Baked potatoes Salad Vegetables Rolls
Sunday	Blueberry pancakes Back bacon Coffee	*	Fish (fried) Hash brown potatoes Salad Rolls
Monday	Omelettes Ham Toast Coffee	*	Beef stew Bread Salad

Tuesday	French toast Bacon Coffee	*	Fish (stuffed lake trout) Baked potatoes
Wednesday	Bacon Eggs Hash brown potatoes Coffee	*	Prime rib of beef Baked potatoes Salad Vegetables
Thursday	Pancakes Back bacon Eggs Coffee	*	Fish (fried) Hash brown potatoes Salad Vegetables
Friday	Fish Hash brown potatoes Coffee	*	Hungarian goulash Noodles Rolls

Looks simple, right? Notice that a couple pieces of cooking equipment, however, may not be available at some outpost cabins. The cabin at Cleveland has a propane barbecue grill stored on the spacious porch overlooking the lake. It also has a four-burner propane stove *and* an oven, as efficient as any in one's own home. Also, the outfitter has provided an excellent assortment of pots, pans, and skillets for cooking. Thus, we could barbecue steaks on a grill, roast a prime rib, bake a stuffed lake trout, and cook a large pot of beef stew. Talk about eating "high on the hog!"

By the way, chef Eveland never touches a soiled dish, piece of flatware, or pot. The washing and drying chores belong to the other anglers. They drink moderately or otherwise amuse themselves while he cooks; he then nurses a B & B while they wash and dry dishes (or else he sneaks off to bed). In similar fashion, everyone on our trips does his share of keeping the cabin immaculately clean and tidy—a prerequisite both for "gracious living" and for an appreciative welcome by outfitter Rob Rowe the following year.

Now, let's return to the menus. The cook must prepare a list of everything to be purchased, including needs other than food. If certain recipes call for particular spices or seasonings (those not available in a small town or village market), it's advisable to bring them from home. In addition, be sure to notice the numerous items which aren't a part of the menus but are needed to do the *total* job of kitchen work (i.e., dish soap, paper towels, napkins, Brillo pads). A careful study of the list will provide reminders of special needs. For example, there is nothing worse for a chef to face than cooking for a week without salt. It actually happened to us one year. It's best to assume the cabin will hold no food or accoutrements.

The list below is presented in alphabetical order. However, when visiting the market, it works better if each member of the fishing party, working from a list, gathers certain types of food and therefore concentrates on only that department in the store. Why? It's amazing how much will be placed in the shopping cart if each person has access to the entire market. Remember that the float plane has only so much room and can carry only so much weight. Beer, wine, liquor, mixers, and soft drinks should be purchased by individuals according to desires. The cook should take care of the meat purchases. Food costs are shared equally among companions.

Grocery list for recipes, snacking, and miscellaneous items for four hungry anglers:

- Bacon (four pounds sliced)
- Bacon, back (three pounds)
- Beef for goulash (three pounds)
- Beef stew meat (three pounds)
- Bell peppers (four—two for stew, two for goulash)
- Blueberries (one package frozen)
- Bread (seven loaves—variety according to preferences of eaters)
- Breading for fish after dredging in egg and milk
- Brillo pads
- Broth for stew and goulash (four cans chicken, four cans beef)
- Butter (four pounds)
- Carrots for stew and nibbling (two bunches)
- Catsup
- Cheese for sandwiches, omelettes, and nibbling
- Potato chips (angler choice and amount)
- Coffee (camper's choice of amount and type; we prefer instant)
- Cornstarch for thickening stew and goulash
- Crackers for stew and nibbling
- Cream, powdered
- Dish soap (two large bottles)
- Eggs (four dozen)
- Fruit (group preference)
- Garlic powder (one jar)
- Ham (a thick slice for each person)
- Hand soap (three bars)
- Hash brown potatoes, frozen (five packages)
- Jam for pancakes (one jar)
- Juice (angler choice)
- Lettuce (six heads)
- Luncheon meat (ten packages)
- Mayonnaise (one jar)
- Milk (three gallons)
- Milk–buttermilk for pancakes (one-half gallon)
- Mustard
- Napkins
- Noodles for goulash (one package)

- Nuts (camper choice and amount)
- Oil, vegetable (one large bottle)
- Onions for sandwiches, goulash, and stew (one dozen)
- Pancake mix, buttermilk (one large box)
- Paper towels
- Pepper
- Pickles (two large jars)
- Potatoes for baking and stew (sixteen)
- Prime rib of beef (six pounds cut)
- Rolls (two dozen)
- Salad dressing (four bottles of campers' choice)
- Salt
- Shrimp and crab for baked trout stuffing (one can of each; may bring from home)
- Spices and herbs, parsley, basil, paprika, (chef preference; bring from home)
- Steaks (six nice ones—Spencer or top sirloin)
- Steak sauce (choice of the group)
- Sugar and/or sweetener
- Syrup for pancakes (consider a container of Canada's superb maple syrup)
- Tabasco sauce
- Tomatoes (one dozen)
- Tomato paste for goulash (one can)
- Tomato sauce for stew and goulash (six large cans)
- Vegetables for three meals (angler choice)
- Vinegar (one bottle)
- Wine—Burgundy for stew

Usually most of the foodstuffs and cabin supplies can be found either in town or at a market near the base camp. In the case of the above list, most of these items may be purchased in the town of Red Lake, just a few miles from Pakwash Lake, where the base camp is situated. The fourteen-passenger plane that takes us from Winnipeg lands at the airfield in Red Lake. Rob Rowe, who owns the base camp, including commercial operating rights for a number of outposts, meets us at the Red Lake airport in his truck. After loading all our bags, he then transports us to the market. (If we arrive after the market closes, our shopping is done the following day. We normally allow an extra day to buy groceries, to unwind from the long trip, or to enjoy a one-day fly-out.)

After loading the food materials, we then proceed to the Pakwash base camp, where Rowe packs the float plane for the flight to the Cleveland outpost cabin early the next morning. Obviously, the entire trip from Southern California must be carefully planned. Timing is essential all along the way. Market hours, plane changes, arrivals, departures—all must be synchronized. If not, we may have to spend the night in Winnipeg, or perhaps reach Red Lake after the grocery store closes. Wherever the departure point, the schedule will need to be worked out with both the travel agent and the owner or manager of the fly-in service.

Some last tips in planning . . . if few clothes are brought, with plans to wash them as they become soiled, be sure to bring a clothes line and laundry soap or detergent. Also, bring bath towels and face towels. Finally, don't be discouraged by all these cautions and words of advice. The trip is really an awesome experience, from beginning to end. Please believe us!

Notes

1. Houston, *Arctic Artist*, 66.
2. Marsh, "James, Thomas," 912.
3. Thompson, "Nature's Nasties," 23-26, 28, 30, 33, 80.
4. Ibid., 80.
5. Ibid., 23.
6. Houston, *Arctic Artist*, 73.
7. Uncommonly troubled by swarms of mosquitoes were members of John Franklin's first Arctic land expedition (1819–22), including Midshipman George Back, whose vividly descriptive journal entries often referred to them. Back's journal includes forty-four references to mosquitoes during the late spring and summer of 1820, 1821, and 1822. In his account of the tragic expedition, he used such colorful language as "a species of guest which comes uninvited—and never ceases to torment one," "vile interlopers," and "never ceasing annoyance" to describe the offensive swarms of mosquitoes that plagued the exploring party, day and night. On July 11, 1821, Back, a superb watercolorist, wrote that teeming cutting insects deterred his artwork efforts:

> Amongst myriads of mosquito's, which in spite of veils, gloves or handkerchiefs stung us in a most unmerciful manner—and quite prevented any attempts to sketch.

See Houston, *Arctic Artist*, 66, 68, 138.

Back (1796-1878), an expert fly fisherman, could readily identify with the need of modern anglers to protect themselves from insect harassment. He left his mark on exploration of the Canadian north. The Arctic grayling, which readily succumbed to his feathered flies, was initially named "Back's grayling" by Dr. John Richardson, Franklin's surgeon-naturalist during both overland expeditions (1819–22 and 1825–27). Also named for him was the Thlew-ee-chow, or Great Fish River, which Back first explored in 1833–35. Back was later knighted and advanced to admiral by the British for his Arctic exploits.

His exquisite watercolor sketches are now held by the National Archives of Canada in Ottawa. Thirty-six of his drawings are color-reproduced in the beautiful book by Houston, *Arctic Artist*.

See Houston, *Arctic Artist*, xxi, 77; Marsh, "Richardson, Sir John," 1582.

Of the four talented British naval officers attached to the first Arctic expedition—Franklin, Richardson, Back, and Robert Hood—only the murdered Hood failed to return. Hood's well-written journal mentions on a number of occasions the onslaught of pesky flies. This excerpt from July 1820, is representative:

> The mosquitoes sought the shade, in the heat of the day, which we felt no inclination to contend with them. . . . Our new assailant, the horse fly, or bull dog, ranged in the hottest glare of the sun, and carried off a portion of flesh at each attack. Another noxious insect, the smallest, but not the least formidable, was the sand fly.

The native peoples refer to the tiny sand flies, which produce a bothersome sting, as "no-see-ums."

The mighty Hood River, named for this young officer, discharges itself into the Arctic Ocean's Bathhurst Inlet south of Victoria Island.

See Houston, *To the Arctic by Canoe, 1819–1821: The Journal and Paintings of Robert Hood,* xxxiv–xxxv, 117.

An 1863 chromolithograph of traders plying Labrador's aptly named Mosquito Lake in birchbark canoes clearly depicts clouds of biting insects surrounding the hooded heads of the harried paddlers. As described at the time:

> All the men were compelled to wear veils . . . and as they paddled mournfully across these little lakes, they looked from a distance like veiled sufferers from snowblindness.

See Newman, "Canada's Fur-Trading Empire," 202, 203.

EIGHT

TROUT TACKLE AND EQUIPMENT

A fishing rod is a stick with a hook on one end and a fool on the other.

—Proverb

The tackle used today is the result of centuries of experimentation, creativity, application, and improvement. Tackle choices made by modern-day anglers are influenced by a number of factors: methods, fish sought, experience, and, of course, personal preference. In this chapter, we share with the reader our tackle choices—as well as those of other laker anglers. Personal preference, of course, is an extremely important ingredient of choice. Our own selections have changed somewhat from trip to trip. One conclusion, however, is certain: Careful selection of equipment or tackle, including rod, reel, line, leader, weights, and lures, is paramount in the final act of catching and landing a big laker. To plan a forktail trip is quite involved and can be expensive. Do yourself a favor: take care in selecting equipment.

Rods

When we were in our youth, most casting rods were made of tubular or octagonal steel. Their action was largely inferior to that of their replacement—fiberglass rods. But today even fiberglass is, to some anglers, primitive when compared to graphite and boron shafts. Considering higher cost of boron, graphite rods usually represent the better arrangement.

Rods of older manufacture, however, are still actually preferred by certain laker anglers today. For instance, some veteran wire-line trollers insist that the octagonal steel rods of yore are best for bottom-hugging forktails. A stiff, medium-length fiberglass model with a roller or hard metal guide tip to withstand wire's constant cutting action also continues to be the rod of choice for many wire-liners.[1]

Taper defines how quickly the diameter of the rod shaft changes from tip to butt. The taper of a rod will, in turn, influence the action and power of the rod. The action of a rod refers to that place on the rod that bends when casting or fighting a fish. Fast action indicates a flexible tip and a fairly stiff butt. Slow action denotes that the rod bends throughout the entire length of the shaft. A rod's power relates to the size of the line and the lures that manufacturers designate for the rod to handle (light casting, medium spinning, heavy casting, and so forth).

The only way to know for certain that a rod has been selected with the right taper, action, and power is to fish with it. At that time, such concerns as sensitivity, casting ease and accuracy, hook-setting, and a comfortable handle will be confirmed—or not confirmed. Handle size, by the way, is far more important than many anglers realize.

For trolling with monofilament line, and deep dragging with braided fiber, lead-core, or steel lines, medium-heavy to heavy action rods from five to seven feet (1.5 to 2.1 m) should normally be used. Dragging a heavy spoon or large plug in front of five to eight ounces of weight (142 to 227 g) attached to 27-pound test (12.2 kg) lead-core or 50-pound test (22.7 kg) wire can result in arm weariness after a time. Although wire cuts through the water with less resistance than conventional lines, all these opposing forces are multiplied when a big laker strikes. A heavy action trolling rod helps to alleviate this problem. Lighter action rods, of course, may be fished when using a downrigger, in which the line uncouples from the heavy weight when a bottom-dwelling laker grabs the lure.

Fly-fishing for gray trout is a growing sport. For this type of angling, heavier, fast-sinking lines to throw larger flies, and longer rods are recommended.

For fishing for winter trout through the ice, many ice anglers use short, stout rods, although others prefer ultra-light tackle or tip-ups.

Reels and Lines

The reels selected for lake trout fishing should balance with the rods of choice. For a laker trip to waters of about 50 to 55 degrees north latitude—lakes we have fished in northwestern Ontario, such as Cherrington, Cleveland, Trout, Dragon, and Sturgeon—several reels and lines are required for the different types of lake trouting encountered. Depending upon the degree of passion for the hobby, the angler's varied equipment will include reels and lines for casting and jigging, shallow and deep trolling, and, if interested, fly-fishing.

While we are lake trout aficionados, our approach to equipment differs. Ed Eveland uses spinning gear for casting, jigging, and, at times, trolling. A Penn trolling reel with level wind is his choice for intermediate angling with weighted or unweighted monofilament (25–30 lb/11.3–13.6 kg test) or lead-core line (27 lb./12.2 kg test). Eveland may utilize a Shimano baitcasting reel with lighter monofilament line for trolling when grays of varying size are near the surface. Shimano level-wind trolling reels loaded with similarly weighted lines are preferred by Ross Shickler when summer forktails seek deep water. Bait-casting reels, also made by Shimano, equipped with 10- to 12-pound test (4.5 to 5.4 kg) monofilament line are his choice for jigging, surface laker casting, and some trolling. To meet the demands of diverse techniques for lakers, each of us stores four or five completely rigged outfits in the boat for a day's fishing.

The diversity of lake trouting situations can result in weight and space problems, particularly for the fly-in angler. Since an outpost cabin on a remote lake reached only by float plane doesn't include a tackle store, tough decisions regarding equipment need to be made. While it's more convenient to carry trolling reels already loaded with monofilament line, super braided, lead-core, or wire, extra spools of line can be stowed in the event that a reel requires relining. Spare reel spools, loaded with line before trip departure, also can save weight and space. But there's always the possibility that a reel may break down, with no way to repair it until the angler returns home. To avoid this eventuality, which could be a serious one indeed for the fly-in fisherman, each of us transports four or five large-capacity trolling reels—two loaded with 25- to 30-pound test (11.3 to 13.6 kg) monofilament line, two spooled with 27-pound (12.2 kg) lead-core, and one packed with 30-pound (13.6 kg) braided super-line. If a reel lined with lead-core becomes inoperative for some reason, this line can be re-spooled on another properly functioning trolling reel from which the monofilament line has been removed.

Seemingly unavoidable incidents do occur, however, causing concern. A few years ago, Shickler lost huge sections of both of his lead-core lines one day apart when trolled lures abruptly caught the bottom of Cleveland Lake. Lead-core liners learn quickly that this line doesn't stretch (as does monofilament), and that the boat must be stopped and motor reversed quickly to save the line. Fortunately, Shickler was still able to catch lakers by trolling—although considerably fewer of them—using heavily weighted monofilament line as a reasonably effective substitute.

One member of our usual fishing party is outfitted for wire-line laker trolling. His hefty rod with modified roller tip and large reel spooled with wire provides a piece of equipment that we can all share in the pursuit of lakers in deep water. This strategy offers a party of four fly-in anglers another way to save weight and space, yet still have a variety of methods available. Of course, if a laker enthusiast prefers wire-lining over other summer lake trouting methods, he or she can cut down on the transport of other deep-water equipment to reduce overall weight for the fishing party.

The micro-fiber super-lines show promise for laker angling. These new lines—uniquely soft, flexible, abrasion resistant, strong, thin, and with virtually no stretch—cast easily and troll nicely. Extremely sensitive, the line communicates lure action to the wrist, and instantly telegraphs a lure-bumped rock or trout strike to the shoulder. At least one professional angler uses super-line for all types of trolling, and even prefers the new line over wire for deep-water fishing.[2]

The terminus of the monofilament leader used with all these lines should be checked regularly for nicks and abrasions during fishing, and retied to the ball bearing swivel, snap, or lure as needed. We retie the knots of trolled rigs by the end of each day's angling, if not more often, as a matter of practice. Aside from the usual line wear, we believe that bottom snags and fighting lakers tighten knots and weaken line strength, necessitating replacing knots daily, or even more frequently. This procedure has worked well for us over the years, with trout seldom lost because of a break at the knot or at some other weak point in the line.

Despite such advice about lines, we don't want to discourage the use of lighter weight monofilament, even for big trout. It's been noted that we may fish lighter action rods and 10- to 12-pound test (4.5 to 5.4 kg) line when lakers are in shallow water. (Even lighter lines may be used, especially with spinning reels.) This smaller diameter of monofilament, of course, is less likely to spook the fish, and more forktails normally are hooked than with heavier line. Of greater importance, however, is that lake trouting in spring or fall provides sensational sport, and the fast action can really test angling skill. In cool waters, these aggressive trout may burst on the scene with great suddenness, attacking casted lures as they splash into the water, assaulting baits on the fast retrieve, or assailing spoons or plugs at the boat.

Lakers are highly active at this time—almost a different fish—and the reel's drag should not be set too tightly. The give-and-take of a good trout on light tackle is exhilarating. The knowledgeable angler skillfully uses rod, reel, and line to bring the lively laker to net, while at the same time respecting the head-shaking fish's quick rushes, evasive twists, and surface rolls. Experienced lake trouters usually win these trying and sometimes protracted battles, with the ultimate goal of releasing the fish.

If a spirited laker does snap the line, we are confident that the stolen lure's barbless hook eventually will drop from the trout's moderately hard mouth, minimizing injury. We have also gained the satisfaction that the use of light tackle has helped to level the playing field between man and fish.

Light lines for big trout? Why not? After all, the current IGFA freshwater line class world records for lake trout are mighty impressive in this regard. A 49-pounder (22.22 kg) was caught in 1987 on eight-pound test (4 kg) line. In 1984, 12-pound test (6 kg) line was used to boat a forktail weighing 50 pounds, 8 ounces (22.90 kg). Both of these giant, ancient fish were taken from that paragon of gray trout waters, Great Bear Lake, in Canada's Northwest Territories.[3]

Laker Lures

Lake trout are enticed by a wide variety of lures, including spoons, plugs, jigs, and flies. But which type of terminal tackle is best to tempt *Salvelinus namaycush* into striking? While local conditions may dictate exceptions, the best all around lure for lakers, according to our angling experience and the literature, is a spoon. Other kinds of baits, of course, are also effective and may even surpass spoons as fish-getters in certain bodies of water. But it is interesting to note that of the nine gray trout lures researched for this book, six are spoons, and have been our favorites for years.

Robert Page Lincoln, a chief of the Chipewyan tribe and travel and fishing service editor of *Fur-Fish-Game* (*Harding's*

Magazine) wrote in 1943: "More than any other fish, the lake trout is attracted by that glint and flash of a lure, let us say, a spoon."[4]

In his classic book, *Musky Fishing*, Lincoln stated that wobbling lures like the Dardevle, Red Eye Wiggler, and Doctor Spoons, in large sizes, were "sure killer" lake trout producers.[5] Ray Bergman, who served as the angling editor of *Outdoor Life* magazine for years, in his famed book *Trout* asserted that in terms of laker bait "almost any sort of a spoon will do, although I would suggest a wabbling or darting type of spoon about four inches long."[6]

Angler-author, John H. Roush Jr. reports that most lake trout in North American waters "are taken on large wobblers and spoons: Eppinger Dardevle, Gibbs-Stewart spoons, Superior Spoons, Redeye, Andy Reeker and McMahon."[7] Mike Rosenthal declares: "Big spoons are best for large lakers and should, if possible, resemble the common bait fish of the waters being fished. But much of this time, color seems to make little difference; I have taken lakers on homemade spoons that resemble nothing the fish have ever seen."[8]

Five of the six lake trout experts consulted in assembling this book, and who spend most of their fishing time on Canadian waters—Lloyd Bull, Bret Everson, Rodney Harback, John Herrmann, and John Rickett—show an overall preference for spoons. Curt Bilbey, the sixth member of the group and a Flaming Gorge Reservoir Mackinaw enthusiast, prefers plugs and jigs. Spoons, particularly Huskie Devles, have always been a favorite of big trout catcher Lloyd Bull while he plies the waters of Great Bear Lake.[9]

One of Bret Everson's pet laker lures is the Abalone Killer, two and one-half inch (6.4 cm) size. The minnow-shaped spoon sports a flared tail fin and is backed by mother of pearl. This unique bait reflects the seemingly endless variety of spoons that are, or have been, on the market. The Killer, not made since the 1960s, was probably an import "knockoff"—a near-duplication of an existing lure, in this case Pflueger's Pearl Minnow, manufactured between 1910 and 1946.[10] Shickler can attest to the efficacy of this lure for catching any type of trout. Everson is also enamored with the use of the Luhr Jensen Krocodile, Doctor Spoon, and the Williams Wabler for gray trout.

If former lake trout world record holder Rodney Harback could only take three lures with him on his next trip to Great Bear Lake, his choices would be the Huskie Devle, Charger Spoon, and large Flatfish.[11]

While John Herrmann recommends the large Dardevle as best all-around laker lure for Nueltin Lake, situated on the border of Manitoba and Nunavut, he also has successfully employed Rapalas, Rebels, Flatfish, and J-Plugs in Nueltin and Lake Michigan. Herrmann has also fly-fished for grays with good results in Alaskan waters.[12]

Central Saskatchewan's Lac la Ronge is the setting of the lake trout angling exploits of John Rickett, whose family owns an island cabin on the lake. Rickett's preferred list of lures for lakers includes the Dardevle, Red Eye Wiggler, Thompson Spoon, half or full wave spoon, Thin Fin plug, and floating jointed Rapala.[13]

The sixth member of the group, Curt Bilbey, selects the Flatfish, Kwikfish, Rapala, and various jigs when fishing Flaming Gorge Reservoir, one of the longest and deepest waterways of the American Southwest. A huge laker caught there by Bilbey in 1988 set a Utah record.[14]

Although the scales are tipped in favor of the spoon for lake trout, it is evident from our discussion that plugs, jigs, and flies are also effective lures. In fact, there are times when the latter baits outperform spoons. But while experience and the literature tell us that the spoon is best overall, sufficient evidence exists in the professional writing that plugs, jigs, and flies should be considered part of the angler's equipment if he or she is to catch lakers consistently under various conditions. For example, tackle recommended for use at northern Manitoba's Nejanilini Lake comprises the Eppinger Huskie Devle, Huskie Devle Junior, Len Thompson spoon (Nos. 2 and 4), T-60 Flatfish, Luhr Jensen J-Plug, and one- to three-ounce (28 to 84 g) bucktail jigs.[15]

Gerald Almy reports that burly lakers grab huge spoons, big diving plugs, and wet and dry flies where Nunavut's historic Back River empties into deep Chantrey Inlet, 1,500 miles (2,400 km) above the United States–Canadian border.[16] Wayne Phillips includes the Thompson spoon and Flatfish among his personal top ten list of lures.[17] Classic lake trout lures with Canadian roots are identified by Craig Ritchie as the Rapala, Williams Wabler, Helin Flatfish, and Canadian Wiggler.[18]

The list of laker lures below is by no means definitive. The choice of these particular baits for consideration is based on the literature and the experience of ourselves and other anglers. Appreciation is expressed to the representatives of the various lure manufacturers for their generosity in sharing historical information, angling tips, and product samples for photographing and evaluating. Our roster of lures is listed alphabetically:

- Charger Spoon
- Dardevle Spoon
- Doctor Spoon
- Flatfish
- Kwikfish
- Rapala
- Red Eye Wiggler

- Len Thompson Lure
- Williams Wabler

Charger Lures
(Lake Products Company Manufacturing, Imlay City, Michigan)

The Charger Spoon was developed by John Rustowicz Sr., a mechanical engineer, in the late 1960s. The unusual looking spoon comes in five sizes, from one and one-fourth to five and one-fourth inches (3.2 to 13.3 cm) in length. Lake Products Company also produces a popular fisherman's knot-tying tool of compact design. In addition to fishing gear, the company does prototype work and metal finishing for the automotive industry.

Rodney Harback rates the Charger one of the most effective lures at Great Bear Lake, often catching lakers when other lures are unproductive. The lure is successfully used in the Great Lakes and elsewhere for trout, including forktails, and salmon.[19]

A number 4 Charger was employed by Lyle McClure on November 14, 1971, to catch a 57.5-pound (25.9 kg) laker at Priest Lake, Idaho. According to data compiled by the National Fresh Water Fishing Hall of Fame, the gigantic fish ranks as both an Idaho and a former United States record for lake trout.[20]

Dardevle
(Eppinger Manufacturing Company,Dearborn, Michigan)

The Dardevle was the brainchild of Lou Eppinger, born in 1877 in Detroit. Operating his own taxidermy shop at the age of 20, Eppinger envisioned a lure that would both cast well and produce good action. In 1906, following a solitary fishing and thinking trip to the Ontario wilderness, the young inventor devised a prototype spoon. Additional years of testing and design modification resulted in the marketing of Eppinger's lure as the Osprey in 1912. Six years later the Osprey, now a proven fish getter, was renamed the Dardevle. The lure's new designation was derived from "Dare Devils," a term respectfully applied by the Allies to hard-fighting American Marines in World War I. "Devil" was changed to "Devle" because a dictionary word could not be used in a trademark.[21]

In the same year, 1918, thirteen-year-old Ed Eppinger joined his uncle in the fledgling lure business, a relationship that was to last forty years. The first year in which the lure was advertised in *Field and Stream* magazine—1923—Dardevle sales jumped 500 to 6,000 annually. By 1928, Eppinger was selling 50,000 spoons a year. After World War II, annual sales reached 200,000 and climbed to 3,000,000 lures per year through the 1980s.[22] *Popular Mechanics* magazine in 1962 chose the Dardevle as one of the all-time greats in American lure history.[23]

Many expert anglers prefer the Dardevle for lake trout. Lloyd Bull, a Huskie Devle advocate, has employed the spoon on most of his twenty-nine expeditions to Great Bear Lake. He also used the lure during two visits to Nueltin Lake and on one sojourn to Chantrey Inlet.[24] Rodney Harback, who has fished Great Bear Lake each year but one since 1977, says the Huskie Devle had been the most consistent producer there over the years, particularly for big fish.[25] Similarly, John Herrmann's success with lakers at Nueltin Lake is attributed in large part to the Huskie

Devle.[26] Both Harback and Herrmann fished the version of the lure colored yellow with red diamonds. Harry Gunter, marketing director at Eppinger, has fished Great Bear, Nejanilini, and Nueltin and agrees that the Huskie Devle is the best size for large fish. Gunter's preferred lure color patterns for lake trout are the yellow with red diamonds, fluorescent orange/black spots, chartreuse/red spots, and hot mackerel.[27]

Eppinger markets a wide variety of lures, including the Skeeter, Lil' Devle, Midget, and Imp; the mid-weight casters Dardevle and Dardevlet; and the heavy, slow trolling spoons Huskie Devle and Troll Devle. The company line also includes the Seadevle, Osprey Notangle and Buel Spinner, Cop-E-Cat and Devle Dog (jigging), Buzz 'N Devle and Mousie Imp (for bass) and Devil Bug Mice and Devil Bug (fly-fishing). Eppinger acquired marketing rights in 1994 for the Red Eye Wiggler.[28]

A Huskie Devle was deep trolled by Jim Sowers of Kittanning, Pennsylvania in 1990 to hook a 46.5-pound (21.1 kg) laker at catch-and-release Nejanilini Lake in north-central Manitoba. The fish is the largest taken from Nejanilini waters to date.[29]

A 57-pound (25.9 kg) laker, a record for Flett Lake in the Northwest Territories, was caught in August 1990 by Mark Podobinski of Chicago, Illinois, using a Huskie Devle Junior (yellow/red diamonds) to boat (and release) his prize. In September 1988 Ted Alsobrook of Woodridge, Illinois, landed an enormous lake trout in the heaving waters of neighboring Snowbird Lake. The fish, believed to weigh at least 60 pounds (27.2 kg), was photographed and released by Alsobrook. This mammoth laker was also enticed by a five of diamonds Huskie Devle Junior spoon.[30]

Doctor Spoon
(Fred Arbogast Company, Akron, Ohio)

The Fred Arbogast Company, founded in 1930, needs no introduction to the veteran angler. Some of the company's most famous baits include the Hawaiian Wiggler Number 2 (1936), Jitterbug (1938), Hula Popper (1941), and Sputtlerfuss (1946).[31] *Popular Mechanics* in 1962 selected the Hawaiian Wiggler Number 2 and the Jitterbug as two of the all-time classic lures produced in America.[32] Arbogast also manufactures the Snooker, A. C. Plug, Fred's Frog, Sputterbug, Mud-bug, Flat Fred, and the Bobber-stop.[33]

The Doctor Spoon was introduced in 1940. The lure was trademarked in 1953 by the Brainerd Bait Company of St. Paul, Minnesota. Brainerd was purchased by the Prescott Spinner Company (founded in 1894 in Prescott, Wisconsin) in 1967 and the Doctor Spoon appeared in its catalog the following year. Arbogast acquired Prescott and the rights to the Doctor Spoon in 1970. Some 35,000 lures are produced annually.[34] The Doctor is a mid-depth lure constructed of solid brass, providing deep luster and positive action. Used for casting or trolling, the darting spoon is an exceptionally effective lake trout bait.

In late September 1992 we and co-workers Roger Cronin and Ron Tessada flew to Cleveland Lake, 110 air miles (177 km) northwest of Pakwash Lake in northwestern Ontario. Our purpose, other than to experience good fishing and fellowship, was to gather research for this book at the time of year when forktails rise onto their spawning beds. When asked a few months prior to the trip which lure to use in the fall, Rob Rowe, our bush pilot, recommended without hesitation the Doctor Spoon. The bait did not disappoint during our five-day stay at Cleveland, with lakers in brilliant spawning colors aggressively striking our barbless Doctor Spoons in shallow water.

We prefer fishing the larger size of spoons for lakers, the "Little Doctor" (P275, 3¾ inches/ 9.5 cm) and "Big Doctor" (P285, 4½ inches/ 11.4 cm).

FLATFISH
(Worden's Lures/Yakima Bait Company, Granger, Washington)

Charles Helin was working at a Detroit auto plant in 1923 when, at the age of eighteen, he began to design work on the famous Flatfish. He kept detailed notes as he carefully tested his lure while bait-casting in lakes located in the northwest section of Michigan's Lower Peninsula. The Flatfish was perfected in 1933 after demonstrating its characteristic swimming action in a bathtub, and patented in 1936. The Helin Tackle Company was founded the following year in Detroit. Charles Helin also developed and marketed the top-water Fishcake in the 1950s and the Swimmerspoon in 1960. The company was acquired by Worden's Lures/Yakima Bait Company in 1989. Millions of Flatfish have been sold since the classic bait was introduced almost 70 years ago.[35] The Flatfish was picked by *Popular Mechanics* in 1962 as one of the most illustrious lures ever produced in America.[36]

Baits in addition to the Flatfish offered by the present manufacturer include the Rooster Tail, Hawg Boss Super Toad, Lunker Licker, Spin-N-Glow, Wonderworm, spinners and spoons. Two single hooks are available for several Flatfish sizes, including the larger models—M2, T50, T55, and T60.[37]

The Flatfish has long been considered an excellent lake trout bait. Rodney Harback rates it as one of his top choices at Great Bear Lake, especially in recent years. When Harback in 1991, caught a 66.5-pound (30.16 kg) laker there, a new IGFA all-tackle world record at the time, the lure used was a metallic silver/blue scale T-60 Flatfish. Harback and his three fishing partners had a big outing that day, boating 52 nice lakers. The 31 largest fish weighed a total of 901 pounds (408.7 kg), an average of just over 29 pounds (13.2 kg) each. With the exception of Harback's recordbreaker, all fish were released. Most of the 52 lakers were caught on T-60 Flatfish.[38]

Kwikfish
(Luhr Jensen & Sons, Hood River, Oregon)

Luhr Jensen, who grew up in Oregon, enjoyed making his own tackle, including wobblers and spinners. His company, founded in 1932, has developed over the years many well-known lures, such as the Krocodile spoon, J-Plug, and that famous fish smoker, the Big Chief Electric Smokehouse. Since 1956, Luhr Jensen & Sons has acquired a number of other major tackle companies. Eddie Pope & Company, of Valencia, California, makers of the Dave Davis Lake Troll, a favorite tackle of Ed Eveland, was purchased in 1974. The South Bend Tackle Company, creator in 1916 of the classic Bass-Oreno and, shortly after World War II, the Nip-I-Deddee, Spin-I-Diddee, and Super Duper, was absorbed in the 1960s by the Glen L. Evans Company of Caldwell, Indiana, producer of, among other baits, the Shyster. The entire Evans line was acquired by Luhr Jensen in 1982. Other acquisitions include the Tony Accetta and Crippled Herring Lure Companies in 1989. The policy of Luhr Jensen is to preserve the autonomy of these legendary manufacturers and their lures.[39]

The Kwikfish, of Canadian origin, was first marketed in the early 1950s. Kwikfish Ltd. of Windsor, Ontario, was procured by Luhr Jensen in 1989.[40] An excellent laker lure, the Kwikfish has been employed with good results, particularly in the American Southwest. One writer has described how a silver jointed Kwikfish (model K8J, 4¼ inches/10.8 cm), deep trolled with a downrigger in south-central Utah's beautiful Fish Lake, was used to boat a 34-inch (86.4 cm), 20-pound (9.0 kg) lake trout.[41] One of the largest lakers ever caught in the United States was taken by Curt Bilbey while wire-line trolling at Flaming Gorge Reservoir in 1988. The fish, weighing 51.5 pounds (23.4 kg), was nailed by a K16 model leopard frog Kwikfish. This model, five and one half inches (14 cm) long and largest in a non-jointed size, closely resembles, in dimension and configuration, the T55 Flatfish. The K16 Kwikfish is narrower, slightly shorter, and features the lure's characteristic large front cavity, a depression at least twice that of the similarly constructed Flatfish model. (The nose ring is affixed to the vertical surface at the rear of this cavity.)[42]

While Bilbey favors the Kwikfish over the Flatfish for use at Flaming Gorge, he is not sure just why the Kwikfish outperforms the latter. Bilbey has caught (and released) many trophy Macs on Kwikfish in his 25 years of fishing at Flaming Gorge.[43]

Rapala

(distributed in the U.S. by Normark Corporation, Minnetonka, Minnesota, and in Canada by Normark Ltd., Oshawa, Ontario)

The Rapala is a truly international lure. Lauri Rapala, born in central Finland in 1905, was a fisherman by trade. Using south-central Finland's Lake Paijanne as his laboratory, Rapala carefully observed the targeting by large predator fish of minnows with a slightly abnormal swimming motion. His research inspired years of carving and experimenting until his lure design resembled that of an erratically swimming bait fish. Rapala's first successful lure was shaped from cork in 1936. When World War II broke out in Europe, shortages forced a switch from imported cork to pine bark. Later he selected balsa, a wood that imparted to the lure a buoyancy and more delicate, quivering action than permitted by a denser, heavier material.[44]

After completion of Rapala's service in the Finnish army in 1945, the lure, now referred to as "Rapala," began to spread across the Atlantic via countrymen who had emigrated to North America. During a Canadian fishing trip in 1959, Ron Weber, a young tackle representative for northern Minnesota and Wisconsin, observed for the first time the effective use of a Rapala, with its life-like action. Since the few anglers who possessed the lures were reluctant to part with them and only a handful were available for sale, Weber placed an overseas order for 500 lures for distribution in the Minnesota area. His order, advertised only by word of mouth, quickly sold out. After establishing a relationship with Lauri Rapala, Weber and Ray Ostrom, a fishing friend and tackle store owner, formed the Normark Corporation to distribute Rapala lures in North America.[45]

The first time we heard of the Rapala—and the first time most anglers of our generation heard of it—was when we were reading an article, "A Lure Fish Can't Pass Up," in the August 17, 1962, issue of *Life* magazine. The article, which referred to catches "breathlessly reported," described how the lures were hand made and individually tested. Accompanying the article was a photograph of a beaming Nick Soteroplos with a 35-pound (15.9 kg) lake trout caught on a Rapala at Ontario's Crow Lake.[46] This issue of *Life*, the now-famous and collectible Marilyn Monroe memorial issue, became one of the popular periodical's all-time best sellers. The instant publicity nearly overwhelmed Normark, quickly exhausting the youthful company's inventory and producing an overnight backlog of orders for three million lures. During this period of incredible demand, enterprising Rapala owners rented their lures (with deposit) and a black market flourished.[47]

Other Rapalas were developed over the years, including the Countdown (1965), Fat Rap (early 1970s), Shadrap (1985) and, a few years later, the Rattlin' Rapala. Fillet knives are also marketed by Normark. Rapala and Normark consolidated in 1990.[48] Normark purchased the Blue Fox Tackle Company of Cambridge, Minnesota, in 1968. Blue Fox Tackle, initially launched in 1933, manufactures the Pixee spoon, well known for its effectiveness as a lake trout lure, particularly in northwestern Canada and Alaska.[49]

Each lure continues to be hand-tested before distribution to guarantee that the swimming action so painstakingly researched and designed by Lauri Rapala is retained. Millions of Rapala lures have been sold worldwide in the past forty years.[50] Every serious gray trout angler should have in his or her tackle box a variety of Rapalas, such as the Floater, Sliver, Countdown, or Magnum models.

The phenomenon of the lake trout feeding frenzy, evidently unique to Snowbird Lake in the southeastern Northwest Territories, occurs when ciscoes, or lake herring are trapped on the surface by hungry lakers. Arctic terns, referred to as "Snowbirds" by Arctic explorer Samuel Hearne in 1770, broadcast the event by repeatedly plunging into the water to snatch injured ciscoes missed by the lakers. Floating Rapalas are superb for casting when this furious feeding occurs.[51]

Red Eye Wiggler
(Eppinger Manufacturing Company, Dearborn, Michigan)

The story of this classic American spoon begins with the establishment of the Hofschneider Corporation in 1926 in Rochester, New York. Dr. Frederick Hofschneider, an invention-minded dentist and angling enthusiast, founded the company to manufacture and distribute dental equipment developed by him. In 1928, the company introduced a spoon designed by Dr. Hofschneider, the Red Eye Wiggler. Strong consumer demand for the new lure induced the company to withdraw from the dental field and devote entire production and sales to the Red Eye Line. Hofschneider continued to operate until 1979 when the Scotch Game Call Company of Elba, New York, acquired manufacturing rights for the complete line of original Red Eye lures. Eppinger purchased Scotch Game Call in 1994.[52]

Lures produced today by Eppinger Red Eye include the Evil Eye Flutter Spoon and Monarch, Sparkle Tail, and, of course, the famous Wiggler.[53]

Correspondence from anglers to the Hofschneider Corporation is replete with examples of exciting lake trout conquests using Red Eye Wigglers. For instance, a letter in 1962 from a Chicago angler tells of catching fish weighing 21, 28, 37, and 42.5 pounds (9.5, 12.7, 16.8, 19.3 kg) during a week's trip to Manitoba's God's Lake. The claim to fame, however, for the Hofschneider Corporation, Red Eye Tackle, Eppinger, and the celebrated lure is Hubert Hammers's 1952 catch of a 63-pound, 2-ounce (28.6 kg) giant in Lake Superior's Canadian waters. Hammers's huge laker, taken on a Wiggler, held the world hook-and-line mark until 1970. The catch remains an Ontario record.[54]

Len Thompson Lure
(Thompson-Pallister Bait Company, Ltd., Lacombe, Alberta)

Len Thompson, a veteran of World War I from Abernethy, Saskatchewan, fashioned his first spoon type lure from an old bean can in the late 1920s. The breakthrough in lure design came in 1929. Spoon patterns were subsequently modified, refined, and tested at nearby Lake Katepwa in the beautiful Qu'Appelle Valley in the southeastern portion of the province. About 150 lures were produced in 1932 and marketed under the name of "Kingfish." Annual production from a shed on the Thompson farm in the years prior to World War II numbered some 300 lures.[55]

Cecil Pallister, father of the company's current president, Rick Pallister, joined the firm in 1947. New spoon designs were added and production by 1950 increased to 40,000 lures. The plant was moved to Lacombe, Alberta, in 1958 to take advantage of improved water and freight facilities. Today the Thompson-Pallister Bait Company, Ltd., boasts a yearly production of about 700,000 lures in various sizes ranging from one to five inches (2.5 to 12.7 cm) in length. Spoons are manufactured from brass and nickel silver because of their combination of superior formability and longevity through a natural capacity to withstand corrosion. A western-oriented distribution of the lure covers British Columbia, the Prairie provinces, the Arctic, Ontario, and the northern United States.[56]

We often have successfully fished Thompson Spoons on fly-in trips to lakes in northwestern Ontario in recent years. We have used the yellow five-of-diamonds—our favorite color—for walleyes and northerns in Meandrine Lake and for lakers in the nearby cool waters of Cherrington Lake, reached by a short portage. Other float plane trips to

Sturgeon and Dragon Lakes (in Woodland Caribou Provincial Park on the Ontario-Manitoba border), Cleveland Lake (northwest of bush pilot Rob Rowe's Pakwash Lake base), and Trout Lake (just north of Pakwash) have yielded excellent laker fishing while trolling Nos. 2 (3¼ inches/8.3 cm) and No. 4 (5 inches/12.7 cm) Thompson Spoons.

The Len Thompson lure received considerable publicity when a trophy laker weighing 62 pounds, 12 ounces (28.5 kg), was pictured on the cover of the seventy-fifth anniversary issue of *Field and Stream* magazine in June 1970. The huge fish, caught at Great Bear Lake, was displayed with the lure that enticed it, a No. 4 yellow five-of-diamonds, hanging from its massive upper jaw. The same model of Thompson Spoon also in 1970 allured a then-world record laker of 65 pounds (29.5 kg). This extraordinary fish also was lifted from the crystal-clear waters of Great Bear Lake.

Williams Wabler
(Breck's International, Incorporated, Sherbrooke, Quebec)

The innovative Williams family, initally associated with prospecting for gold in the Klondike over 100 years ago and, later, the dental industry, entered the fishing tackle business quite unexpectedly early in the twentieth century. It began, according to company archives, when a youngster dropped his silver lunch spoon into the water while boat fishing. To the lad's surprise, a giant trout grabbed the spoon before it sank into the depths. Cameron Williams, who had been an eager fisherman since his youth in the Yukon, upon hearing the story, began experimenting with silver-plated lures. These baits turned out to be quite successful. From these rather unusual beginnings came in 1932 the tackle enterprise of the Williams Gold Refining Company. Design modifications in the spoon resulted in a raised, anti-spin rib down the middle of the lure's proven shape. This rib, along with the highly reflective gold or silver plating, continues to characterize these unique spoons.[57]

The lure division of the Williams Gold Refining Company of Fort Erie, Ontario, was acquired in 1989 by Breck's International, and operations were moved to Sherbrooke, Quebec. The Williams line includes the famous Wabler and Li'l Bud (named after Cameron Williams's son), Trophy II, Quick Silver, Thinfish, Whitefish, Flasher, and Dartee. The shape of the Trophy II, according to a company executive, is reminiscent of that lost lunch spoon that launched the company so many years ago.[58]

The Williams Wabler has long been known for its effectiveness as a lake trout lure. In July 1990, Rick Krawec of Weirdale, Saskatchewan, used a barbless Wabler while trolling with a downrigger to boat a near-record laker for Saskatchewan waters, a fish weighing 50 pounds, 13 ounces (23 kg), at Nemeiben Lake in the central portion of the province.[59]

It often has been said that big fish prefer big lures. But how big is *big*? Rodney Harback, that hunter of trophy fish, tells us that while large lures don't always catch big fish, the use of sizable lures reduces the number of smaller fish caught. Big lake trout, in his view, are looking for one big meal, and hefty lures are needed to satisfy the hefty laker's appetite.[60] Many fishermen, however, prefer to use smaller lures to increase the numbers of their catch while hoping that a lunker will occasionally strike. After all, some huge fish have been caught on tiny lures. So if you want to catch big lakers, how large a lure should you use, and why?

To answer this question, it is instructive to compare the eating habits of two North American freshwater game fish known to reach 100 pounds (45.4 kg)—the muskellunge and the lake trout. A three-pound (1.4 kg) pike was found in the stomach of a 78-pound (35.4 kg) deceased Wisconsin muskie in 1923.[61] Robert Page Lincoln, in his classic book, *Musky Fishing*, observed that muskrats, mink, chipmunks, squirrels, rats, mice, ducklings, coots, shorebirds, snakes, turtles, and large bullheads all have been found in the stomachs of ravenous muskellunge.[62]

The large lake trout, spending more time in deeper water than does the muskellunge, feeds almost exclusively on other fish. The preferred natural food of the north country laker is the cisco or lake herring (*Coregonus artedii*). While most ciscoes are just a few inches or centimeters in length, large specimens weighing five pounds (2.3 kg) or more have been recorded. A hefty Mackinaw can easily engulf a fish of this size. Huge lakers, in fact, prey on large representatives of their own kind.[63]

Lake trout that have been introduced seem able to take advantage of other types of food fish. A two-pound (.9 kg) kokanee was found in the stomach of a big laker that had resided in Flaming Gorge Reservoir.[64] Biologists have recently confirmed that predaceous lake trout have invaded the icy blue waters of Yellowstone Lake, set amid snowy peaks at 7,733 feet (2,357 m) in Yellowstone National Park. The intruding lakers, perhaps surreptitiously planted by renegade anglers in one of the largest high-altitude lakes on the North American continent, threaten the existence of the native cutthroat population for which the lake is famous.[65]

The voracious appetites of large muskellunge and lake trout have led anglers such as Robert Page Lincoln, Lloyd

Bull, and Rodney Harback to conclude that large lures are necessary to catch big fish. Lincoln was one of the best muskie fishermen of his day; Bull and Harback are highly successful in their quest for big lakers today. (Bull employs large spoons with a single bent-barb hook to facilitate laker catch and release.)

So how big is big enough? One writer has described deep trolling at Nejanilini Lake with a 15-inch (38.1 cm) Dardevle spoon (available on special order from Eppinger).[66] While a lure of this size is probably too large for most of us, we feel that the baits in the products' largest sizes—with strong consideration given to barbless hooks—are appropriate for big lakers: No.s 4 or 5 Charger, Huskie Devle (and Junior), P285 Doctor Spoon, T50-55-60 Flatfish, K16 Kwikfish, Model 18 Rapala, 3R Red Eye Wiggler, Number 4 Thompson spoon, and the W70 Williams Wabler.

In the final analysis, however, lure size is up to the angler.

Swivels

We have special concern about choosing swivels for the terminal tackle used in lake trout fishing, especially when trolling. Great Bear Lake veteran Lloyd Bull strongly recommends the use of large, quality, ball bearing swivels, especially for lunker lakers. Since Great Bear's powerful fish can break open snaps during a tough fight—taking valuable big spoons with them—Bull suggests that fastenings be pinched to spoons with pliers prior to leaving home. To change a spoon, he advises, tie on a new one, complete with clamped swivel.[67] Of course, the consistent use of quality ball bearing swivels—regardless of size—should prevent line twisting and kinking when trolling wobbling spoons.

Does the use of a ball bearing snap swivel with a spoon affect the action? Tiny Bennett, in *The Art of Angling*, contends that a swivel impedes the natural action of a spoon. He recommends that both split ring and swivel supplied by the manufacturer should be removed to sharpen the spoon's action. He suggests that the angler tie on a snap that has no swivel and use this as connector to the spoon.[68]

However, Richard Pallister, president of the Thompson-Pallister Bait Company, Ltd., states that a ball bearing snap swivel should always be used with his company's lures. In his view, the belief that a direct tie-on or snap-on without a swivel improves a spoon's action is "just another one of those myths!"[69] Harry Gunter, Eppinger's marketing director, also stresses that a ball bearing snap swivel should be attached directly to a Dardevle, without a split ring. Gunter goes a step farther, suggesting that a three-foot steel leader be used if a spoon is bounced off bottom rocks while fishing for lake trout. This would help allieviate any line abrasion problem.[70]

With regard to the Flatfish, Roy Houle, field researcher for the Yakima Bait Company, says that the line should be tied directly to the nose ring in lieu of a snap.[71] However, Rodney Harback, who caught a former world record laker on a Flatfish, uses a large ball bearing swivel with coast-lock snap when trolling this lure. Harback feels that it is simply more convenient to switch lures using this arrangement. The swivel attachment evidently works for Harback who consistently catches big lakers on Flatfish at Great Bear Lake.[72]

John Rickett, when plug trolling for lakers at Saskatchewan's Lac la Ronge, prefers to forego a snap or swivel and tie directly to the lure. The knot should form a large open loop in the leader to promote best action.[73]

In our opinion, the angler, if in doubt how to proceed, should fish favorite lures with or without a swivel to determine which works better. While we normally employ large, high-quality, ball bearing swivels, the issue is really a matter of individual choice.

Boats, Boating, and Related Gear

Boats for lake trout fishing need to be comfortable and roomy, especially if a guide is employed to show two anglers where the lakers are to be found. Powerful and reliable outboard motors or inboard engines are required to propel sturdy craft over expansive bodies of water. Such waters include west-central Moosehead Lake in Maine; Lake Champlain, bordering northeastern New York, northwestern Vermont, and southern Quebec; Flaming Gorge Reservoir, stretching from northeastern Utah into southwestern Wyoming; Nueltin Lake in Manitoba and Nunavut; Great Bear Lake in the Northwest Territories; and, of course, the Great Lakes.

Proprietors of camps, lodges, and marinas on gray trout lakes in the United States and Canada provide a wide variety of equipment to enhance the experience of the laker angler. Bob Lawrence, owner of Lawrence's Lakeside Cabins and Guide Service on Maine's Moosehead Lake, supplies boats ranging from 14 to 16 feet (4.3 to 4.9 m) long and fitted with 10-horsepower motors to 25-foot (7.6 m) charter boats powered by large inboard engines. Two anglers can troll satisfactorily using the smaller craft, while up to four can comfortably drag lures from aboard a charter. Charter boat equipment provided includes rod holders, rods, reels, lures, computer-controlled downriggers, depth/fish-finders, and radios. Moosehead, an irregularly-shaped wilderness lake, extends some 40 miles (64 km) long and up to 20 miles (32 km) wide. Longer excursions on Maine's biggest lake require larger craft for reasons of safety and comfort.[74] Another such well-experienced proprietor is Casey Creber, at Lake Simcoe, Ontario, who has offered lake trout charter service for over thirty years.[75]

The lodge at 39-mile-long (62.8 km) Nejanilini Lake located in north-central Manitoba advertises that anglers fish for lakers from 16-foot (4.9 m) boats with swivel seats and powered by 25-horsepower motors.[76] A brochure for Treeline Lodge on Nueltin Lake, states: "Guests will fish in a comfortable 16.5-foot Pro-Guide Alumarine boat specially designed for Nueltin Lake. The boats are equipped with comfortable swivel seats, cushions, lifejackets, fishfinders, nets, paddles, etc. We equip all our boats with brand new 20-horsepower Mercury motors every year."[77] North of Sixty Fishing Lodges, Ltd., in the Northwest Territories, reports: "Boats at Obre Lake are all 18 feet long, with padded swivel seats, fish locators, wood floors, and 30-horsepower Yamaha outboards. Fly-out boats are 16.5 feet long, with padded swivel seats and 20-horsepower Yamahas."[78] At Plummer's Great Bear Lake Lodge, anglers are provided with new 18-feet (5.5 m) aluminum boats, padded swivel seats, 25-horsepower Mercury motors, and four-horsepower backups.[79] As stated before, Great Bear is home to trophy lake trout, and another all-tackle world record in 1995.

Boating safety involves careful planning and good judgment. As we have seen, many gray trout lakes are of considerable size and may present difficult challenges to the intrepid fisherman. Anglers who outboard many miles or kilometers from docks or cabins to choice fishing spots may encounter sudden storms, experience mechanical breakdown, suffer injury or boat damage from submerged rocks, or become lost.

The danger of high winds that seemingly come out of nowhere, cannot be overemphasized. During a recent trip to northwestern Ontario's Cleveland Lake, strong mid-day winds forced us to shore for a break in the angling action. While Ross Shickler and fishing companion Frank Thometz were cleaning lake trout and walleyes for dinner, a strong gust abruptly snapped off a 30-foot-tall (9.1 m) birch about five feet (1.5 m) from the ground. The heavy tree fell on Thometz, knocking him off his foot. Fortunately, he suffered only minor cuts and scrapes.

Submerged or partially submerged rocks also can present serious hazards for the angler. Familiarity with a lake or river certainly helps to avert them, but this knowledge is tested when rocks appear and disappear with variations in water level from trip to trip. Polarized sunglasses help boaters to spot them when light is sufficient. When entering a narrow channel or passing through another location where rocks just under the surface are known or suspected, teamwork is essential. Moving at a lower speed, both the angler in the front of the boat and the motor operator can watch carefully.

Such diligence can pay big dividends in safety and peace of mind. Despite precautions, outboard motors used by us have struck submerged rocks, nicking the props. Today's motors are engineered to bounce backward on heavy impact, then drop back into position, and continue running. Motor damage, however, can range from bent props and sheared pins to wrecked drive gears in the lower unit and bent or cracked casings. We have even heard of transoms being ripped out and anglers and equipment thrown into the water when rocks are struck at high speed. If the accident occurs at some distance from the dock or cabin, a backup motor keeps an angler unstranded, but if the fisherman doesn't have an auxiliary motor, then hopefully he or she has remembered to bring paddle or oars for the long return trip. (And it is hoped such a trip is blessed with daylight and a little aft wind.) We once towed back to camp two disgruntled anglers who had experienced outboard mechanical problems far from home. It is recommended that high speeds be confined to open water, and that the throttle be slowed in shallow, unfamiliar waters.

Maps, Radios, and GPS Receivers

Good maps can be indispensable tools for the boating angler. For example, in unfamiliar waters the location of rocks can be noted on maps by outfitters or other anglers. It has been our practice for years to obtain topographic maps of Canadian lakes. An index to maps of the National Topographic System of Canada may be obtained from the Department of Energy, Mines and Resources in Ottawa, Ontario. Maps of lakes in the United States are available from state governments. Proprietors of lodges at Nueltin Lake, Obre Lake, and Nejanilini Lake provide official topographic maps. The Snowbird Lake edition includes Obre, Atzinging, Wholdaia, and Sherwood lakes, bodies of water in the southeastern Northwest Territories that offer outstanding lake trout fishing.

Northwestern Ontario's Meandrine Lake, a favorite outpost of ours, has to be one of the most unusual-shaped lakes ever surveyed. Resembling a river more than a lake, it meanders in virtually every direction during its 17-mile (27.4 km) length. With its shape described variously as a carelessly tossed string of pearls or a runaway inkblot, Meandrine even sends crooked fingers into Manitoba, where it eventually feeds the Meandrine River. Its many islands and varying width, from about a mile (1.6 km) to that of one's living room, provide protection from wind and storms and enable anglers to fish under most conditions. While Meandrine may look strange on the map, it is a lake of unspoiled beauty and provides exceptional fishing for ravenous walleyes and big northerns.

Our first exploration of Meandrine a few years ago required expert navigation skills. Hank Garcia, a navy veteran of World War II, religiously followed map and compass readings to get us from end to end. It was his idea to attach pieces of fluorescent yarn to branches of trees that had toppled into the lake to provide easily recognizable features for the return trip. We learned that the unfamiliar territory looked even more so when traveling in the opposite direction. The three of us also carried an auxiliary motor in the event of outboard mechanical failure or damage. We had been told that even native peoples who trap in the area each fall have become lost at times.

We did become temporarily lost during one of our first visits to Meandrine. The three of us traveled in two boats, with Garcia and a reserve motor occupying one craft. We had planned to keep both boats together, or at least within sight, as we coursed this unusual-shaped lake. After lingering at one of Meandrine's many narrows to fish, we slipped quietly away, while Garcia remained at the productive spot, marked by huge granite boulders that had once tumbled from the massive shoulder of a steep, forested hillside into the restricted passage. Catching a glimpse of Garcia's boat about a quarter-mile (.4 km) away as we rounded a point leading to the lake's wide midsection, we continued to work some small bays with which we were largely unacquainted at the time.

We had figured that Garcia would catch up to us, but, after concentrating on fishing for about forty-five minutes, we observed that he was nowhere in sight. We suddenly realized that we not only didn't know where he was, but weren't aware of our own location either! Becoming lost can call up intense emotions—fear, doubt, helplessness, and disorientation. Our unfamiliar environment consisted of bays, islands, and expanses of new water; map and compass readings seemed blocked out by a lack of clear-mindedness and calmness.

It took us about twenty minutes to get our bearings, and to tentatively decide to proceed westward in an effort to retrace our movements. In doing so, we came upon a narrow passageway reaching to the north—and there was Garcia, still fishing in the same spot! Abruptly, it seemed, the landscape was again recognizable and our confidence restored. While we were relieved to be reunited, Garcia was not pleased to have been separated from his fishing buddies in unaccustomed surroundings at a remote, fly-in lake, even though the two boats were probably not more than a half-mile (.8 km) apart. He related later that when he became aware of being alone, he decided in logical fashion to "stay put." He realized that the narrows were the return route to the outpost cabin, and eventually we would find him. Thereafter, our boats were virtually always kept in view of each other.

The experimental use of a referee-type whistle as a signaling device during a subsequent trip had to be abandoned, however. We learned that the outboard's engine noise, even when operated at quieter trolling speed, drowned out the shrill sound of the whistle even when boats were in sight of one another. In later years, we added compact, lightweight portable two-way radios to help us keep in touch and facilitate safety and enjoyment. Radios also have been used by members of our fishing parties to communicate between different bodies of water, such as Meandrine and Cherrington, the nearby laker lake reached by easy portage.

Because lake trout anglers navigate large and perhaps unfamiliar bodies of water and journey to remote lakes by trail, losing one's way can result in dire consequences. Although keeping boats in sight and using radios facilitate communication, such strategies, while important, do not fix position nor reveal the course back to camp or vehicle. The familiar landmark for an outpost camp on a large lake, such as low hills that can be observed even at a distance of many miles or kilometers, can suffice for positioning purposes if visibility is good. However, an obscuring mist, rain, fog, or darkness can thoroughly confuse the laker angler on his precise location, particularly when confronted with strange surroundings.

Today's lake trout angler can rely on satellite navigation technology, alleviating fear of becoming lost. A lightweight, rugged, and surprisingly affordable handheld receiver takes signals from the United States Air Force's global positioning system (GPS), a worldwide satellite and ground station network used to triangulate the receiver's position with remarkable accuracy. The extremely popular GPS device not only provides accurate position fixes 24 hours a day in all weather, but also directs the user to a destination, with information on distance, direction, and time needed to reach a pre-selected waypoint. A member of our fishing party now carries one of these amazing GPS units—a piece of equipment that brings a degree of welcome assurance in the wild.

Photographic Equipment

Since lake trout live in great places, a camera to record catches (prior to release) and the beautiful scenery is a must. Some anglers are better photographers than others, and some are blessed with better equipment. But since today's inexpensive cameras and fine-grain color film produce such surprisingly good results, fancy equipment is no longer essential.

The new camcorders are excellent, and today many anglers use both still and action photography. Camcorders provide a wonderful film and sound record of laker catch-and-release, fellow anglers at work, and choice locations. The battle and boating of Rodney Harback's then–all-tackle world record lake trout, caught at Great Bear Lake in 1991, was videotaped by a fishing partner. Using a copy of this tape for research purposes, we were pleased to share in the thrill of catching a record fish that weighed 66.5 pounds (30.16 kg).

Tackle Boxes

The large tackle boxes used by the two of us are basically similar for lake trout fishing. But our walleye lures differ in some respects. Eveland, who employs a spinning rod, prefers jigs, while Shickler, a baitcaster, likes both jigs and deep diving plugs such as the Rapala Fat Rap (a lure that also entices lakers when they're on the surface). We also have a supply of floating Rapalas and Rebels for shallow water trolling. (Lakers will grab these lures in just a few feet or meters of water early and late in the season.) But since we prefer angling for lakers (mostly trolling), walleye fishing actually represents a diversion for us. Two or three times during a week's stay we enjoy a mess of these delicious fish for dinner. Eveland, a gourmet cook, knows how best to prepare them, too.

Each of us carries four or five casting, jigging, and trolling rods and reels in the boat. A portable Humminbird fish/depth-finder is also utilized. Downriggers are not used by us, largely because of overall weight restrictions for fly-in trips. For walk-in gray trout lakes, such as Cherrington, or one-day fly-outs to other lakes in northwestern Ontario, like Sturgeon, Dragon, or Trout, one tackle box serves both of us.

Notes

1. Dawson, "Wire-Lining: A Time-Tested Tactic for Lake Trout," 20.
2. Linder, "Perspective from Al," 132.
3. *World Record Game Fishes*, International Game Fish Association, 1999 ed., 158.
4. Lincoln, "Spring Lake Trout Fishing," 4.
5. Lincoln, *Musky Fishing*, 94.
6. Bergman, *Trout*, 378.
7. Roush, *Enjoying Fishing Lake Tahoe, the Truckee River, and Pyramid Lake*, 195.
8. Rosenthal, *North America's Freshwater Fishing Book*, 161.
9. Bull, personal telephone conference, 1998.
10. Everson, "Lake Trout Fishing Experiences," 1992 (audiocassette recording); Manns, personal telephone conferences, 1992–93.
11. Harback, personal telephone conference, 1992.
12. Herrmann, "Lake Trout Fishing in Nueltin Lake, Manitoba/Northwest Territories, Canada," 1992 (audiocassette recording).

13. Rickett, "Personal Experiences on Lake Trout Fishing at Lac la Ronge in Northern Saskatchewan," 1992 (audiocassette recording).

14. Bilbey, personal correspondence, 1992.

15. Malz, "Manitoba's Nejalini Lake," 56.

16. Almy, "Back River Char and Lakers," 55–57, 91–92.

17. Phillips, "The Most Wanted Lures," 53–54.

18. Ritchie, "Lures that Endure," 30–33.

19. Harback, personal telephone conferences, 1992–93.

20. *Charger Lures*, Lake Products Company, 1986; *Official World and U.S.A. State Fresh Water Angling Records*, National Fresh Water Fishing Hall of Fame, 1999 ed., 63.

21. Kaminsky, "Dardevle—An American Success Story," 94–95.

22. Ibid., 95.

23. Kirkpatrick, "Fishing's Deadly Dozen."

24. Bull, personal telephone conference, 1997.

25. Harback, "Reflections on Trips to Great Bear Lake in the Northwest Territories," 1992 (audiocassette recording).

26. Herrmann, "Lake Trout Fishing in Nueltin Lake, Manitoba/Northwest Territories, Canada," 1992 (audiocassette recording).

27. Gunter, personal telephone conference, 1992.

28. *Eppinger Catalog*, Eppinger Manufacturing Company, 1996.

29. Malz, "Manitoba's Nejalini Lake," 56.

30. Frederickson, "For the Record . . . ," *North of Sixty News*, 9.

31. "Backgrounder," Fred Arbogast Company, 1.

32. Kirkpatrick, "Fishing's Deadly Dozen."

33. *Fred Arbogast Company Catalog*, 1996.

34. Kiel, facsimile transmission, 1992.

35. *Flatfish, Fishcake, Swimmerspoon,* Helin Tackle Company Catalog, 1973–74; Burton, personal telephone conference, 1992.

36. Kirkpatrick, "Fishing's Deadly Dozen."

37. *Worden's Lures/Yakima Bait Company Catalog*, 1992.

38. Harback, "Reflections on Trips to Great Bear Lake in the Northwest Territories, Canada," 1992 (audiocassette recording); Harback, "Trophy Lodge: 901 Lbs. of Fish in One Day and a New World Record," 1991 (videocassette recording).

39. *Luhr Jensen & Sons, Company History*, 1995, 1–8. The popular Little Chief model, acquired from a California company in the 1960s, preceded the Big Chief Home Electric Smokehouse, developed by Luhr Jensen in 1991.

40. Ibid., 8.

41. Thomas, "Fish Lake Lakers," 92.

42. Bilbey, personal telephone conference, 1993.

43. Ibid.

44. "Making of a Legend: The Normark/Rapala Story," Normark Corporation, 1991; Weber, "The Lure Fish Can't Pass Up," 1–5.

45. "Making of a Legend: The Normark/Rapala Story," Normark Corporation, 1991; Weber, "The Lure Fish Can't Pass Up," 6–7.

46. "The Lure Fish Can't Pass Up," 39, 41, 44.

47. "Making of a Legend: The Normark/Rapala Story," Normark Corporation, 1991, 8.

48. Ibid., 9–11.

49. Ibid., 11.

50. Weber, "The Lure Fish Can't Pass Up," 9.

51. "Snowbird Lake Lodge—Housekeeping in Style," 3; Grooms, "Snowbird Lake Dream Trip."

52. Burke, "The Stirring Story of Mrs. Hofschneider . . . No. 1 Mother and Manufacturer"; Dippel, "Short and Sweet Success Story Belies Hofschneider History," 27–28; Scrivener, "Hofschneider Corporation Story," 8–9.

53. *Eppinger Catalog*, Eppinger Manufacturing Company, 1996.

54. Speckerman, correspondence to Hofschneider Corporation, 1962; Hammers, correspondence to Norman E. Gauch, Hofschneider Corporation, 1953.

55. Hope, "Fishing Lure's Success Persists."

56. Ibid.

57. *Williams Catalog*, "The Accident That Inspired a Company," 1997, 3.

58. Daigle, personal correspondence, 1992; Gautrey, personal telephone conference, 1993; *Williams Catalog*, 1997.

59. Phillips, "Near Record Laker."

60. Harback, "Reflections on Trips to Great Bear Lake in the Northwest Territories," 1992 (audiocassette recording).

61. Atwill, "Wisconsin Muskies," 90.

62. Lincoln, *Musky Fishing*, 14.

63. Scott and Crossman, *Freshwater Fishes of Canada*, 225.

64. Bilbey, personal telephone conference, 1993.

65. Milstein, "Lake's Cutthroat Competition Rises."

66. Agnew, "Bright Nights, Big Critters," 36.

67. Bull, "Those Giant Fish of the Arctic," 4.

68. Bennett, *The Art of Angling*, 97–99.

69. Pallister, personal telephone conference, 1992.

70. Gunter, personal telephone conference, 1992.

71. Houle, personal telephone conference, 1992.

72. Harback, personal telephone conference, 1992.

73. Rickett, "Personal Experiences on Lake Trout Fishing at Lac la Ronge in Northern Saskatchewan," 1992 (audiocassette recording).

74. Lawrence, personal telephone conference, 1994.

75. Creber, personal telephone conference, 1993.

76. *The "New" Nejalini Lake Resort,* 4–5.

77. "Treeline Lodge," *Nueltin News,* 3.

78. "Obre Lake—The Main Lodge," *North of Sixty News,* 3.

79. *Fly-In! Fish . . . Fabulous Great Bear Lake!* Plummer's Lodges.

NINE

MACKINAW METHODS

> Innocence is a wild trout. But we humans, being complicated, have to pursue innocence in complex ways.
>
> —Datus C. Proper

During the first Franklin expedition, British naval officer Robert Hood meticulously recorded in his journal that Cree Indians preferred an eagle's claw to a hook and often caught lake trout "with a stick, to which the line is fastened in the middle, and also slightly at one end. The bait covers the stick, and the fish gorging it, the upper end is detached by a jerk of the line, and falling across within his jaws, he is easily taken."[1] Hood penned his observations during the bitterly cold winter of 1820–21 while headquartered at Fort Enterprise, about 200 miles (322 km) southeast of Great Bear Lake.

Lake trout anglers have come a long way since the days of early nineteenth century Arctic exploration. Today, roomy, comfortable, stable, and multi-featured boats equipped with powerful, dependable, and technologically advanced outboard motors speed us to abundant fishing grounds. Innovative fish-finders chart boat speed, depth, water temperature, bottom structure, and trout location. Rods, reels, and other equipment of exceptional performance are utilized to troll, cast, jig, fly- or ice-fish for lakers. Tough new fishing lines and high quality lures with strong, super-sharp hooks help bring Mackinaw to the boat. After all, a variety of gear is needed, since the forktail, depending upon latitude and season, can be found from top to bottom in the deep, cool North American lakes it naturally inhabits. From fly-lining to wire-lining, today's angler is well-equipped to employ a variety of successful strategies in seeking what Canadians respectfully refer to as "the monarch of the northern lakes." Truly, the lake trout is a fish for all seasons.

Trolling

Trolling is the most effective method of taking lake trout. While some anglers dismiss it as unchallenging and unduly repetitive, Ray Bergman, one of the outstanding angler-writers of the twentieth century, takes a higher view of the practice:

> Successful trolling is more a matter of thoughtful experience with different boat speeds, various fishing depths, and an assortment of lures. . . . The masters of this fish-taking system of angling are as meticulous and thoughtful in their style of fishing as those who take their fish with dry flies.[2]

The legendary Bergman sees advantages in trolling for fish in general, and lake trout in particular. His thoughts, as well as those of other writers and fishermen, including ourselves, are incorporated into this discussion.[3] Trolling does the following:

- Employs a basically simple approach in which a lure is pulled behind a moving boat in hopes that a lake trout will strike. By trolling, novice anglers may catch as many forktails as experienced trouters seated in the same boat. However, to consistently catch large numbers of sizeable trout, trolling, like most fishing techniques, becomes more sophisticated when used to its fullest potential. Trolling various spoons, plugs, spinners, and flies requires divergent approaches that can depend upon complex factors, such as lake knowledge, latitude, season, weather, water temperature, forage fish, and thermocline location. An assortment of tackle is utilized, ranging from medium- to heavy-action rods, and trolling, casting, or spinning reels spooled with monofilament line when lakers are on or near the surface in fall or spring, to specialized bottom equipment for reaching the domain of deep dwelling lakers in summer.
- Sanctions virtually any type of craft for the purpose, from a canoe or inflatable boat to a charter cruiser.
- Empowers lake trouters to pinpoint scattered fish populations in large bodies of water with a minimum of effort.
- Provides the opportunity for more fish to see the bait. Unlike casting and retrieving, the troller's continually moving craft covers considerably more territory, including a great variety of depths, shallows, and structures, faster, easier, and more completely. The lure is left where trout can attack it—in the water.
- Allows two fishermen to fish simultaneously with different lures at dissimilar depths and speeds—if lazy-S patterns are employed—to determine trout preference and position.

- Lets anglers reach deep-water or bottom-hugging lakers with appropriate tackle, such as weighted lines, downriggers, or large, heavy spoons.
- Permits a trolled lure to be kept continually in motion near the bottom where summer forktails are found in many lakes. On the other hand, a casted bait employed to reach the same bottom-abiding trout spends an inordinate amount of time in the air, sinking to the depths, or being retrieved through unproductive water.
- Captures larger lake trout. Trolling furnishes the opportunity to drag bigger lures, keep the bait close to forage and to big fish-frequented structures, maintain appropriate depth, and take advantage of a distinctive forktail practice of trailing a spoon or plug, sometimes for a considerable distance.
- Enables the angler to establish proper boat speed by sensing lure action through the rod or by directly observing plug or spoon swimming motion alongside the boat.
- Gives anglers the opportunity to work the lure, following short pauses. Lurching a lure, of course, is not a new idea, the maneuver having been employed for decades by Mackinaw fisherman.
- Presents unusual trout-catching possibilities that might not happen with other methods, such as casting or live-baiting. We have noticed on numerous occasions that when one of us hooks a fish, the partner's bait is also belted, either immediately or while the lure is being retrieved in preparation for netting. Often the second strike transpires in the motor's wake or beside the boat, the hard-hitting trout appearing suddenly. The phenomenon of the subsequent strike or strikes

may be due to encountering a school, or to other trout becoming excited by a fighting fellow fish or spinning outboard prop—or both of these.

- Accommodates differing angling inclinations. Such cooperation assumes, of course, that boating partners are mutually respectful of, and attentive to, sporting idiosyncrasies. While the authors are good friends, we are not fishing clones and, aware of this, endeavor to oblige differing backgrounds and interests. Eveland possesses the greater passion for trolling and is perfectly content to spend long hours at it. Shickler, on the other hand, enjoys dragging lures for a while—and changing them often, especially if the action is slow—but occasionally likes to stop and cast or jig, particularly when concentrations of trout are located. When beginning a troll, Eveland prefers that the motor be accelerated briefly to facilitate quick release of the desired amount of line as he gently thumbs his spool. Shickler chooses to check lure action at boatside each time prior to a gradual issue of line. While each would like the other to adopt his method, we manage to make the adjustment in a cooperative spirit.

Still, some anglers perceive drawbacks to trolling for trout. Thus, either they don't fish moderate climate lakes in summer at all, or, if they do, they see trolling as one-dimensional—like a baseball team that patiently waits for a home run to power the offense—or as excessively tedious. We remind detractors of trolling that there are exciting games within the game, such as the selection of equipment to employ; the choice of lure, including size and color; trolling depth; and boat speed. As for the claim of boredom, we suggest that trollers drink in the overall trouting experience and not just the dragging of a spoon.

Many anglers view solo trolling as another drawback, desiring a companion to assist with running the motor and netting the fish. But, with practice, a person can troll by himself or herself, and successfully net a weighty fish. An experienced angler can facilitate the netting by tiring the fish prior to netting, or tossing rod and reel into the boat at a propitious moment and grabbing the net handle with both hands (the latter admittedly a tricky procedure). Despite a lack of appeal for some, many trouters prefer to fish alone, especially if living or vacationing close to lakes or at lakeside cottages. Most use the latest equipment, while a few outboarders still employ the old-style hand line, slowly swinging the arm in rhythmic fashion to flutter and tumble the spoon. Of course, a huge advantage of single trolling is the freedom to fish how, when, and where one chooses.

Not a few temperate zone lake trouters are bothered by an inherent risk of deep trolling: losing expensive tackle. While no one likes to sacrifice valuable equipment, if the lure is not occasionally grabbing the lake floor, the angler is not fishing deeply enough. Lake trout, particularly in summer, sojourn near bottom structure, and this is where the bait needs to be to hook them. The use of a depthfinder alleviates the problem of sudden snags. Another effective means of avoiding bottom hookups (one regularly used by us) is the three-way brass swivel, from which a sinker is dropped. The sinker, suspended from the dropper eye by a short length of monofilament, lesser in strength than line or leader, breaks off if it catches a crevice, thereby saving line, leader, and lure.

Summer Shifts

When spring shifts into summer, lake trout shift from the shallows to the depths, and the angler must shift strategies to relocate them. This seasonal transformation in habitat—referred to as "scattering" by laker expert John Rickett—occurs in North America in stages according to latitude. Normally, bottom-bumping for Mackinaw is the midsummer rule for lakes that exhibit thermal stratification in the southern portion of their range. In other words, trout dwelling in lower latitude lakes scatter sooner than do those in the more northern parts of their Canadian realm.

Anglers, however, have used a downrigger to reach big grays crowded together in 90-foot (27.4m) holes at northern Manitoba's Nejanilini Lake, positioned in latitude at 59.33° north, 7°, or 480 miles (772 km) below the Arctic Circle.[4] Particularly intriguing about this fishing venture in early August was that the ice had broken only three weeks earlier, with spring-like conditions prevailing in midsummer. Of course, most anglers plying cold, higher latitude waters find plenty of lake trout near the surface in summer and successfully use monofilament line for trolling purposes. The Nejanilini example is distinctive in that even forktails that inhabit cold lakes will go deep to find comfort zones offering the desired temperature, oxygen, light, security, and forage. The seasonal movement of these trout is a fascinating phenomenon, a migration perhaps as enigmatic as that of the Arctic tern, barren land caribou, or monarch butterfly.

In the lakes of Canada's far north, monofilament, fusion, or lead-core line may be employed in July and August when forktails are usually found no deeper than 20 feet (6.1 m). The Nejanilini illustration—and we could cite other instances of midsummer trough trout at Great Bear, Nueltin, and Snowbird Lakes, situated all or in part above the sixtieth parallel—demonstrates the need for assisted depth trolling (or jigging) to get the lure down as needed. Weights from one to six ounces (28 to 170 grams) could be used with monofilament or fusion line, and less weight or none at all dragged with lead-core line.

While monofilament is fine for near-surface fishing, problems develop when this line is used with weight for deep water trouting. Combined with the tendency of monofilament to stretch and constrain hook sets, water pressure produces a convex bulge in the line, a lifting effect that is only exacerbated as more monofilament is released.[5] In our view, fusion line is more dependable. It offers near-zero stretch, solid hook sets, extremely low line drag, and exceptional sensitivity.

We have used lead-core line for years with excellent results. This time-tested line, with a lead center inside a nylon sleeve, is dandy for intermediate-depth trolling. Weight may be added as needed. The 27-pound test (12 kg) lead-core which we use is color-coded—a different color every ten yards (9.1 m)—helping anglers remember the length of line trolled. Many lake trouters troll lead-core line because it is user-friendly and highly versatile. Water from shallow to quite deep can be accessed by lures during a day's fishing simply by controlling the amount of line dragged behind the boat. If necessary, backing may be employed to help reach deep dwelling forktails.

While we usually choose a simple, three-way swivel with a sinker to assist in dropping a trolled lure to the laker's lair, other means of reaching the depths are similarly effective. The Dan Gapen Bait-Walker serves as a nearly snag-free, bottom-walking sinker. The manufacturer recommends for deep water lake trout weights ranging from three-and-a-half to ten ounces (99.2 to 283.5 g). A drop-back swiveled leader about three feet (.91 m) long completes the trout rig. The leaded weight is suspended from one end of the L-shaped wire form, the leader attached to the other tip, and rod line connected to the safety-pin-style, fulcruming point.

Efficient trolling/diving sinkers manufactured by Luhr-Jensen include the Deep Six and Pink Lady. Featuring adjustable easy-trip action, the Deep Six, depending upon size, dives to 90 feet (27.4 m). The forty-five degree diving angle of the Pink Lady, which can take a lure down to 100 feet (30.5 m), is maintained by onrushing water pressure at normal trolling speeds. When a gray strikes, the sinker slip-trips and quickly planes to the surface; slack line resets the diving position. About five feet (1.5 m) of leader is secured to the rear of the instrument.

Several years ago, the authors planned a one-week fishing trip at the beginning of August to the Meandrine Lake outpost cabin in northwestern Ontario, reached by float plane from the base camp at Pakwash Lake. The overall scheme included a one day fly-in to Sturgeon Lake (also known as Upper Kilburn) the day prior to the Meandrine departure, weather permitting. A principle of physics had application to trouting during this Sturgeon visit—an enterprise that at first punctured Shickler's pride and pocketbook, yet ultimately provided a scientific rebuke that has brought rewards in subsequent fishing success.

After a long series of flights from Los Angeles to Red Lake on a Friday, arrangements were finalized with bush pilot Rob Rowe for the Sturgeon sojourn early Saturday morning. With abundant sunshine forecast, we looked forward excitedly to the long-awaited return to this beautiful, laker-loaded waterbody in Woodland Caribou Provincial Park, a trip forestalled two years earlier by stormy conditions.

As we eagerly packed our gear that night, Shickler observed Eveland seating reels filled with lead-core line to both trolling rods. Shickler pondered the initial trip to Sturgeon in mid-July four years earlier when we had caught 30 trout with ease, trolling with lightly-weighted monofilament line despite any previous angling knowledge of the lake. Figuring this visit would prove even better, although it occurred in late July, he shrugged off any doubts about line weight and quickly fastened monofilament-spooled trolling reels to a pair of medium-heavy action rods, attached a three-way rig, and knotted large coast-lock swivels to the leaders. He then placed by the cabin door the rod setups and his tackle box—the one that both would use the next day in the cramped quarters of the Zodiac inflatable boat—and fell into bed. After all, he thought before drifting off to sleep, wasn't this spring-nourished little gem a tad cooler than other northwestern Ontario lakes which they had fished for forktails?

Around seven-thirty the next morning, the floats of Rowe's de Havilland Beaver touched down smoothly on Sturgeon's serene surface. We were trolling less than 45 minutes later, seated comfortably in an inflatable boat powered by a Mercury outboard. However, when Eveland boated the first five lakers and lost a few others—with Shickler experiencing only a strike or two—Ross quickly realized that something was terribly wrong. Normally, we matched each other fish for fish, especially over a span of days. But this outing was rapidly proving otherwise. Shickler checked his tackle box for additional weight, but found only a few one-ounce (28.4 g) sinkers in a top tray. He suddenly recalled to his horror that an extra bag of sinkers had been left in the duffle back at the cabin. We now realized that Shickler's tackle box, normally well-stocked, held only a handful of weights to serve both of us, placing our fishing success at risk, particularly if we would lose sinkers on snags. This was July 31, 1993, not July 15, 1989, and the trout were obviously deeper than during our previous visit. Eveland, continuing to hook trout, anxiously noted with his first fish the absence of a net, the lack of which could seriously compromise the boating of slippery lakers. Concern was also expressed about safety, with lakers being dragged over the Zodiac's bulging sides rather than netted, and the unwelcome possibility of hook points catching in tube fabric and puncturing air chambers. Were we amid a comedy of errors?

Shickler moved quickly to make needed adjustments. Available weights were added in an attempt to drop his monofilament line into the depths, and rocky shoals were avoided to preserve the precious supply of sinkers. He tried large, heavy spoons such as the Red Eye, Doctor, Huskie Devle, and Thompson, along with deep-diving, sinking plugs like the Rapala Magnum and Sliver, but nothing really worked for him, even though some of the same lures performed well for Eveland, and the grays were concentrated in the same spots as four years earlier (only holed up this time). Borrowing one of his lead-core rigs was really not an option, as neither of us as a matter of practice preferred to risk damaging or losing the other's tackle.

Frankly, Shickler was devastated by a huge error in judgment that could easily have been avoided. After all, his equipment included two reels loaded with lead-core—but all this weighted line was packed away on dry land. He could, in fact, have flown in one reel of each line, which probably would have proven sufficient.

With Eveland catching most of the trout and his partner serving mainly as motor operator and innovative fish lander, Shickler had plenty of time to think about the fine mess into which he'd got himself. While he didn't know the full answer at the time, it was obvious that serious lake trouters needed to pay very close attention to the interaction between line and water, and, most importantly, the physics of lake stratification in summer. By the end of the day, we tallied almost three dozen lakers without incident. Although Shickler rallied somewhat, hooking trout usually coincident with the other's strikes, Eveland soundly outfished him by better than three to one. A humbling experience had to be taken in stride.

We concluded later that more stratification had taken place at Sturgeon Lake this time than on our earlier visit, with the added two weeks of summer heating clearly making a difference. Thermal stratification in temperate zone lakes, caused by the relationship between water temperature and density, produces three characteristic layers that remain identifiable throughout summer and early fall: the epilimnion, thermocline, and hypolimnion. Sturgeon's epilimnion—the upper layer of warm water that responds to wind action and air temperature—probably increased in thickness by the end of July, depressing the thermocline, or zone of rapid temperature drop and sufficient oxygen, and into which the epilimnion abruptly grades. In a large lake, the thickness of the epilimnion in early summer may be 30 feet (9.1 m), but by early autumn can be as much as 70 feet (21.3 m). The thermocline makes a transition rapidly into the hypolimnion, a region where minimum temperatures prevail and an oxygen deficit may exist.[6]

In colder regions, deep lakes may receive insufficient heat in the short Arctic summer, so that stratification is reduced or doesn't occur. In the northern section of elongated Nueltin Lake, for example, thermoclines don't develop.[7] But Sturgeon Lake does stratify, and by the end of July, layering apparently was more fully developed than on our previous visit in mid-July.

One of us paid the price for inadequate preparation, but he would not make the same mistake again. During our visit to Sturgeon in the last week of June 1997, stratification evidently hadn't happened yet, with trout actively feeding near the surface. Both of us had learned an invaluable, first-hand lesson about this marvel of lake physics, a scientific wonder that profoundly influences the distribution of lake trout and methods of taking them in summer.

Woodland Caribou Provincial Park, in which Sturgeon is situated, straddles the Ontario-Manitoba border. The park's southern limit lies about 70 miles (112 km) north of the renowned Lake of the Woods, a sprawling water body that crosses the Ontario-Minnesota boundary. Sturgeon, in the park's southeastern corner, is 50 air miles (80 km) west of Pakwash Lake's Snake Falls base camp. Narrow and aligned east-west, the lake stretches about three miles (4.8 km) long with a maximum depth of 120 feet (36.6 m). Day-use park fees are charged, with permits obtained through the Ministry of Natural Resources at nearby Red Lake.

Sturgeon, like most lakes in the park, is accessible primarily by aircraft. Water access is also available, with canoeists following travel routes used by prehistoric peoples. The Palaeo people, the first park dwellers, lived and hunted along the shorelines of retreating glacial Lake Agassiz some 9,000 years ago. In the late seventeenth and early eighteenth centuries, the park was the site of intense fur trading competition between the Hudson's Bay Company and the North West Company. The two rival organizations merged under the name of the Hudson's Bay Company in 1821.[8]

Of some 100 named park lakes, 35 hold lake trout, 19 of these containing only trout and northern pike populations. These 19 bodies of water, including Sturgeon, are grouped in the southern sector of the park, a lake productivity and deep water phenomenon associated with Woodland Caribou's geologic past.[9] (See chapter 2 notes for further information on the park's geology and its effect on lake trout distribution.)

Table 9.1 provides a statistical summary of five floatplane trips to Sturgeon Lake over a ten-year period. The data show that, with one exception, more forktails were caught by us in early summer, despite less time on the lake and varied weather conditions. In addition, a substantial number of gray trout were hooked and lost. Cooler water and near-surface-feeding fish strongly influenced the increase in laker numbers during the 1997 trip, a fly-in that occurred at the beginning of summer and just three and a half weeks after ice breakup. In 1999, unsettled weather, including potent thunderstorms, likely lowered the trout tally. We should note, however, that we have never intensively fished this overlooked little lake, preferring to mix piscatorial business with pleasure. In addition to trolling for trout, we've explored shorelines, bays, and islands; inspected an abandoned native trapper's shanty; probed inflowing streams; observed the abundant wildlife; studied ancient glaciated rocks; observed the dominant jack pine forest; stopped to enjoy a tasty lunch

Table 9.1. Data Summary for Five Fly-in Visits by the Co-Authors to Northwestern Ontario's Sturgeon/Upper Kilburn Lake in Woodland Caribou Provincial Park (Latitude 50.44° N/Longitude 94.57° W/Elevation 1,155 ft. [352 m])

Date of Fly-in	*Weather*	*Hours on Lake*	*Number of Lake Trout Caught*
July 15, 1989	Overcast/ showers	9	30
July 31, 1993	Sunny skies	8	34
July 7, 1995	Sunny skies	7	37
June 25, 1997	Partly cloudy/ showers	5	41
June 23, 1999	Partly cloudy/ thunderstorms	5	23

in the boat or on shore; recorded our adventures on film; and delighted in having the lake all to ourselves.

Most of Sturgeon's trout apparently are not large, with those caught by us ranging to about ten pounds (4.5 kg). Ministry netting surveys, however, indicate that some genuine trophies inhabit this lake.[10] While the majority of Sturgeon's lakers may not be tackle-busters, they more than make up for smaller size with their numbers and scrappiness. The famished, energetic forktails in this spring-fed lake hit hard, fight furiously, and refuse to quit at the net. Uncharacteristically, these feisty fish occasionally jump in their efforts to throw the lure. Seated on upturned plastic crates in the inflatable boat, we've been startled by hooked trout springing above eye level, then forcibly dropping to continue the battle under the surface. Indeed, lakers inhabiting cooler surface waters behave much differently than those in warmer water.

Some lakes in the southern part of the park, as mentioned, include forktails and northerns only—no walleyes. Two of these water bodies, Haggart and Bulging, each larger than Sturgeon, are clustered near the park's western boundary. Accessed by Red Lake–based Green Airways, which has long maintained an outpost camp at Haggart, both lakes are known for their great lake trout fishing. Moose, bear, and woodland caribou may readily be observed from the remote Haggart Lake outcamp.[11]

Wire-lining is the classic method to reach deep-dwelling Mackinaws, particularly those of trophy size. The technique has been around for a long time. The 1936 James Heddon and Sons catalog pictures a large, disk-shaped, skeleton frame Winona trolling reel capable of holding 450 feet (137.2 m) of 50-pound test (22.7 kg) wire line. Resembling a miniature amusement park Ferris wheel with the cross plate side-fitted to the reel seat, the now-vintage product features a thumb-drag brake and trumpet-style agatelike line guide.[12]

Benefits of dragging with steel include the ability to fish deep water; no-stretch line; superior feel in terms of lure action, bottom-bumping, and strikes; and the opportunity to hook the larger lake trout that are deep-dwellers in summer. While experienced wire-liners prefer the method, many anglers—especially beginners—are deterred by a number of associated problems. Frankly, wire novices should engage a practiced guide.[13]

Wire-lining can be a trying technique. A great deal of trolling wire may be needed to reach bottom—500 feet (152.4 m) or more. Large, heavy trolling spoons should be worked constantly. Wire is abrasive, grooving line guides if a levelwind reel is used, and cutting rod blade and tip guides of lesser toughness. Metal line kinks easily, producing weak spots. An abrupt bottom snag or hard strike from a trophy trout can nearly yank a troller from his or her boat seat if the reel's drag is set too tightly. Uncontrolled free-spooling can produce serious line overrun, resulting in the mother of all tangles.[14]

Trolling with steel, however, serves as an extremely efficient system that has been successfully employed by both freshwater and saltwater anglers for decades. The stratagem has proven deadly for delivering huge lakers from the depths. Seasoned wire-liners usually eliminate, or at least alleviate, the various difficulties encountered. Any weariness is reduced by experienced expectancy, serious attentiveness, and active engagement. Some proven techniques: bottom-bouncing the lure or sinker and then reeling in a few turns to decrease hang-ups; pumping the rod to manipulate the spoon; winding and releasing line to relieve any buildup of wire fatigue at the roller or hard metal guide tip; watching for and smoothing out kinks if they develop; checking the drag setting, thumbing a gradual release of line; and realizing that, if big grays are to be found, occasional bottom obstacles are part of the wire-dragging game.[15]

Wire-liners prefer rigid or heavy duty five- to seven-foot (1.5 to 2.1 m) trolling rods with solid metal tip guides. Many anglers modify stiff action rods by installing a high-strength roller guide tip. The round or octagonal steel rods of yesteryear remain the tackle of choice for some seasoned steel trollers. Suggested reels include the Penn-manufactured GTi level-wind series and Senator sequence, such as the wire-friendly Mariner 49L. For trolling with wire, Penn recommends its new black Sabre E-glass rods, equipped with carbide ring guides and roller tip top. A sinker with a three-way rig or a bottom-walker may be employed to reach suspended or bottom-hugging lake trout. Lures that work well with wire are the large wigglers, Flatfish, Kwikfish, Rapalas, and big wobbling spoons like Red Eyes, Huskie Devles, and Thompsons.[16]

The downrigger, aptly named and ingeniously designed, represents a particularly effective means to reach deep dwelling lakers in midsummer. Now popular for freshwater use, the downrigger was originally developed by West Coast salmon fishermen in the 1950s.[17] The boat-mounted system includes a weight or cannonball up to ten pounds (4.5 kg) that is either lowered or raised manually or electrically by a short boom and oversized reel spooled with stainless steel cable. Before lowering the weight to the desired depth, the leader and lure are attached by a breakaway coupling or line release, and the rod handle placed in a tube-like holder adjacent to the cable reel (or else the rod is hand-held). When a fish strikes, the line is pulled free and the battle is fought without the encumbrance of the heavy downrigger weight.

Downrigger advantages include light tackle access to deep water trolling, capability to fish directly under the boat, precise depth control, and a sporting method. A disadvantage might be the need for another fisherman to work the unit or units, or to operate the craft and outboard. A depth-finder locates schools of lake trout or preyfish, and the downrigger is positioned to operate at the determined depth. Spoons, such as the Thindevle or Williams Wabler, and plugs, like the Flatfish or Rapala—often preceded by dodger or flasher units—trail the weight from 10 to 100 feet (3 to 30.5 m) or more and serve as notable lake trout producers. The Dave Davis lake troll is famed for attracting forktails in downrigger fishing.

Anglers around the world have used jigs for centuries. One can almost picture Canada's native peoples jigging for lake trout, causing a lure crudely fashioned from bone or shell to sink, hop, dash, pause, or otherwise imitate a struggling bait fish. The modern angler must similarly manipulate a jig to induce forktails to strike.[18]

We prefer bait-casting gear when vertically jigging for gray trout. A medium- to-stiff-action rod is needed for solid setting of hooks. A bait-casting reel offers more precise line control than does a spinning reel, and avoids problems generated by an unexpected strike with the bail open. A spinning reel may provide a more rapid drop, however. A large capacity spool loaded with 10- or 12-pound monofilament line (4.5 to 5.4 kg) or thin, no-stretch super-line completes the outfit.[19]

Depending upon depth, various jig weights are used. Jigs of two ounces (56.7 g) or more may be employed when lakers are belly-bumping at around 80 feet (24.4 m), with heavier lures if the fish are deeper. We opt for maximum depths in the range of 70 to 90 feet (21.3 to 27.4 m), finding that vertical line control often becomes an issue beyond this level. In addition, dropping and retrieving jigs too deeply can consume time and reduce the extent of productive water covered.[20]

Vertical jigging is not a particularly difficult method to master, and resembles lure-jigging while ice fishing. Keeping the line between rod tip and lure as plumb as possible, the jig is dropped rapidly to the bottom. A varied jigging stroke, ranging from aggressive to passive, is applied near the lake floor, especially during the first 20 feet (6.1 m) where many strikes occur. Starting the rod tip about a foot (.3 m) from the surface and lifting to waist level will jump the jig off the bottom. Dropping the tip while cranking slack line flutters the spoon or dances the jig. We normally choose a forceful action immediately after the bottom bounce. The trick is to maintain an almost slack-free line for best detecting strikes. The entire water column is repeatedly worked in a series of drops, retrieves, and jig snaps. Lakers suspended near schools of ciscoes are reached in this manner.[21]

The tendency of a gray to hit a sinking jig can be somewhat unsettling to any angler, especially one who is inexperienced in the technique. The problem is that the take can be no more than a slight twitch or line hesitation, even with large lake trout. When this occurs, the alert angler should instantly engage the spool and vigorously set the hook, overcoming with rod and human muscle 80 feet (24.4 m) of monofilament stretch.[22]

Lures used include small, heavy spoons—large, fluttery ones may take too long to sink—lead jigs, Buzz-Bombs, Zzingers, Airplane Jigs, Swedish Pimples, Crippled Herrings, big blade baits, and Mr. Mean soft plastic jig bodies for suspended lakers. Some anglers tip jigs with sucker belly or end-forked pork rind as additional enticements. To avoid line twists, black barrel swivels may be tied 18 inches to 3 feet (45.7 to 91.4 cm) above the lure.[23]

Hook sharpness is vital. The hook of a free-falling jig can be multi-angled to the direction of the rod, reducing the percentage of effective penetration, particularly if the hook point is blunted. Lac la Ronge laker expert John Rickett stresses the importance of needle-sharp points for another reason. When deep jigging, lures often grab rocky structure, dulling hook points. A hook sharpener utilized as needed helps to alleviate this problem. Rickett also recommends washing hands with soap to preclude transferring to lures outboard motor gasoline or other impurities. As he puts it, "So often it seems that it's the little things that make a difference."[24]

Electronic devices that find fish and structure have revolutionized fishing, specifically Mackinaw angling. Summer lakers are niche fish, corralled into deep water holding spots, such as basins, holes, or trenches where forage and proper temperature are found. But to jig for them, these compact concentrations of trout must first be located. A fish-finder with properly mounted transducer is a must in seeking out lakers in hiding.[25]

We experienced transducer adherence problems with our usually reliable Humminbird portable fish-finder. On occasion, when attempting to view an unreadable display screen, we found that the transducer unit, suction-cupped to the wet, slick surface of the aluminum transom of the boat, had slipped into the motor's wash. Midway through one Canadian trip, the prop sliced off the trailing power cord and attached transducer, effectively ending fish-finder operation. The problem was nicely solved on the next visit by installing a portable transducer bracket mounted vertically on the transom. Clear readouts then were consistently available, even at high boat speeds. Positioning the craft directly over sonar-spotted lakers is an indispensable tool to successful vertical jigging.

Topside Trout

Spring and fall are our preferred times for forktail angling—with the earlier season favored. These are the periods when lakers congregate in cool, surface waters. We're referring, of course, to temperate zone lakes, such as the gray trout water bodies we've visited in northwestern Ontario. Arctic region lakes can experience spring-like conditions in July and August. While lake trout fishing can be outstanding during these seasons—when the fish are exceptionally hard-hitters—there are downsides to these times, too.

Problematic are the spandex-tight windows of opportunity for angling following ice breakup and preceding and following the autumn spawn. An arrival too soon after ice-out may find lakers huddled in deeper water, far from the surface where they might be expected to be, because of a paradox in freshwater physics. Fresh water is most dense at 39.2°F (4°C), and water below this temperature becomes lighter and rises as it approaches the freezing point. Because of this phenomenon, the lightest and coldest water lies directly under the late-winter ice cover, and denser water that is less cold forms a layer deeper in the lake. Thus many lake trout, while not particularly content with the water temperature below, seek this level since the depths are somewhat warmer than water that rests just under the ice. Similarly, fresh meltwater may also be colder than deeper water, precluding laker activity on the surface for several days after the ice breaks up.[26]

Tough winter conditions of extremely frigid water, reduced oxygen, and dearth of food also weaken many forktails, with some fish dormant at ice-out. With melting of the ice cover, the situation begins to improve for both fish and fisherman. Spring warmth and winds mix the ice-chilled surface waters with the relatively warmer waters below. Light penetration helps to stimulate life, lakers begin to look for food, and the fish move to the surface. It may take a couple of weeks for all this to take place in moderate climate lakes, but lake trout fishing over the ensuing two weeks can be superb.[27]

Topside trouting is not without its drawbacks with regard to other life forms that appear at this time. Black Flies, principal pests of northeastern Canada and northernmost United States, emerge in enormous numbers about the same time that laker fishing peaks in spring. Yet many gray trout anglers in this geographical area actually prefer this time of year, despite the torment of these tiny, winged biters.[28]

The most serious handicap facing such trouters is the menace of downright miserable weather—the Darth Vader of spring and fall angling in the north. We prefer spring fishing because warmer and longer days are approaching and, hopefully, good weather follows the seasonal trend. But the transition from spring to summer is not without the possibility of inclement weather. Some anglers have sustained fog, cold rain, blinding snow, sleet, and high winds—in wild combinations—and still experienced great surface-fishing for lakers.[29]

Fall weather also can worsen abruptly and threaten the success of a fly-in fishing trip. Several years ago we flew by float plane to northwestern Ontario's Cleveland Lake in late September. In the middle of our five-day stay, gray clouds lowered and a strong, chilly north wind developed. By early evening, cold, driving rain had been replaced by blowing snow. The quickly moving snowstorm departed before dawn, however, and the relieved anglers happily passed the nippy, early morning hours successfully spoon-casting bouldered shallows for hard-fighting, pre-spawn lakers. Fortunately, the icy wind had exited with the previous night's storm, although the air shortly after sunrise that day is remembered as particularly frosty. A warming trend for the balance of the visit enhanced our angling enjoyment. Unpredictable weather during spring or fall forktailing certainly dictates the need for proper rain gear and warm clothing.

The tight top-water trouting window in spring and fall can be widened somewhat with careful planning and experience. When a month or so has passed after ice-out in lower latitude lakes, many lake trout seekers turn to other fish rather than deal with the summer shift to deep water. Such action is unfortunate. Grays can still be found in the shallows in early summer and even later, if anglers know when and where to look for them. Shickler first experienced this apparent peculiarity of lake trout behavior many years ago, but at the time the event seemed a mystery.

In late June 1960, he journeyed with Bret Everson, Jim Concilla, and Louie Mangano to Hollow Lake in southeastern Ontario, north of Lake Simcoe. The brief visit introduced Shickler to lake trout fishing. The foursome spent most of its fishing time trolling the main water body with lead-core line between rocky points and islands, boating several lakers. Beginning a troll perpendicular to shore early one morning, instead of gradually releasing line, Shickler threw a small spoon near the bank where a shoal broke off into deepish water. Immediately, a fat five-pound (2.3 kg) forktail hit the spoon. The trout surprised members of the party. What was a laker doing in shallow water at this time of year in this lake? After all, ice had broken up more than two months earlier, and trout should have been in deep water by now. Believing the catch to have been a fluke, the anglers did not follow up on shoreline fishing for the remainder of the stay. However, Shickler mentally filed the incident away as a puzzle to be solved.

After a number of trips to northwestern Ontario in recent years, we have found that lake trout do indeed cruise the shallows long after ice-out, especially early in the morning when air is cooler and light diminished. Choice travel locations for summer lakers include bouldered shorelines, rocky points, and granitic islands where the edges of shallow shelves fall off sharply into deep water. Warm weather forktails also may be found feeding along windward shores where strong winds stir up plankton and forage. Shallow cruising may occur throughout a cloudy day. Although most gray trout caught in this manner usually are less than trophy size, occasionally a big fish shows up. Light tackle may also be used at the juncture. Other outdoor writers verify our findings, that anglers may take advantage of a lengthened spring forktail period at this latitude. As stated previously, lake trout may be caught near the surface throughout the summer months in the chilly waters of the far north.[30]

We have visited Cleveland Lake five times since construction of the island cabin in 1991. These trips covered the third and fourth weeks of June, the first and second weeks of July, and the third week of September. As shown in table 9.2, Cleveland's ice breaks about late May, so the July outings took place some five or six weeks after ice-out.

The early morning hours through the first half of July were our most productive summer trolling times at Cleveland, a small lake some seven miles long (11.2 km) with a maximum depth of 150 feet (45.7 m). Trolling alongside shoreline reefs, the edges of islands or surface-breaking rocky spines, and steep rock faces that plunged into deep water, we have enjoyed fruitful lake trouting prior to ten o'clock in the morning. Later in the day, action dropped off in these areas, probably because trout retreated to deeper water for greater comfort. Depth trolling with weighted lead-core line in wider sections of the lake produced fish during the heat of the day. On occasion, nice grays were captured paralleling the west-facing beach end of a bubble-shaped bay

Table 9.2. Geographical Factors, Spawning Periods, and Icing Conditions of Selected Lake Trout Lakes in the United States and Canada[31]

Lake	*State/Province/ Territory*	*Latitude*	*Longitude*	*Elevation*	*Spawning*	*Ice In*	*Ice Out*	*Maximum Ice Thickness*
Cleveland	Ontario	52.20° N	93.57° W	1135 ft/ 346 m	Early Oct	Early Nov	Late May	4 ft/ 1.2 m
Fish	Utah	38.35° N	111.43° W	8700 ft/ 2652 m	Oct	Dec/ Jan	Mid May	3 ft/ 0.9 m
Flaming Gorge	Utah/ Wyoming	41.15° N	109.30° W	6040 ft/ 1841 m	Oct/ Nov	Dec/ Jan	Late March	1 ft/ 0.3 m
Great Bear	N.W.T.	66.00° N	120.00° W	512 ft/ 156 m	Aug/ Sept	Late Nov	Early July	5 ft/ 1.5 m
Jackson	Wyoming	43.51° N	110.64° W	6770 ft/ 2064 m	Oct/ Nov	Late Dec	Late May	1 ft/ 0.3 m
Nueltin	Manitoba/ Nunavut	60.30° N	99.30° W	912 ft/ 278 m	Aug/ Sept	Mid Sept	June 15– July 7	5 ft/ 1.5 m
Placid	New York	44.17° N	73.59° W	1858 ft/ 566 m	Mid Oct	Mid Dec	Late April	2 ft/ 0.6 m
Raquette	New York	43.52° N	74.38° W	1762 ft/ 537 m	Mid Oct	Mid Dec	Late April	2 ft/ 0.6 m
Simcoe	Ontario	44.26° N	79.09° W	718 ft/ 219 m	Early Oct	Early Jan	Late March	2 ft/ 0.6 m
Tahoe	California/ Nevada	39.07° N	120.03° W	6226 ft/ 1898 m	Sept/ Oct	—	—	—

where compact turns were negotiated along a deep water troll. On especially breezy days, feeding bait fish apparently gathered there and lakers moved in to feast. Eveland, who consistently uses lead-core line, achieved particular success in this pass while dragging a large Doctor Spoon over gravelly bottom in about eight feet (2.4 m) of water. Catches of this type—initially real eye-openers to us—provided another piece of solid evidence that lakers shift to shallow water in summer under special conditions.

Our sojourn to northwestern Ontario in 1997 enabled us to sample for the first time cool water forktail fishing at three fly-in lakes: Cleveland, Trout, and Sturgeon (or Upper Kilburn). We spent three and a half days at Cleveland, arriving on June 20, a couple of days before spring officially merged into summer in the northern hemisphere and about three weeks after ice broke. Bush pilot Rob Rowe returned early June 24 to Cleveland Lake and flew us to Trout Lake for a day's fishing there. We were flown on June 25 from the Pakwash Lake base camp, where we spent the night, to Sturgeon Lake for our final day of lake trouting. We had considered a day of leisure between trips, but with improved weather forecast, Rowe thought it best to depart the next day. We agreed with his experienced judgment. Rain on June 26 could have washed out the Sturgeon trip altogether. Although the week's wet weather was the soggiest we had encountered, the lake trout fishing proved to be as good as it gets.

The three lakes differed in size, shape, temperature, fish population and location, and color. Trout, a big lake, dwarfed both Cleveland and tiny Sturgeon. Of the two spring-fed lakes, Sturgeon seemed colder than Trout; both appeared slightly cooler than Cleveland. Cleveland and Trout yielded lakers, walleyes, and northern pike; Sturgeon, only forktails and pike. At Cleveland and Sturgeon, trout were dispersed widely in the shallows near shorelines; at Trout, lakers also gathered in shoal water, but clustered in definite locations. Gray trout at all three lakes were found no deeper than about 20 feet (6.1 m). Each water body featured in varying degree the distinct brown tint—often described as the tea color of bog waters—characteristic of many northern lakes. This hue, produced by peat deposits at the bottom and margins, influences the shading of trout and other fish in the lakes.[32] Reflecting the degree of water stain, forktails ranged in tinge from lightest toning in Trout Lake to darkest coloring in Sturgeon.

When we arrived at Cleveland, smiling members of an outgoing party of four reported that walleye and lake trout action had begun to heat up toward the end of the week. This was welcome news indeed for us, who keenly awaited our first visit to northwestern Ontario in two years. Cleveland proved a much different lake the third week in June as compared to the first two weeks of July. The situation might be described as a forktail flip-flop, with late spring fish habitat completely reversed from that of early summer. Lakers this time were found in places where we had not previously located them in July, at least in large numbers—off rocky points, around islands, in shallow inlets, and close to inflowing streams—often in water no deeper than six feet (1.8 m).

Summertime fish normally caught in deep water haunts, such as the main body of water, now patrolled the top 20 feet (6.1 m) of mid-lake expanse. But most of these last-half-of-June lakers collected in sheltered shoal water warmed by nearby landforms and feeder creeks. Our fish-finder, which alerted us to potential snags in the shallows, also revealed an absence of bottom-dwelling trout anywhere in the lake, even in favorite summer jigging locations. The warmer shallows must have been a welcome refuge for winter-stressed lakers at this time of year. Gray trout grouped on shoals throughout the day, regardless of weather conditions, which ranged from partly cloudy to rainy and from calm to breezy during our stay. About one fish in five was a lake trout, with pike and particularly walleyes preponderant in the same warm spots. Cleveland's forktails, however, dominated in size those of other lakes, although we did pick up some big walleyes—a couple of which provided a delicious dinner—from a small, seldom-fished, walk-in lake.[33]

Rapalas, those baits with the signature minnow-shaped bodies, proved particularly effective on this outing. Jointed models such as the five and one-quarter-inch (13 cm) Floater and eight-inch (20 cm) Sliver were trolled. Forktails lurking near rockbound structures pounced on the jointed Floater with a vengeance. Fluorescent-finished Rapalas were dynamite fish catchers for both walleye and trout. Also excellent for lakers were Thompson and Doctor Spoons. A sinker, when used, weighed no more than one ounce (28.3 g).

We shared a memorable experience on our last full day at Cleveland Lake. That afternoon, Eveland trolled a shallow, dark-bottomed back bay where forktails had been taken the previous two days. Gray trout evidently assembled here because the darker surroundings absorbed spring solar heat and winding shorelines and islands shielded the inlet from the cold of the larger lake.[34] Suddenly, an electrifying strike almost jerked him from his bucket boat seat. Eveland and his Power Stick battled a titanic trout that behaved more like a moving lake bottom than a fish. The jumbo laker slowly turned the boat as Shickler readied the net. Just as Eveland gained some line, the taut leader parted with a loud "ping!" at the unweighted, three-way swivel, and the now-unburdened swivel and line whipped around the rebounding rod tip. For a few moments, we stood silently in the boat and reflected on the experience, rod and net hoop resting on the gunwale. A 20-pound (9.1kg) leader had unexpectedly snapped five feet (1.5 m) above the lure. A trophy trout had been lost, the largest either of us had hooked at Cleveland. We tipped our caps to this lunker and moved on.

After a final dinner at Cleveland, we surveyed a molten-glass-like surface from the porch of the pine-sided cabin. A cloud-filtered sunset backlighted the ripple and splash of trout and other fish, perhaps rising for mayflies.

Trout Lake was next on the agenda. The lake lies 90 miles (145 km) south of Cleveland, a distance normally covered by float plane in about 50 minutes. But in order to skirt scattered showers and hill-hugging fog, the zigzag flight path covered nearly 140 miles (225 km) and took 75 minutes. Since we delighted in the splendid panorama unfolding below, the delay didn't bother in the least. Veteran back-country fliers never really tire of surveying the breathtaking Canadian bush from the air. A "Kodak moment" view swept by below—a lush forest carpet of variegated greenness, punctuated by countless mirror lakes, rivers, streams, marshes, swamps, and sporadic ridges of sparsely-wooded, glacially polished bedrock. Northwestern Ontario's timbered areas are thickly covered with balsam, tamarack, spruce, ash, poplar, aspen, birch, and jack pine.

Stepping from the plane onto the dock, we were introduced by Bernie Harapiak, manager of Trout Lake Lodge, to our guide, Jason Green, son of Jack and Heather Green, owners of the lodge and a flying service. Fifteen minutes later, with tackle, rain gear, and lunch transferred to the boat, we were underway. Five minutes from the lodge, a sharp strike on Eveland's trolled spoon disclosed that forktails were swimming at about the same depth as at Cleveland, and that similar tactics should suffice.

Since we had only one day to fish a substantial lake with 383 islands, our guide's skills were paramount to fishing success. Unlike smallish Cleveland, where forktails scattered in the shallows, Trout's lakers bunched in discrete locations. Green, who often had fished Trout's northern reaches, knew where the lakers collected in mid to late June and led us to these hot spots. A particular troll parallel to an island not far from the lodge proved especially fruitful. Effective lures, dragged with lead-core line or super-line, included the jointed Rapala Sliver and Doctor, Thompson, and Huskie Devle spoons. While we didn't take any trophy trout—the lake record is a 55-pounder (24.9 kg)[35]—we boated and released plenty of fish. Heavy rainfall, including a brief thunderstorm, drenched us, but trolling and trout catching continued without interruption.

That evening, Harapiak graciously invited us to dine with lodge guests for "Eye Night"—a marvelous banquet of deep-fried walleye strips and charbroiled rib eye steak. After dinner, as light rain fell, we bush-hopped from the island outcamp to Pakwash Lake to prepare for Sturgeon, our last stop.

With spotty showers and partly cloudy conditions predicted for the next day, Rowe flew us in the morning from the Pakwash base to Sturgeon for our final hours of forktailing. Most of Sturgeon's trout, like those at Cleveland, congregated near rocky points, islands, and shorelines. However, trolling from one landform to another we found a number of fish near the surface over deep water. We enjoyed our best-ever outing at Sturgeon, boating over 40 beautiful, battling lakers with bodies bedecked in olive-brown and beige spots. And we probably lost half again that many in only a short span of fishing (see table 9.1).

Cruising into a shallow inlet at the lake's western end, we observed clearly a cobble bottom in water the color of diluted coffee. Any movement on our part sent skittish grays darting away in all directions from the inflatable boat. Had we packed a casting rod or two, we would have experienced great sport tossing small spoons toward a bouldered bank. In any case, limited Zodiac floorspace usually restricted the transport of rods to a pair of trolling rigs each. Unstable air produced dramatic weather changes. A brightening sky of towering cumulus clouds and anvil-topped thunderheads brought intervals of sparkling sunshine, sharp showers, and brilliant rainbows. In spite of the rainy weather, this trip was especially remembered for its trouting success at all three backwoods lakes.

During the corresponding period in 1999, we again flew by float plane to Sturgeon and Cleveland Lakes but replaced Trout with Dragon Lake, another lake trout and northern pike fishery in Woodland Caribou Park. Shallow water angling proved excellent, despite a wide spectrum of weather from sunny skies to cold, blowing rain and occasional thunderstorms. Dragon, new to us, was a pleasant surprise. The lakers here ran larger than those at Cleveland and Sturgeon on this trip. Rowe flew us to Sturgeon, Dragon, and Cleveland, in that order, with the Cleveland outpost stay covering three days.

Intense weather probably reduced the fish count at normally fruitful Sturgeon (see table 9.1). Shortly after arrival, dark clouds rolled in, accompanied by lightning strikes and thunderclaps that resounded among the ridges encircling the lake. A powerful thunderstorm that suddenly developed over the water body nearly swamped us, and we promptly outboarded to a nearby cove to beach the inflatable boat. We rode out nature's brief bombardment, cowering among shoreline trees.

Beautiful weather welcomed us at Cleveland, but the wind shifted to the east the next two days, bringing with it teeth-chattering, driving rain and a slowdown in trout activity. While the atmospheric instability cut into lake-trouting success at Sturgeon and Cleveland—walleyes remaining reasonably active at Cleveland—we voiced no complaints. Although changing meteorological patterns again had produced variable angling conditions on this outing, our love of fly-in bush country laker fishing has endured.

A high level of trip satisfaction results when the visit is of sufficient length and variety to accommodate bad weather, and angling companions agree fully on an itinerary of lakes with varying environments. The one-day fly-in to Dragon Lake, a body of water previously unknown to us, proved to be a vacation highlight.

Determining which of the park's lakes to fish required a bit of homework. Initially, Sturgeon seemed a relatively easy choice, since both Rowe and the previous owner of the Snake Falls Camp and Flying Service, Walt Jones, had visited the lake. As for Dragon, Jones never had fished it and Rowe only became aware of it about a month before our arrival. An older ministry canoe route map of ours did not identify the lake by name. But canoeists whom Rowe had flown into Woodland Caribou in May had fished several interconnected lake trout waters and told him that Dragon yielded more hefty forktails than did other lakes. The second-hand information helped us to settle on Dragon, rather than one or two other better-known, productive fly-in lakes in the park.

Bright, early-morning sunshine bathed us as the floats of Rowe's de Havilland Beaver skimmed Dragon's rippled surface. The lake, just west of Sturgeon and similarly sized, probably was named for its serpentine shape. As soon as pilot and passengers climbed off the plane, we realized that Dragon offered an unspoiled wilderness scene, a step back in time. The thick, old-growth jack pine and deciduous forest that ringed the lake, untouched for decades by burns, grew atop rugged, Precambrian bedrock, a continental foundation some three billion years old. The narrowness of Dragon magnified the relief of steep glaciated granitic cliffs and huge lakeshore rockfalls. We found ourselves immersed in a gorgeously aesthetic landscape!

While we knew that Dragon held lakers, we didn't know where to fish for them. With interior space at a premium, we hadn't included portable sonar gear for fishing from an inflatable boat, so finding the fish involved trial and error, not a particularly difficult endeavor for smaller lakes. Having launched the Zodiac at Dragon's northern end, we trolled close to the eastern shore where a multicolored igneous rock wall suggested deeper water nearby. By lunchtime, a few large aggressive fish had been taken along this stretch and by crisscrossing the lake between bouldered points. The water became shallower as we motored southward and strikes dropped off. We hadn't really found the trout yet, and sensed that Dragon's northern reaches held more promise.

About midafternoon we located a significant concentration of lakers around a pine-crowned island near the spot where the plane touched down. As we circled the island at varying distances from its shoreline, strong trout smacked our big spoons and gave frenzied battle. For a lake this size, all of these wild fish were surprisingly large, averaging about ten pounds (4.5 kg). We sensed that most of the dark-bodied beauties inhabiting these pristine waters never before had seen a lure.

On this trip, the trout were inclined to dine on sizeable spoons, such as Doctors, Thompsons, and Huskie Devles. When trolling, Eveland utilized lead-core line with no additional weight; Shickler employed super-line with a one-half-ounce (14 g) sinker. We eagerly anticipated a future round of terrific early season forktailing at these and other Canadian fly-in lakes. Clearly, Woodland Caribou offered both extraordinary scenery and superior lake trout angling.

Important to our discussion of topside trouting is the way that two record-breaking anglers, Rodney Harback and Lloyd Bull, approach forktail fishing in the shivery waters of Great Bear Lake. Both are Great Bear veterans of many years, employ trolling as a technique, and consistently catch big fish. But the similarities end there. Harback usually visits the sprawling water body in early July, just after ice-out; Bull visits a month later when the big trout rise from deeper water to spawn. In recent years, Harback has spooled heavy monofilament line to explore shallow sand flats with a pebble-scraping T-60 Flatfish. Bull loads his reels with sturdy lead-core line and probes offshore reef structures that border deep water. A Huskie Devle is Bull's bait of choice. The tactics of these knowledgeable, sporting, and successful lake trouters have evolved over time. Bull and Harback have lifted the two largest lakers from these fertile waters. Bull set the current IGFA record in 1995 (72 pounds/32.65 kg), besting Harback's 1991 mark (66.5 pounds/30.16 kg).[36]

By late summer in the northern hemisphere, lake trouters experience Goldilocks conditions—surface air and water neither too hot nor too cold. As the days of early fall grow shorter, weather and water cool, especially after sunset. When lake stratification breaks down and surface temperature approaches 50°F (10°C), forktails move onto rocky reefs. During this period, the spawning mechanism is triggered, with both temperature and light believed to be influential.[37]

Like spring surface forktailing, opportunities in fall are brief. Anglers should be aware of spawning and freeze-up times for particular lakes. Trout are active near the surface before and after the spawning interval, with short stretches of relative inactivity associated with the generative process. An angler who arrives too early in autumn could find lake trout still in deep water. A fall lake trouter who reaches a destination too late might discover forktails, but also skim ice and finger-numbing cold. Male trout, preceding females, clear the spawning areas and a few days later spawn with females over a rubble bottom. Because of instinctive fixation on spawning tasks, lakers at this juncture may be somewhat passive, with short periods of activity by some fish between grounds cleaning and spawning. Following the spawn, liveliness picks up again. The angler who visits a laker water body during the actual spawning procedure may experience few strikes at this ticklish time.

Spawning and ice-in periods are shown in table 9.2. Non-listed lakes with latitudes similar to those listed can be expected to exhibit comparable periods. While geographical latitude is the single greatest cause of temperature contrasts, elevation is another factor to be considered (see table 9.2). Local anglers and outfitters may be contacted for spawning and icing information for lakes of choice.[38]

The opening of the Cleveland Lake outpost in 1991 extended the fishing season there. Before then, outfitter Rob Rowe offered occasional fly-in tent camping at Cleveland. With a wood-burning stove for heat, the comfortable, solidly-built island cabin now provides refuge from the elements and biting insects. During our initial stay at the nearly-completed outcamp in early July of that year—before the siding was finished a few months later—we decided to return for the pre-spawn period the following fall. While Cleveland seldom had been fished in autumn, our outfitter thought that lakers probably spawned there around October 1. Testing the waters at that time should provide more definite answers.

Later in the year, Rowe sent us a videocassette recording of Pakwash Lake and fly-out fishing highlights during the five-month season. In early October, during a break from cabin work, he videotaped two angler-builders wearing heavy sweatshirts and raincoats catching frenzied lakers in nearby island shallows. Eggs protruding from a flopping female suggested that spawning time was near. One beaming fisherman excitedly remarked on tape that he had boated the first laker in his life on his second cast. Carefully considering spawning information, vacation timing, and concerns about the possibility of deteriorating fall weather conditions, we booked a reservation at the island outpost for September 20–25, 1992.

Weather on the trip ranged from calm to stormy. Midway through our visit, a bone-chilling wind brought rain in the afternoon and snow overnight. The morning following the sudden snowfall, we surveyed from our boat a leaden sky, bluish-gray water, and whitened shoreline dotted with slate-colored, snow-capped boulders. Accenting this winter-like scene, a forest of pine and white-trunked birch glowed with shades of green, gold, and orange. Multi-hued spawning lakers caught early that day complemented the flame of boreal color. The crisp, morning scene seemed dream-like, as if we were tiny figures fishing in a surreal painting.

If the weather proved inconsistent, so did the lake trouting. It varied from extraordinary to ordinary. We had learned that waters on the northern side of a small, craggy island about a quarter-mile (.40 km) south of the cabin were preferred spawning grounds. The reefs fronting the two islands and the deep trough separating both provided classic, year-round lake trout water. We visited this spot many times, but found grays in large numbers on only a few occasions. Most of the action took place early in the day, with lakers present for just brief periods. We speculated that this apparently rhythmic, in-and-out movement of fish, usually just after daybreak, might somehow be linked to nocturnal spawning behavior.

While we caught some nice fish on the shoals at first light after the snowstorm, we really got into them early another morning. This time, trout were all over the shelf, even breaking in the shallows. With a placid surface, we fished the reef from the outside inward so as not to startle any lakers in shoal water. First, paralleling the island, we spoon-trolled about 200 feet (61.0 m) from shore. After netting some terrific battlers on several passes, we cut the motor and slowly and silently approached the northern point. Forktails continued to seize spoons as we casted parallel to the shore on either side of the boat. Eveland threw a large silver-and-blue Doctor Spoon toward the bouldered bank, and fin-deep lakers, snatching the lure, exploded into airy leaps. At the same time, Shickler, also casting a Doctor, probed water about ten feet deep (3.0 m) on either side of the boat. We experienced several doubles during the heated action. Shickler, switching to a deeper-diving Rapala Fat Rap, then hooked tussling lakers and walleyes on alternate casts. When the spurt slowed, we motored elsewhere.

Weather conditions determined how we approached the island spawning grounds. Lakers were less jumpy with a choppy surface, so we could come from virtually any direction on these occasions. The post-storm morning provided a good example. Rolling swells screened the boat's motion, enabling us to surprise lively pre-spawners in the shallows. We located skittish forktails on the reef another time, around noon on a particularly breezy, overcast day.

Other than the fish moving onto the island's spawning beds, we found few lakers elsewhere in the lake. Mysteriously, water lying off points, around other islands, and inside wind-protected coves proved relatively unfruitful. Cleveland's narrows, usually productive, seemed barren of gray trout. Our companions, Roger Cronin and Ron Tessada, worked the island shoals in our absence, but did not match our reef successes. They did take some good fish in other spots, however. Various islands surrounded by rock and cobble bottoms looked promising, but pre-spawners were not present in significant numbers, at least when these locations were visited.

It took us a while to properly assess this autumnal venture, quasi-successful in terms of fish caught. We had anticipated a trip of consistently excellent fall fishing. Ultimately, we concluded that if had we arrived a week later—closer to the spawning by Cleveland's lakers—our expectations probably would have been realized. While the trouting pace ranged from fast to slow, we did boat a good batch of lakers overall. Besides the fishing, fixed in our memories were the colorful foliage, an unexpected snowstorm, and valued camaraderie.

Few lake trouters take advantage of the narrow time slot between spawning and ice-in, especially for north country fly-in lakes such as Cleveland, Great Bear, and Nueltin (see table 9.2). With the tourist season ended by mid-October, outfitter Rob Rowe removes his float plane from Pakwash Lake by this time. Since spawning at Cleveland usually has been completed by the end of the first week in October, about three weeks of open water remain before ice-over. However, with winter approaching and bush flying for angling purposes concluded for another year, a potentially productive period of topside trouting is lost because remote Cleveland is not routinely accessible by air then.

Fly-Fishing

> Flies may also be used for this surface lake-trout fishing. In my experience the best patterns have been streamers and bucktails, the same used for landlocked salmon fishing in the East.
>
> —Ray Bergman
> *Trout* (1952)

An early reference to fly-fishing is found in Aelian's *De Natura Animalium*, written in the third century A.D. In his book, Aelian describes how Greek river fishermen of that day deceived insect-loving "spotted fish" (brown trout) with colorful dry flies.[39]

In the intervening centuries, much more has been written about tossing a line into the water with an artificial fly tied on the end. And, of course, fly casting tackle has improved considerably. But very little information appears in the angling literature concerning fly-fishing for lake trout. In the early 1960s, A. J. McClane, celebrated angling authority and former executive editor of *Field & Stream* magazine, described how he took cruising inshore Macs to 27 pounds (12.2 kg) on dry flies at Great Bear Lake. The lake, a reservoir colossus, was largely unknown to the fishing fraternity at the time.[40] A quarter of a century later, writer and fisherman Gerald Almy depicted the use of spurted wet and skittered dry artificial flies in fly casting for forktails at Chantrey Inlet, where the storied Back River plunges into the Arctic Ocean.[41]

Impressive IGFA fly rod weight records have been established in recent years, with hefty lakers taken from Quebec to the Yukon (see table 5.4.) But relatively few anglers currently fly-fish for gray trout. In the words of Bruce Ranta, Ontario biologist, fisherman, and writer:

> Other than trolling with the odd streamer, fly-fishing has not caught on with Ontario's spring lake trout anglers. Some great opportunities are being missed.[42]

John Herrmann, one of the six lake trout experts chosen to contribute to this book, resumed fly-fishing a few years ago after a long hiatus. His adrenalin-inducing account of fly casting for lakers during an early-season trip to southwestern Alaska is a story well told:

> My angling buddy, Martin Hamar, and I had been fishing for a week at Crystal Creek Lodge in Alaska during the second week of June. We had had good luck with the kings, char, grayling, and rainbows. On our last day we flew out to a river in the Nushagak Basin for some spectacular rainbow fishing. During lunch the pilot, Steve Nicoll, and our guide, Jim Eberhard, asked if we would like to try some lake trout fishing with fly rods in the afternoon. Would we ever! Marty and I had been talking for some time about taking a special trip to try for lakers in northern Manitoba at the very beginning (ice out) or end of the season when they are in shallow water.
>
> After lunch we flew about twenty minutes to a place called Goodnews Lake, in the Togiak National Wildlife Refuge. It is located in a spectacular setting—in a bowl surrounded by snow-covered, glacially carved mountains with some of the best cirque basins I have ever seen. Goodnews Lake is really two small lakes connected by a deep and fast-moving river. At this time of the year the lake trout are concentrated in the river, feeding on the salmon smolt which are moving in schools downstream.

Marty fished the lower end of the river and I worked the top.

I was using a Sage Graphite III RPL, nine-foot, five-weight rod, courtesy of our guide, Jim. We were casting into the wind, and my rod could not punch through it. The stiffer Sage made a big difference. I had on a floating line and needed to get down to the fish, so I put on an Orvis 24-inch Mini Lead Head above a seven and one-half foot, 2X leader with a 3X tippet. We used a blue and green weighted smolt pattern on a No. 6 hook.

I cast across and slightly upstream, and let it drift down while stripping in. Just as it reached the end of the drift and started to rise, I had a fish on! For the next two hours, I was hooked up more than I was casting. The fishing was absolutely fabulous. Early on I got a hit on every second or third cast. They tended to just bump it, and I missed a fair number of strikes. We were not using indicators, and the water was too deep to see the fish, so we had to go by feel. During about two hours of fishing, I caught and released eight or nine fish, some of which gave protracted battles. Never once did any of the fish try their typical tactic of rolling up on the line. The fish were quite thin after the long winter, but fought very well—more so than fish of the same size in a lake. This could be due to a higher oxygen level in the river. About fifteen minutes before we had to leave to fly back to the lodge, the fishing shut off.

This type of fishing for lake trout is possible only for a very short period of time during the year. We were at the point between ice-out and the strong salmon runs, when the main food supply for the lakers (as well as the other fish) was the smolts making a run for the sea. As the smolts travel down the rivers in schools, the fish gang up on them. We had seen some awesome boils of Arctic char feeding on smolts from below while sea gulls attacked from above. The boils would move down the river with the migrating smolt. Spectacular! Marty, down river from me, saw some similar boils of lake trout. At the end of the trip Marty and I decided that "it's tough being a smolt."

Once the salmon start laying their eggs, this becomes the main food for the lake trout, followed by salmon flesh. Later, of course, the trout go deep for colder water.[43]

For all-around topside trout fly casting, we recommend a high-performance nine-foot (2.7 m) rod for 7/8 weight lines. Many innovatively designed and technically superior reels are available to provide a balanced outfit. The Orvis Odyssey + II, for example, may be spooled with Depth Charge sinking line, 250 grains, and 20-pound (9.1 kg) braided Dacron backing. Big Game XT IGFA-rated knotless leaders combined with Mirage Shock tippets, also by Orvis, produce a specialty package for versatile laker fly-fishing. Simple, large-pattern streamers, size 2/0 to 4/0, are suggested. Local fly shops should be contacted for fly casting advice. The key to forktail fly-fishing in lakes and rivers is to use lengthy rods of sufficient power for long casts—even in windy conditions—and weight forward lines with fast-sink-rate that drop big flies to productive depths. Premium casting equipment may be obtained through other established companies, such as Winston, Thomas and Thomas, L. L. Bean, and Scott. Various rod and reel combinations may be integrated to fit anglers' budgets and levels of experience.

Ice Fishing

While still fishing with minnows and frozen baits has its charms, nothing beats the power of a winter lake trout hitting a jigged spoon. In ice fishing, there's no greater thrill.

—Gord Ellis
Ontario Out of Doors
(March 1998)

Ice fishing in portions of the United States and Canada has long enjoyed widespread popularity. In recent years, however, lake trout have emerged as an extremely desirable hard-water quarry. Table 9.2 lists selected North American lakes where fishing for ice lakers is popular: Fish Lake in Utah, Flaming Gorge in Utah and Wyoming, Great Bear in the Northwest Territories, Jackson in Wyoming, Raquette in New York, and Simcoe in Ontario. Winter lake trout are in demand in Ontario at big waters, such as Lake of the Woods/Whitefish Bay, Simcoe, and Temagami, and a host of smaller lakes where ice huts may be rented. This latter group of water bodies includes Bark, Boshkung, Diamond, Dunlop, Herridge, Jumping Caribou, Kamaniskeg, Maple, Muskoka, Mount, Restoule, Ten Mile, Twelve Mile, and Lake of Bays. While a few of the lakes mentioned here are fished only by locals, most draw ice anglers from afar.[44]

Advances in equipment have helped to fuel interest in frozen top-water fishing. Power ice drills and improved warm clothing have led the way. The list of other new items for the winter angler to consider is impressive: portable shelters, high-performance snowmobiles, sturdy all-terrain vehicles, versatile sleds, ice fishing rods and reels, ice-friendly sonar gear, GPS units, propane heating and cooking stoves, and underwater cameras.

Cold and hungry British explorers and native people who gathered at Fort Enterprise, south of Point Lake—a notable lake trout fishery—in the Northwest Territories early in the nineteenth century certainly could have benefited from the fast-cutting technology of a power auger, rather than the laborious axe chopping of an ice opening by hand for their wintertime fishing. Available to today's winter anglers, for instance, is a Jiffy auger, energized by a three-horsepower Tecumseh gasoline engine with a precision drill assembly that cuts the eight- to ten-inch (20.3 to 25.4 cm) holes required for forktail fishing. This sophisticated gear would greatly have facilitated access by expedition members to gray trout habitat lying beneath a daunting seven feet (2.1 m) of lake ice! John Richardson, Franklin's surgeon-naturalist on both overland journeys (1819–22 and 1825–27), recorded ice of such thickness in his journal on April 27, 1821.[45] Data suggest much colder temperatures at that time than are experienced in the region today.[46]

The dynamics of ice formation for particular lakes are well known to winter lake trouters who fish them. Huge reservoirs positioned north to south, such as Flaming Gorge and Nueltin, otherwise geographically dissimilar, freeze over first in their northern sections. At Flaming Gorge, most Mackinaw ice fishing during the three-month winter season occurs at the northern end, with holes drilled above summer trolling runs and familiar underwater structure. Nueltin, situated nearly 20 degrees higher in latitude, is covered for more than eight months of the year by ice of a maximum thickness five times that of higher-elevated Flaming Gorge. Ice on Nueltin is still strong in May. The few folks who fish this remote setting just weeks prior to the open water season enjoy excellent hard-water laker fishing in shirtsleeve, bug-free weather (see table 9.2).[47]

Great Bear and Cleveland, lakes that vary widely in latitude, size, depth, and duration of freeze, surprisingly accumulate similar ice thicknesses (see table 9.2). Exposed to extremely strong winds in November, Great Bear's ice formation is delayed, with any ice skin alternately formed and then broken up. By late November, bitter cold has set in and icing is underway. Powerful wind action in late fall reduces Great Bear's freezing period, and limits ice thickness to a maximum of five feet (1.5 m). Smallish elongated Cleveland, cradled by low forested hills, is largely shielded from blustery winds. Having flown to the lake in three seasons and talked to others about winter conditions there, we believe that ice growth is enhanced by the long freezing time that results from the lake's relative protection from these pre-winter blasts.[48]

Reached primarily by a temporary ice road over frozen tundra in subzero weather, the Great Bear wilderness is bitterly cold and unforgiving in the winter months. Yet some residents of Deline (formerly Fort Franklin) take pleasure in productive lake trouting. Drilling holes with power augers about one and one-half miles (2.4 km) up-lake from the nearby outlet of the fast-flowing Great Bear River, winter fishermen have caught through the ice a number of lakers weighing 40 pounds (18.1 kg) or more. Evidently, the big fish follow their preferred forage, lake herring or ciscoes (*Coregonus artedii*) to the river. Silver-finish spoons jigged in 25 to 30 feet (8.4 to 9.1 m) of water are effective trout catchers in this unsullied environment.[49]

Cleveland Lake, an isolated outpost, is ice fished for gray trout infrequently, at most. An account reported by outfitter Rob Rowe about the lake's untapped hard-water forktail fishing is both captivating and humbling, especially considering the tackle used. In April 1991, Rob, his father, Larry, and a load of building materials were flown to Cleveland in a ski-equipped Green Airways de Havilland Otter aircraft to construct the island cabin. The plane returned nearly a week later to transport the pair back to Pakwash Lake. Taking a break from cabin labor on the first day, Rob penetrated four feet (1.2 m) of heavy ice by power drilling and finally thrusting with a pipe about 60 feet (18.3 m) from shore to try lake trouting. For his rod, the resourceful outfitter—admittedly not an ardent angler—cut a short branch from a shoreline willow and tied a length of line to the tip. The lure he used, a lead-head jig slipped inside a plastic tube body and tipped with frozen minnow, located bottom at 35 feet (10.7 m). Fishing with his makeshift outfit just above rocky structure, he immediately caught several obviously famished lakers. While father and son resumed work on the cabin, the butt-end of the stick was anchored in spring snow slush piled around the opening in the ice. Occasionally a dancing willow tip brought Rob scrambling to the hole to set the hook. The pair fished, on and off, for a couple of days during the stay, keeping a few lakers for the table. The largest weighed seven pounds (3.2 kg).[50]

After ice forms, then begins winter temperature stratification—the inverse of summer layering. A layer of dense water about 39°F (4°C) builds near the lake bed, with less dense water approaching the freezing point rising to the top. During the early ice period, golden active post-spawning fish thriving in a stable temperature and oxygen environment may be found anywhere under a gradually thickening ice ceiling. However, as winter deepens, dissolved oxygen levels decline from top to bottom in eutrophic (high nutrient) and mesotrophic (moderate nutrient) lakes where shallow plants decay. In oligotrophic water bodies, having low fertility, water clarity, and deep rock-studded basins, suitable oxygen levels continue all winter. Metabolism slows and forktails sometimes become difficult to locate and catch in mid to late winter.[51]

A laker's marked affinity for structure is a year-round phenomenon. Knowledgeable hard-water trouters drill holes off sandy beaches, steep cliffs, rubble-strewn shorelines, river mouths, and shoals near points and islands. They also cut these openings over deep holes, troughs, humps, saddles, boulder fields, rock bars and reefs, and habitat transition zones. Valuable aids include lake familiarity, depth contour charts, power augers, and portable sonar units. Because gray trout are migratory, several holes may be cut in a day's efforts to follow the fish.[52]

Vertical jigging with artificial baits is the technique used by most winter lake trout enthusiasts. An advantage of ice fishing is that the jigger does not have to contend with boat movement. Because below-ice temperature is roughly uniform, the entire water column may be fished. Although water just under the frozen surface is a little colder than that farther below, the oxygen count is higher and considerable activity may occur in this unlikely zone, even in the dead of winter. Plankton production, stimulated by light penetration, attracts bait fish, and, ultimately, predacious grays cruising just under the ice.[53]

Jigging ice rods, usually 36 to 48 inches long (91.4 to 121.9 cm) and with plenty of backbone for setting the hooks, are equipped with bait-casting or spinning reels, according to preference. If using monofilament, ice trouters normally spool up with 150 yards (137.2 m) of 10- to 12-pound test (4.5 to 5.4 kg) line sufficiently abrasion-resistant to preclude nicks from forktail head armor, gill plate edges, and underwater cover. Anglers also may use non-stretch fused superline, with a thirty-six-inch (91.4 cm) fluorocarbon leader added for less visibility in winter's clearer water.[54]

A wide variety of spoons, jigs, and blade baits are dropped through ice holes by laker anglers. Productive jigging spoons with flash and vibration embrace the Buzz Bomb, Swedish Pimple, Little Cleo, Rattlin' Snakie, Hopkins, Gibbs Minnow, Kastmaster, Crippled Herring, and Williams Whitefish or Wabler. The Airplane Jig and various lead-head jigs also are effective, along with blade baits such as the Cicada and Heddon Sonar. Spoons and jigs may be covered with tube bodies or tipped with live minnows or cut bait. Jigged baits, generally three-eighths to three-fourths ounce (10.6 to 21.3 g), and line strength can be scaled down to entice finicky forktails as winter progresses. To probe bottom composition in really deep water, lures weighing up to two ounces (56.7 g) may be fished. To reduce line twist, a black barrel swivel should be added 18 to 36 inches (45.7 to 91.4 cm) up the line.[55]

Winter lake trout are more active in the early morning hours, although these light-sensitive fish may be mobile throughout snowy, overclouded days. Most fishing occurs in less than 60 feet (18.3 m) of water, the depth at which most ice grays are taken. Depending upon level of fish activity and the time of the ice season, jig presentation varies from a vigorous approach to one with probably more finesse than in summer. Jigged artificial baits are systematically worked from bottom to top, with the ice angler employing a drop-lift-pause-jiggle technique. Jigging motions are enhanced by the use of flashing, fluttering spoons and tube-bodied, lead-headed jigs that provide a gentle, spiraled fall. Gold, silver, and chartreuse are effective finishes for spoons. For jigs, white and other light colors seem to work best. Lure action and the degree of laker interest may be observed on a portable sonar screen.[56]

Time-honored strategies, such as flag-type tip-ups and floats for live or dead bait, can work better than lure-jigging at times. In fact, some anglers take advantage of both methods using a pair of adjacent holes. A few years ago, Rob Rowe and a group of fishing friends traveled by snowmobile two hours through northwestern Ontario's midwinter back country to Trout Lake. After cutting openings through three and one-half feet (1.1 m) of ice, they sank hooks baited with sucker meat to depths of 50 feet (15.2 m). A number of ravenous, scent-enchanted lake trout were captured, including some approaching trophy size.[57]

The lake trout is a complex species dwelling in an ever-changing watery world. Science, history, and generations of experience have taught anglers much about how to beguile this vermiculated beauty. The prize awaits those who patiently persevere in studying the laker literature, understanding the fishing environment, talking to experts, and practicing their techniques.

Notes

1. Houston, *To the Arctic by Canoe, 1819–1821: The Journal and Paintings of Robert Hood,* 76.
2. Janes, *Fishing with Ray Bergman*, 191, 192.
3. Bergman, *Trout*, 381, 391; Bull, "Those Giant Fish of the Arctic," 1–8; Harback, personal telephone conference, 1992; Harback, "Reflections on Trips to Great Bear Lake in the Northwest Territories, Canada," 1992 (audiocassette recording); Janes, *Fishing with Ray Bergman*, 187–195; Scott and Crossman, *Freshwater Fishes of Canada*, 225; *Technology Report No. 5: Lake Trolling Techniques for Trout*, Luhr Jensen & Sons, 2, 4; Webster, "Thermal Stratification," 1033.
4. Agnew, "Bright Nights, Big Critters," 35–36.
5. *Trophy Lake Trout Tactics*, 1990 (videocassette SLT01, 31:47–32:11).

6. Webster, "Thermal Stratification," 1031–1033.

7. *Nueltin Lake*, Nueltin Fly-In Lodges, no date.

8. *Woodland Caribou Provincial Park*, Ontario Ministry of Natural Resources (brochure and canoe route map).

9. "MNR Fish Community/Yield Report A," 1986, 97–106; Quewezence and Thiess, personal correspondence, 1997; *Woodland Caribou Provincial Park*, Ontario Ministry of Natural Resources (brochure and canoe route map); *Woodland Caribou Provincial Park: Background Information*, Ontario Ministry of Natural Resources, 1986; "Woodland Caribou Provincial Park: Lakes and Fins," no date.

10. Gerrish, personal telephone conference, 1998.

11. *Green's Fly-In Camps*, 1996; "MNR Fish Community/Yield Report A," 1986, 97–106; Quewezence and Thiess, personal correspondence, 1997; *Woodland Caribou Provincial Park*, Ontario Ministry of Natural Resources (brochure and canoe route map).

12. *Heddon Catalog*, 1936 ed., 27; Luckey, *Old Fishing Lures and Tackle*, 32–33, 69.

13. Bergman, *Trout*, 388–394; Dawson, "Wire-Lining: A Time-Tested Tactic for Lake Trout," 18–20, 55–56; Journey, "Lakers East to West," 69, 108–109; *Trophy Lake Trout Tactics*, 1990 (videocassette SLT01, 23:10–35:45).

14. Ibid.

15. Bergman, *Trout*, 388-394; Dawson, "Wire-Lining: A Time-Tested Tactic for Lake Trout," 18–20, 55–56; *Trophy Lake Trout Tactics*, 1990 (videocassette SLT01, 23:10–35:45).

16. Bergman, *Trout*, 388–394; Dawson, "Wire-Lining: A Time-Tested Tactic for Lake Trout," 18–20, 55–56; Journey, "Lakers East to West," 69, 108–109; *Penn Catalog*, 1997 ed., 19, 25, 58; *Trophy Lake Trout Tactics*, 1990 (videocassette SLT01, 23:10–35:45).

17. Rosenthal, *North America's Freshwater Fishing Book*, 243.

18. McClane, "Jig/Jigging," 501–503.

19. Golad, "Hunting and Fishing Tips," 67.

20. Rosenthal, *North America's Freshwater Fishing Book*, 162.

21. Bailey, "Vertical Jigging for Summer Lakers," 27, 28, 50; McGary, "Mighty Niagara River Lakers Simply Awesome," 41–42; Rickett, "Personal Experiences on Lake Trout Fishing at Lac la Ronge in Northern Saskatchewan, Canada," 1992 (audiocassette recording).

22. Gierach, "Snowbird and the Kazan: Still Pumping Out Big Fish," 2; McGary, "Mighty Niagara River Lakers Simply Awesome," 41–42; Rosenthal, *North America's Freshwater Fishing Book*, 162; Sura, "Stout Trout," 150; *Tech Bulletin*, "Flaming Gorge," Luhr Jensen & Sons.

23. Bailey, "Vertical Jigging for Summer Lakers," 28, 50; McGary, "Mighty Niagara River Lakers Simply Awesome," 40–42; Rickett, "Personal Experiences on Lake Trout Fishing at Lac la Ronge in Northern Saskatchewan, Canada," 1992 (audiocassette recording); Sura, "Stout Trout," 150.

24. McClane, "Jig/Jigging," 503; Rickett, "Personal Experiences on Lake Trout Fishing at Lac la Ronge in Northern Saskatchewan, Canada," 1992 (audiocassette recording).

25. Sura et al., "Stout Trout," 146, 148.

26. Ranta, "Spring's Blackfly Lakers," 38, 40, 42, 64; Webster, "Thermal Stratification," 1031–1032.

27. Ibid.

28. Ranta, "Spring's Blackfly Lakers," 38, 64.

29. Bergman, *Trout*, 378–388.

30. Bennett, *The Art of Angling*, 255–256.

31. For Cleveland Lake: Rowe, personal telephone conference, 1998.

For Fish Lake: Hepworth, personal telephone conference, 1998. Because of depth and stored thermal energy, Fish Lake does not freeze over until late December or early January, despite high elevation. Smaller Mackinaws are caught by ice anglers, with most larger fish taken in spring and summer. Big forktails inhabiting this smallish natural water body appear to be wary and present a challenge to the lake trouter.

For Flaming Gorge: Brayton, Personal Telephone Conference, 1998.

For Great Bear Lake: French, personal telephone conference, 1998; Plummer, personal telephone conference, 1998. Bay ice at Great Bear breaks up in early July, with the last ice chunks in the lake proper usually gone by mid-July.

For Jackson Lake: Kiefling, personnel telephone conference, 1998; Kiefling, facsimile transmission, 1998. Jackson is described as a two-story fishery, with cutthroat and browns in surface waters and lake trout underneath. Walk-in ice fishing occurs close to the dam, and at Catholic Bay near Signal Mountain, Colter Bay, and adjacent Swim Beach.

For Nueltin Lake: Gurke, personnel telephone conference, 1998. A lake trout ice fishing venture initially offered by Nueltin Fly-In Lodges during the first two weeks of May 1994 was ultimately phased out because of a lack of angler interest. Evidently, fishermen preferred to spend their far north vacation dollars during the open water season.

For Lake Placid: Schoch, personnel telephone conference, 1998. Since Placid is designated as a "trout water" (chiefly rainbows), ice fishing is prohibited.

For Raquette Lake: Preall, personal telephone conference, 1998; Preall, *Lake Trout Monitoring Report*, P 293, 1991, 5. Raquette's forktail ice fishing occurs at the south end of the lake, which is shallow and readily accessible. Spring lake trouting takes place in the north segment's upper basins. Raquette Lake serves as the egg source for all Adirondack strain lakers stocked in New York.

For Lake Simcoe: Power, personal telephone conference, 1998.

For Lake Tahoe: Roush, personal telephone conference, 1998. Tahoe, North America's third deepest lake, does not develop surface ice, except at the edges on occasion. Emerald Bay froze over once years ago, according to John Roush, author and Tahoe Mackinaw veteran. Stored summer heat and massive upwelling preclude ice formation for the main water body.

32. Welch, *Limnology*, 387.

33. Coleman, "Goodbye Winter . . . Hello Trout!" 63; Ranta, "Spring's Blackfly Lakers," 42.

34. Coleman, "Goodbye Winter . . . Hello Trout!" 63.

35. *Welcome to Trout Lake Lodge Ltd.*, 1996.

36. Bull, "Those Giant Fish of the Arctic," 1–8; Harback, "Trophy Lodge: 901 Lbs. of Fish in One Day and a New World Record," 1991 (videocassette recording).

37. Scott and Crossman, *Freshwater Fishes of Canada*, 222.

38. Bergman, *Trout*, 385–387; Scott and Crossman, *Freshwater Fishes of Canada*, 222–223; Trewartha, *An Introduction to Climate*, 4, 5, 36.

39. McClane, "Fly-Fishing," 368.

40. McClane, "Topside Togue," 29–31, 54–56.

41. Almy, "Back River Char and Lakers," 55–57, 91–92.

42. Ranta, "Spring's Blackfly Lakers," 64.

43. Herrmann, personal correspondence, 1993.

44. Kerr, "1998–1999 Ice-Hut Rundown," 28–31.

45. Dorn, "Augers . . . on the Cutting Edge," 40–41; Houston, *Arctic Ordeal*, 33; Wilson, "Making a Point . . . ," 56–57.

46. Houston, *Arctic Artist*, 323.

47. Brayton, personal telephone conference, 1998; Gurke, personal telephone conference, 1998; "The Ultimate Ice-Fishing Trip," *Nueltin Notes*, May 1993.

48. French, personal telephone conference, 1998.

49. French, personal telephone conference, 1998; Scott and Crossman, *Freshwater Fishes of Canada,* 236–243.

50. Rowe, personal telephone conference, 1998.

51. McGary, "Ghost Busters: Lake Trout May Be Toughest Winter Target," 47–50; Quinn, "Understanding Ice Calendar Periods," 10–13.

52. McGary, "Ghost Busters: Lake Trout May Be Toughest Winter Target," 47–50; Ranta, "Ice Lakers Away from the Crowds," 34–37; Ranta, "Ice-Fishing Tackle and Tactics: Lakers," 23.

53. Linder, "Nontraditional Tactics for Lake Trout," 80–83; McGary, "Mighty Niagara River Lakers Simply Awesome," 40–42.

54. Straw, "Ice Line Choices (Simplified?)," 46–47; Straw, "Ice Rods: Cutting Edge Gear for Today," 28–30.

55. Ellis, "Soft-Plastic Baits for Winter Lake Trout," 59, 60, 62, 66; Ellis, "Spooning for Winter Lake Trout," 30, 34, 37, 42; Hoffman, "Jigging Lures for Predators: Categorizing the Options," 48–51; Linder, "Nontraditional Tactics for Lake Trout," 80–83; Ranta, "Ice Lakers Away from the Crowds," 34–37; Ranta, "Ice-Fishing Tackle and Tactics: Lakers," 23.

56. Linder, "Nontraditional Tactics for Lake Trout," 80–83; Quinn, "Understanding Ice Calendar Periods," 10–13; Ranta, "Ice-Fishing Tackle and Tactics: Lakers," 23.

57. Ellis, "Spooning for Winter Lake Trout," 30, 34, 37, 42; Hoffman, "Tip-Up and Floats: Who's Who and What's New," 34–35; Rowe, personal telephone conference, 1998.

TEN

THE FUTURE OF LAKE TROUT

Catch and release is both a personal philosophy and a common sense conservation strategy.

—*Three Men—Three Rivers* (videocassette recording)

Montana Department of Fish, Wildlife, and Parks (1993)

"The Future of Lake Trout Fishing is in Our Hands"

As professional educators, we believe that education is the key to an appreciation of the lake trout and its delicate environment and, therefore, the future of laker fishing. Topics covered in this chapter—technological advances, catch and release, and preservation and protection—are critical to this educational mind-set. We think you'll agree that the following discussion shows that the gray trout is indeed worthy of special treatment as an irreplaceable ecosystem resource.

Technological Advances

Despite technical improvements in equipment and methods, the lake trout is still considered a challenge to catch. Anglers have gained considerable proficiency in recent years. Techniques practiced today include jigging; downrigging; trolling with monofilament, fusion, lead-core, or wire lines; bait or spin casting; fly-casting; and ice fishing. Angling equipment is of superior quality. Temperature probes and fish- and depth-finders are utilized. Chartered jet aircraft transport anglers to isolated lodges in northern Canada where full accommodations and guided world-class lake trout fishing are offered. Bush pilots fly them to remote laker fishing spots for a day or a week. All of this progress and sophisticated angling imposes a special responsibility. What can we do to ensure quality gray trout fishing for the future?

Catch and Release

The catch-and-release ethic, a recurring theme of this book, has gained force as a movement. Catch-and-release lake trout angling is practiced at major fishing sites in northern Canada, including Nejalini Lodge, at Nejanilini Lake in north-central Manitoba near the border of Nunavut Territory; Nueltin Fly-In Lodges, on the shores of trans-boundary Nueltin Lake; and North of Sixty Fishing Lodges, in the southeast Northwest Territories, with the main lodge at Obre Lake and outpost camps at Flett, Wholdaia, and Anaunethad Lakes. Nueltin became Canada's original catch-and-release lake in 1979. A brochure of Nueltin Fly-In Lodges states: "Over 98 per cent of all the lake trout, northern pike, and Arctic grayling caught on Nueltin have been released since

1979. And this includes thousands of trophy sized fish!"[1] Nejanilini Lake adopted the catch-and-release rule in 1985.[2] The vast region served by North of Sixty Fishing Lodges attained catch-and-release standing in 1988.[3]

Catch limits for Great Bear Lake in the Northwest Territories, the premier trophy fishery for lake trout, have decreased substantially in the past twenty years. Plummer's Arctic Lodges, at Great Bear Lake, Great Slave Lake and Tree River, promote a policy of "Hug and Release," particularly for trophy fish. It has met with wide acceptance among anglers.[4]

The catch-and-release ethic for lake trout in Manitoba has been embraced by a high percentage of anglers, according to early 1990s editions of the booklet *Manitoba Fishing and Hunting Adventures.* A change reflecting this conservation principle has been implemented for the province's Master Angler Awards Program. In 1990, when anglers submitted applications by weight for these awards, 87 percent of the lake trout had been released after the catches. (The 504 lake trout registered for the awards program in that year ranged from 19.84 pounds, or 9.00 kg, to 41.67 pounds, or 18.90 kg.) By 1991, Master Angler Award applications were submitted by length, rather than weight, since Manitoba resource officials had decided that measuring length is quicker, whereas suspending a heavy specimen from a scale can stress or even kill the fish. (Lake trout listed for the 1991 and 1992 awards programs ranged from 39.37 inches or 100 cm to 49 inches or 124.46 cm.) The combined rate of release for lake trout in 1991 and 1992 was 92 percent, a 5 per cent increase over 1990. A recognition certificate and distinctive release crest were awarded by the province of Manitoba to anglers for releasing Master Angler fish.[5]

The weight of a lake trout can quickly be computed by using of a length and girth chart kept in the boat, thereby precluding injuring the fish through actual weighing. A tape is used to measure the length and girth of the fish, and the weight is calculated from the measurements. For example, Nueltin Lake's largest lake trout of 1990 measured 43 inches (109.2 cm) long with a girth of 27 inches (68.6 cm). The fish's weight, read from the chart, was 39.2 pounds (17.75 kg). Mechanical engineer John Herrmann, who caught this big laker at Nueltin, developed the formula upon which the chart is based:

$$\text{weight} = \frac{\text{length} \times (\text{girth})^2}{800}$$

Although the weight of lake trout determined by this method is relatively accurate, the procedure does not meet certification standards of the IGFA, National Fresh Water Fishing Hall of Fame, and Canadian National Fish Registry, which require physical weighing of the fish.

Barbless or bent-barb hooks can be used when angling for gray trout. Barbless hooks enhance catch-and-release fishing, and find a growing acceptance among conservation-minded anglers.

Those who practice hook barb-bending stress the ease of sharpening, more effective penetration, quick removal (from both fish and angler!), simple fish release, and the good feeling generated by watching an unharmed fish swim away. Some opponents, however, allege that barbless hooks can penetrate the fish too deeply, causing brain and gill damage.[6]

During Lloyd Bull's initial visits to Great Bear Lake in the early to mid-1970s, he discovered that big lakers often deeply engulfed small spoons, with hooks sometimes catching in the gills. To increase fish survival, he switched years ago to very large spoons with a single barbless hook, such as the Huskie Devle. In 1995, Bull's 72-pound (32.65 kg) record-breaker was enticed by a Huskie Devle with a bent-barb hook, a device that helped to facilitate the ultimate release of the giant fish.[7]

While the barbless hook ethic needs more study, *Sports Afield* magazine writer Homer Circle sees a trend in that direction:

> Today it is rare to visit a camp which doesn't foster conservation of sport fishes. Manitoba has taken the lead in Canada with a new law that requires barbless hooks for all recreational fishing. If the results are positive on fish and fishermen, then this movement is bound to grow as concerned anglers spread the gospel.[8]

We recommend that barbless hook users for lake trout maintain tight control over the rod tip at all times, avoiding slack line that might permit a fighting fish to throw the lure. Confidence has grown as we have observed that our laker-catching ability has not been adversely affected through the use of barbless or bent-barb hooks.

The use of unbarbed hooks for forktails, by the way, evidently is a long-time practice. The captivating journal of Arctic explorer George Back describes what may be its earliest recorded lake trout application near Lac de Gras in the Northwest Territories. His account, dated May 7, 1821, depicts an Inuit who "caught ten large trout at the rapid with a hook without a barb—fixed in a piece of horn."[9]

Which is the best method to handle a fish that an angler intends to release unharmed? Dan Sura, angler and staff member of *In-Fisherman* magazine, says jumbo lake trout are especially difficult to maneuver without risking injury to the fish, even when employing the familiar landing net:

> A conventional landing net seems safe. However, it can harm the fish because it curls the fish tightly, removes

> protective slime, damages scales, splits fins, and may even injure the gills if they become tangled in the net. And that's not to mention the problems that the hooks can cause if they get hung up in the netting.[10]

A laker slated for release might be left in the water alongside the boat while hooks are removed. A device helpful for handling a large lake trout at this juncture is the fish cradle, a net supported by two parallel poles or rods. Both cradle and fish could be weighed, then the laker released without stress or injury.[11]

Preservation and Protection

The lake trout is the largest of the chars. It has the widest natural range of salmonids in Canada, reaching all provinces and territories and some low-latitude Arctic islands, and has been transplanted widely in the United States and elsewhere. The laker is the char most valuable in commercial and sport fisheries. Catches, however, have declined in some areas since the early 1960s.[12] Biologists believe that the Atlantic sea lamprey has contributed to the decline of lake trout in the Great Lakes, and the American and Canadian governments have implemented a program to reduce the lamprey population.[13]

By the late 1950s, commercial over-fishing, pollution, and the lamprey eel had seriously depleted Lake Erie's stock of lake trout. Since then, much has been done by biologists, industry, and local communities to restore the lake to the status that it once enjoyed as a superb fishery. Erie's forktails are once again an important game fish.

Not too many years ago, anglers returned from lake trout fishing trips laden with trophy specimens for mounting or large quantities of fillets for home cooking. Since the removal of trophy lakers can harm a fishery, and the taste of fillets that are too old or had been frozen cannot match that of freshly caught fish, a meal of smaller gray trout in the wilderness offers both a viable alternative and an unforgettable experience. It would be a shame indeed if the quality of lake trout fishing ever declined to the point that future generations could no longer partake of that memorable event offered by a number of northern Canadian lodges—the shore lunch. John Gierach describes one of the highlights of a trip to Snowbird Lake:

> Fresh lake trout is one of the best tasting fish you'll ever find, especially when prepared shore-lunch style. The pleasures of a Northwest Territory shore lunch can only be hinted at to those who have never had one. Imagine fresh chunks of pink lake trout fillets rolled in corn meal and deep fried, with fried potatoes, onion rings, baked beans, thick slices of homemade bread, and strong coffee, served on the rocky beach of a wild lake hundreds of miles from civilization.[14]

The importance of selective harvest to lake trout evolution is expressed by Ontario biologist Bruce Ranta:

> We need to be more selective in our harvesting of lake trout. Rather than keeping big fish and releasing smaller fish, it should be the other way around. Taking larger fish puts tremendous natural-selection pressures on smaller fish to become big fish.[15]

Ranta, also a field editor of *Ontario Out of Doors* magazine, issues an ominous warning:

> Lake trout are a species easily exploited by humans, and are also very sensitive to changes in their fragile,

> nutrient-poor environment. Unless we as humans can quickly modify our own destructive habits, I fear the lake trout may soon join the likes of the Lake Erie Blue Walleye and the Labrador Duck.[16]

The closing statement of the excellent *In-Fisherman* videocassette recording *Trophy Lake Trout Tactics* is instructive, with wise counsel on the future of laker angling:

> Lake trout grow very slowly in the cold, infertile waters of the Canadian north. A large fish may be fifty, sixty years old, or more. Each is a valuable member of the resource community and should be treated as such. Lake trout populations are threatened by the dual specter of acid precipitation and angler harvest. Most of these infertile lakes have little ability to buffer the effects of acid rain, and many are already stressed beyond the breaking point. And when you consider how vulnerable lake trout are to ice fishing and the easy snowmobile access to once-remote areas today compared to the past, it's critical to limit the harvest of these dynamic fish. Catch-and-release is an important aspect of lake trout angling. We, as concerned anglers, should do our utmost to preserve and protect this unique fishery. It's fine to catch and enjoy these ancient fish as long as you carefully release them back into the system, particularly the larger ones. Don't think of them as food fish. Each and every one is a trophy to be revered, respected, and remembered.[17]

To paraphrase a statement of the Ontario Ministry of Natural Resources: The future of *lake trout* fishing is in our hands!"

Notes

1. *Nueltin Lake*, Nueltin Fly-In Lodges, no date.

2. Benson, personal telephone conference, 1993.

3. Frederickson, personal telephone conference, 1992.

4. *Fly-In! Fish . . . Fabulous Great Bear Lake!* Plummer's Lodges, no date.

5. *Manitoba Fishing and Hunting Adventures*, Travel Manitoba, 1991, 1992, 1993.

6. Circle, "The Barbless Hook Ethic," 107–109.

7. Bull, "Those Giant Fish of the Arctic," 2.

8. Circle, "The Barbless Hook Ethic," 109.

9. Houston, *Arctic Artist*, 120.

10. *Trophy Lake Trout Tactics*, 1990 (videocassette SLTO1, 51:38–51:55).

11. Ibid., 52:27–52:36.

12. Lane, "Char/Lake Trout," 317.

13. Vladykov, "Lamprey," 970.

14. Gierach, "Snowbird and the Kazan: Still Pumping Out Big Fish."

15. Ranta, personal telephone conference, 1993.

16. Ranta, personal correspondence, 1993, 2.

17. *Trophy Lake Trout Tactics,* 1990 (videocassette SLTO1, 52:39–53:56.)

BIBLIOGRAPHY

"Accident That Inspired a Company, The." *Williams Catalog*. Breck's International, Sherbrooke, Quebec 1997.

Agnew, Ron. "Bright Nights, Big Critters." *Outdoor Canada* (May 1989): 35–36, 43.

Alberta Guide to Sportfishing. Fish and Wildlife Division, Edmonton, Alberta 1993: 50.

Almy, Gerald. "Back River Char and Lakers." *Sports Afield* (August 1987): 55–57, 91–92.

Atlas of the World. 6th ed. Washington, D.C.: National Geographic Society 1990.

Atwill, Lionel. "Wisconsin Muskies." *Sports Afield* (September 1989): 90–95, 120–121.

"Backgrounder." Fred Arbogast Company, Akron, Ohio (June 1, 1991): 1–2.

Bailey, Bob. "Vertical Jigging for Summer Lakers." *Ontario Out of Doors* (June 1997): 27–28, 50.

Bailey, Gilbert E. *California: A Geologic Wonderland*. Los Angeles: Times-Mirror Press 1924.

Balford, Dave. Fisheries Biologist. Game and Fish Department, Cheyenne, Wyoming. Personal telephone conference (March 29, 1993).

Beamish, Richard. "An Embattled Wilderness." *National Parks* (September/October 1992): 36–41.

Bennett, Tiny. *The Art of Angling.* New York: Prentice Hall 1988.

Benson, Marvin. Owner/operator. Nejalini Lodge, Nejanilini Lake, Manitoba. Personal telephone conference (February 9, 1993).

Bergman, Ray. *Trout*. New York: Alfred A. Knopf 1952.

Bilbey, Curt. Personal correspondence (July 1, 1992).

———. Personal telephone conference (July 18, 1993).

Bockstoce, John. "Changing Images of the Northwest Passage." *National Geographic* (August 1990): 2-33.

Boonstra, Rudy. "Beaver." *The Canadian Encyclopedia*. Vol. 1. Edmonton, Alberta: Hurtig 1985.

Boyce, Farrell M. "Lake." *The Canadian Encyclopedia*. Vol. 2. Edmonton, Alberta: Hurtig 1985.

Boyer, David S. "Minnesota, Where Water Is the Magic Word." *National Geographic* (February 1976): 200–229.

Brayton, Steve. Project Leader, Flaming Gorge/Green River. Division of Wildlife Resources, Dutch John, Utah. Personal telephone conference (April 13, 1998).

Brown, Jim. Assistant to the President. International Game Fish Association, Pompano Beach, Florida. "Seventy-two-pound trout, lake, caught on August 19, 1995." Correspondence to Lloyd E. Bull (January 21, 1996).

———. Personal telephone conference (April 4 and August 24, 1993).

Bull, Lloyd E. "Catching the 72¼ Pound Current World Record Lake Trout" (January 1999): 1–3.

———. Correspondence to Michael Leech, President, International Game Fish Association, Pompano Beach, Florida (October 26, 1997).

———. Personal correspondence (October 26 and December 15, 1997).

———. Personal telephone conference (September 30 and November 9, 1997; January 1, 1998).

———. "Those Giant Fish of the Arctic" (1997): 1–8.

Burke, Roland. "The Stirring Story of Mrs. Hofschneider . . . No. 1 Mother and Manufacturer." *Sporting Goods Dealer* (August 1949).

Burton, Pam. Marketing Director. Worden's Lures/Yakima Bait Company, Granger, Washington. Personal telephone conference (August 17, 1992).

"Canadian National Fish Registry." *Canadian Sportfishing* (November 1998): 56.

Carlander, Kenneth D. *Handbook of Freshwater Fishery Biology*. Ames, Iowa: Iowa State University Press 1969.

Charger Lures. Lake Products Company, Imlay City, Michigan. Catalog 1986.

Circle, Homer. "The Barbless Hook Ethic." *Sports Afield* (November 1992): 107–109.

———. "We Caught 'Em by the Ton." *Sports Afield* (June 1963): 60–63, 125–127, 128.

Coleman, Geoff. "Goodbye Winter . . . Hello Trout!" *Canadian Sportfishing* (March 1998): 62-64.

"Cover Story: Lake Trout Release." *Splash*. National Fresh Water Fishing Hall of Fame, Hayward, Wisconsin. Vol. 13, No. 1 (1989): 7.

Creber, Casey. Operator, Charters and Guiding Service. Lake Simcoe, Ontario. Personal telephone conference (July 5, 1993).

Daigle, J. P. Vice President, Sales and Promotions. Breck's International, Sherbrooke, Quebec. Personal correspondence (August 6, 1992).

Dawson, Blair. "Wire-Lining: A Time-Tested Tactic for Lake Trout." *Ontario Out of Doors* (July 1994): 18–20, 55–56.

Dipple, Clem. "Short and Sweet Success Story Belies Hofschneider History." *Fishing Tackle Trade News* (March 1966): 27–28.

Dorn, Mark. "Augers . . . on the Cutting Edge." *Ice Fishing Guide 1999*. In-Fisherman/Primedia (November 1998): 40–41.

Drolet, Jean-Paul. "Mineral Resources." *The Canadian Encyclopedia*. Vol. 2. Edmonton, Alberta: Hurtig 1985.

Dunbar, Carl O. *Historical Geology*. New York: John Wiley 1963.

Ellis, Gord. "Soft-Plastic Baits for Winter Lake Trout." *Ontario Out of Doors* (February 1994): 59–60, 62, 66.

———. "Spooning for Winter Lake Trout." *Ontario Out of Doors* (March 1998): 30, 34, 37, 42.

Eppinger Catalog. Eppinger Manufacturing Company, Dearborn, Michigan 1996.

Evans, David. "Nueltin Lake." *The Canadian Encyclopedia*. Vol. 2. Edmonton, Alberta: Hurtig 1985.

Everson, Bret. "Lake Trout Fishing Experiences." Audiocassette recording (January 1992).

"Far Northern Outpost Camps." *North of Sixty News*. Vol. 4, No. 1 (January 1991): 4.

Fergurson, Ernest B. "Lake Tahoe: Playing for High Stakes." *National Geographic* (March 1992): 112–132.

Final Report: XIII Olympic Winter Games. Lake Placid, New York (February 13–24, 1980).

Fishing Lake Placid and Surrounding Waters. Chamber of Commerce, Lake Placid, New York. Pamphlet (no date).

Flatfish, Fishcake, Swimmerspoon. Helin Tackle Company, Detroit, Michigan. Catalog 1973–74.

Fly-In! Fish . . . Fabulous Great Bear Lake! Plummer's Lodges, Northwest Territories. Brochure (no date).

Fowler, John. "You Shoud Know About Lakers." *Outdoor Life* (July 1960): 48–51, 81–82.

Francis, Daniel. "Amundsen, Roald." *The Canadian Encyclopedia*. Vol. 1. Edmonton, Alberta: Hurtig 1985.

———. "Dease, Peter Warren." *The Canadian Encyclopedia.* Vol. 1. Edmonton, Alberta: Hurtig 1985.

———. "Lac La Ronge." *The Canadian Encyclopedia.* Vol. 2. Edmonton, Alberta: Hurtig 1985.

Fred Arbogast Company Catalog. Akron, OH 1996.

Frederickson, Dave. "For the Record . . ." *North of Sixty News.* Vol. 4, no. 1 (January 1991): 9.

———. Co-Owner/operator. North of Sixty Fishing Lodges Ltd., Northwest Territories. Personal telephone conference (August 17, 1992).

French, Howard. Angler and Manager, Community Development Corporation, Deline/Great Bear Lake, Northwest Territories. Personal telephone conference (April 11 and 13, 1998).

Gautrey, Sharon. Controller. Breck's International, Sherbrooke, Quebec. Personal telephone conference (July 19, 1993).

Geology of the Fish Lake Area. U.S. Department of Agriculture, Forest Service. Fishlake National Forest, Richfeld, Utah. Pamphlet 1979.

Gerrish, Lee. Information and Planning Supervisor. Ministry of Natural Resources, Red Lake, Ontario. Personal telephone conference (March 18, 1998).

Gierach, John. "Snowbird and the Kazan: Still Pumping Out Big Fish." *Fishing World* (June 1983).

Golad, Frank S. "Hunting and Fishing Tips." *Sports Afield* (Almanac) (July 1992): 67.

Graham, Jane E. "Pond, Peter." *The Canadian Encyclopedia*. Vol. 3. Edmonton, Alberta: Hurtig 1985.

Greene, C. W. "Lake Trout." *New York State Conservationist* (April–May 1955): D-11, D-12.

Green's Fly-In Camps. Red Lake, Ontario. Brochure 1996.

Grooms, Steve. "Snowbird Lake Dream Trip." *Fins and Feathers* (February 1978).

Gunter, Harry. Marketing Director. Eppinger Manufacturing Company, Dearborn, Michigan. Personal telephone conference (April 1, 1992).

Gurke, Shawn. Operations Manager. Nueltin Fly-In Lodges, Manitoba/Northwest Territories. Personal telephone conference (April 6 and 13, 1998).

Hammers, Hubert H. Correspondence to Norman E. Gauch, Hofschneider Corporation (April 21, 1953).

Hansen, Wallace R. *The Geologic Story of the Uinta Mountains*. U.S. Department of the Interior. Geological Survey Bulletin 1291, 1983.

Harback, Rodney. Personal telephone conference (July 14 and August 3, 1992; July 21, 1993).

———. "Reflections on Trips to Great Bear Lake in the Northwest Territories, Canada." Audiocassette recording (June 15, 1992).

———. "Trophy Lodge: 901 Lbs. of Fish in One Day and a New World Record." Videocassette recording (July 19, 1991).

Heddon Catalog. James Heddon's Sons, Dowagiac, Michigan 1936.

Henderson, Dave. "Anglers Hook Two World Records: Lake Trout Mark to N.Y. Man." *Press and Sun-Bulletin* (Endicott, New York) (October 16, 1996).

Hepworth, Dale. Aquatics Program Manager. Division of Wildlife Resources, Cedar City, Utah. Personal telephone conference (May 20, 1992; April 16, 1998).

Herrmann, John. "Lake Trout Fishing in Nueltin Lake, Manitoba/Northwest Territories, Canada, July 1990 and June 1991." Audiocassette recording (March 20, 1992).

———. Personal correspondence (August 11, 1993).

Hoffman, Steve. "Jigging Lures for Predators: Categorizing the Options." *Ice Fishing Guide 1999*. In-Fisherman/Primedia (November 1998): 48–51.

———. "Tip-Ups and Floats: Who's Who and What's New." *Ice Fishing Guide 1999*. In-Fisherman/Primedia (November 1998): 34–35.

Hope, Marty. "Fishing Lure's Success Persists." *Calgary Herald* (March 29, 1986).

Houle, Roy. Field Researcher. Worden's Lures/Yakima Bait Company, Granger, Washington. Personal telephone conference (June 8, 1992).

Houston, C. Stuart, ed. *Arctic Artist: The Journal and Paintings of George Back, Midshipman with Franklin, 1819–22*. Montreal and Kingston: McGill-Queen's University Press 1995.

———. *Arctic Ordeal: The Journal of John Richardson, Surgeon-Naturalist with Franklin, 1820–22*. Kingston and Montreal: McGill-Queen's University Press 1985.

———. *To the Arctic by Canoe 1819-21: The Journal and Paintings of Robert Hood, Midshipman with Franklin*. Montreal and Kingston: McGill-Queen's University Press 1975.

Information about History, Recreation, Trails, and Management of the Fish Lake Basin. U.S. Department of Agriculture, Forest Service. Fishlake National Forest, Loa, Utah. Pamphlet 1989.

Janes, Edward C. *Fishing with Ray Bergman*. New York: Simon & Schuster 1970.

Johnson, Gaylord, and Irving Adler. *Discover the Stars*. New York: Sentinel Books 1965.

Journey, Bud. "Lakers East to West." *Outdoor Life* (February 1989): 69, 108–109.

Journey through the Past: A Geologic Tour. Grand Teton National Park, Moose, Wyoming. Folder 1992.

Kaminsky, Peter. " Dardevle—An American Success Story." *Field and Stream* (May 1984): 94–95, 177.

Kerr, John. "1998-99 Ice-Hut Rundown." *Ontario Out of Doors* (December/January 1998–99): 28–31.

Kiefling, John. Regional Fisheries Supervisor. Game and Fish Department, Cheyenne, Wyoming. Facsimile transmission (April 13, 1998).

———. *Jackson Lake Completion Report*. Game and Fish Department, Cheyenne, Wyoming (April 1981).

———. Personal telephone conference (April 13, 1998).

Kiel, Beulah. Administrative Assistant. Fred Arbogast Company, Akron, Ohio. Facsimile transmission (March 4, 1992).

Kirkpatrick, Dick. "Fishing's Deadly Dozen." *Popular Mechanics* (May 1962).

Kupsch, Walter O. "Richardson, Sir John." *The Canadian Encyclopedia.* Vol. 3. Edmonton, Alberta: Hurtig 1985.

Lane, E. David. "Char/Lake Trout." *The Canadian Encyclopedia.* Vol. 1. Edmonton, Alberta: Hurtig 1985.

Lawrence, Bob. Owner/Operator. Lawrence's Lakeside Cabins and Guide Service, Moosehead Lake, Maine. Personal telephone conference (October 17, 1994).

Lee, David. "Matonabbee." *The Canadian Encyclopedia.* Vol. 2. Edmonton, Alberta: Hurtig 1985.

Leech, Michael. President. International Game Fish Association, Pompano Beach, Florida. "Seventy-two-pound Lake Trout Caught on August 19, 1995." Correspondence to Lloyd Bull (December 30, 1997).

Levy, Howard M. *Man against Musky*. Harrisburg, Pennsylvania: Stackpole 1962.

Lincoln, Robert Page. *Musky Fishing*. Harrisburg, Pennsylvania: Stackpole 1952.

———. "Spring Lake Trout Fishing." *Fur-Fish-Game* (May 1943): 3–5, 23–25.

Linder, Al. "Nontraditional Tactics for Lake Trout." *Ice Fishing Guide 1999*. In-Fisherman/Primedia (November 1998): 80–83.

———. "Perspective from Al." *In-Fisherman* (February 1996): 132.

Lindsey, C. C. "Lake Trout." *McClane's New Standard Fishing Encyclopedia*. New York: Holt 1974.

Luckey, Carl F. *Old Fishing Lures and Tackle*. Florence, Alabama: Books America 1996.

Luhr Jensen & Sons Company History. Hood River, Oregon 1995: 1–8.

"Lure Fish Can't Pass Up, A." *Life* (August 17, 1962): 39, 41, 44.

"Making of a Legend: The Normark/Rapala Story." Normark Corporation, Minneapolis, Minnesota (October 1991): 1–11.

Malz, Carl. "Manitoba's Nejalini Lake." *Fishing Facts* (April 1992): 54–57.

Manitoba Fishing and Hunting Adventures. Travel Manitoba, Winnipeg, Manitoba 1991, 1992, 1993.

Manns, Hobart. Antique Lure Authority. Portland, Oregon. Personal telephone conference (July 25 and August 11, 1992; July 11, 1993).

Marsh, James. "Athabasca, Lake." *The Canadian Encyclopedia*. Vol. 1. Edmonton, Alberta: Hurtig 1985.

———. "Back River." *The Canadian Encyclopedia*. Vol. 1. Edmonton, Alberta: Hurtig 1985.

———. "Back, Sir George." *The Canadian Encyclopedia*. Vol. 1. Edmonton, Alberta: Hurtig 1985.

———. "Bush Flying." *The Canadian Encyclopedia.* Vol. 1. Edmonton, Alberta: Hurtig 1985.

———. "Champlain, Lake." *The Canadian Encyclopedia.* Vol. 1. Edmonton, Alberta: Hurtig 1985.

———. "Coppermine River." *The Canadian Encyclopedia.* Vol. 1. Edmonton, Alberta: Hurtig 1985.

———. "Dubawnt River." *The Canadian Encyclopedia.* Vol. 1. Edmonton, Alberta: Hurtig 1985.

———. "Franklin Search." *The Canadian Encyclopedia.* Vol. 2. Edmonton, Alberta: Hurtig 1985.

———. "Great Bear Lake." *The Canadian Encyclopedia.* Vol. 2. Edmonton, Alberta: Hurtig 1985.

———. "Great Slave Lake." *The Canadian Encyclopedia.* Vol. 2. Edmonton, Alberta: Hurtig 1985.

———. "Hearne, Samuel." *The Canadian Encyclopedia.* Vol. 2. Edmonton, Alberta: Hurtig 1985.

———. "Hudson, Henry." *The Canadian Encyclopedia.* Vol. 2. Edmonton, Alberta: Hurtig 1985.

———. "James, Thomas." *The Canadian Encyclopedia.* Vol. 2. Edmonton, Alberta: Hurtig 1985.

———. "Lake of the Woods." *The Canadian Encyclopedia.* Vol. 2. Edmonton, Alberta: Hurtig 1985.

———. "Richardson, Sir John." *The Canadian Encyclopedia.* Vol. 3. Edmonton, Alberta: Hurtig 1985.

———. "Shield." *The Canadian Encyclopedia.* Vol. 3. Edmonton, Alberta: Hurtig 1985.

McClane, A. J. "Fly-Fishing." *McClane's New Standard Fishing Encyclopedia.* New York: Holt 1974.

———. "Jig/Jigging." *McClane's New Standard Fishing Encyclopedia.* New York: Holt 1974.

———. "Topside Togue." *Field and Stream* (February 1963): 29–31, 54–56 .

McGary, Bob. "Ghost Busters: Lake Trout May Be Toughest Winter Target." *Canadian Sportfishing* (November 1998): 47–50.

——. "Mighty Niagara River Lakers Simply Awesome." *Canadian Sportfishing* (November 1997): 40–42.

McNicholl, Martin K. "Tyrrell, Joseph Burr." *The Canadian Encyclopedia*. Vol. 3. Edmonton, Alberta: Hurtig 1985.

McPhail, J. D., and C. C. Lindsey. *Freshwater Fishes of Northwestern Canada and Alaska*. Ottawa: Fisheries Research Board of Canada. Bulletin 173, 1970.

Milstein, Michael. "Lake's Cutthroat Competition Rises." *Los Angeles Times* (November 22, 1994).

"MNR Fish Community/Yield Report A." Ontario Ministry of Natural Resources (September 3, 1986): 97–106.

Mouat, Lucia. "N.Y.'s Adirondack Park Celebrates 100 Years." *Christian Science Monitor* (May 21, 1992): 10–11.

Murphy, Dudley, and Rick Edmisten. *Fishing Lure Collectibles*. Paducah, Kentucky: Collector Books 1995.

Neatby, Leslie H. "Arctic Exploration." *The Canadian Encyclopedia*. Vol. 1. Edmonton, Alberta: Hurtig 1985.

——. "Franklin, Sir John." *The Canadian Encyclopedia.* Vol. 2. Edmonton, Alberta: Hurtig 1985.

Nejalini Lodge—In Canada's Tundra Land. Nejanilini Lake, Manitoba. Brochure (no date).

——. Folder 1993.

"New" Nejalini Lake Resort, The. Nejanilini Lake, Manitoba. Brochure 1995.

Newman, Peter C. "Canada's Fur-Trading Empire." *National Geographic* (August 1987): 192–229.

Nueltin Lake. Nueltin Fly-In Lodges, Manitoba/Northwest Territories. Brochure (no date).

"Obre Lake—The Main Lodge." *North of Sixty News*. Vol. 3, no. 1 (January 1990): 3.

O'Brien, D. S. "Northwest Territories." *McClane's New Standard Fishing Encyclopedia*. New York: Holt 1974.

Official World and U.S.A. State Fresh Water Angling Records. Hayward, Wisconsin: National Fresh Water Fishing Hall of Fame. 1995 and 1999 eds.

Ontario Record Fish Registry. Ontario Federation of Anglers and Hunters, Peterborough, Ontario 1992.

Opre, Tom. "Great Bear's Great Fishing." *All About Fishing with Eppinger's Famous Dardevles*. Eppinger Manufacturing Company, Dearborn, Michigan 1969: 8–11.

Pallister, Cecil. President. Len Thompson Lures, Lacombe, Alberta. Personal telephone conference (August 1, 1992).

Parsons, John. "Cabot, John." *The Canadian Encyclopedia*. Vol. 1. Edmonton, Alberta: Hurtig 1985.

Penn Catalog. Penn Fishing Tackle Manufacturing Company, Philadelphia, Pennsylvania 1997.

Phillips, Wayne. "The Most Wanted Lures." *Western Sportsman* (August/September 1991): 52–54.

——. "Near Record Laker." *Western Sportsman* (October–November 1990).

Plummer, Chummy. President, Plummer's Lodges, Great Bear Lake, Northwest Territories. Personal telephone conference (April 7, 1998).

"Potential New IGFA All-Tackle Record." *Arctic Lure*. Plummer's Lodges (Fall 1996): 4.

Power, John. Lake Simcoe Fisherman and Outdoor Writer. Beaverton, Ontario. Personal telephone conference (April 17, 1998).

Preall, Richard. *Lake Trout Monitoring Report, P 293—Raquette Watershed, Hamilton County*. Department of Environmental Conservation, Inland Fisheries, Region 5, Ray Brook, New York 1991: 1–61.

——. Senior Aquatic Biologist. Department of Environmental Conservation, Ray Brook, New York. Personal telephone conference (March 10, 1993; April 13, 1998).

Prorok, Paul. "Rick Clunn and Bill Murphy Talk Crankbaits." *In-Fisherman* (February 1993): 68–73.

Quewezence, Claire, and Al Theiss. Assistant Superintendent and Superintendent. Ministry of Natural Resources, Red Lake, Ontario. "Lake Trout in Woodland Caribou Provincial Park." Personal correspondence (July 11, 1997).

Quinn, Steve. "Understanding Ice Calendar Periods." *Ice Fishing Guide 1999*. In-Fisherman/Primedia (November 1998): 10–13.

Ranta, Bruce. "Ice Lakers Away From the Crowds." *Ontario Out of Doors* (February 1995): 34–37.

———. "Ice-Fishing Tackle and Tactics: Lakers." *Ontario Out of Doors* (December/January 1995–96): 23.

———. Field Editor, *Ontario Out of Doors*; Angler; Biologist, Ministry of Natural Resources, Kenora, Ontario. Personal correspondence (July 27, 1993): 1–2.

———. Personal telephone conference (July 6, 1993).

———. "Spring's Blackfly Lakers." *Ontario Out of Doors* (April 1995): 38, 40, 42, 64.

Ray, Arthur J. "Hudson's Bay Company." *The Canadian Encyclopedia.* Vol. 2. Edmonton, Alberta: Hurtig 1985.

"Record-Breaking Lake Trout Released." *North of Sixty News.* Vol. 2, no. 1 (January 1989): 1.

Rennicke, Jeff. "America's Deepest Canyon." *National Geographic Traveler* (March/April 1993): 110–121.

Rickett, John. "Personal Experiences on Lake Trout Fishing at Lac la Ronge in Northern Saskatchewan." Audiocassette recording (August 1992).

Ritchie, Craig. "Lures That Endure." *Outdoor Canada* (April 1992): 30–33.

Rollefson, Max, and Jon Erickson. "Jackson Lake's Big 'Macks.' " *Wyoming Wildlife* (September 1963): 20–24.

Rosenthal, Mike. *North America's Freshwater Fishing Book*. New York: Charles Scribner's Sons 1989.

Roush, John H. Jr. *Enjoying Fishing Lake Tahoe, the Truckee River, and Pyramid Lake.* Chicago: Adams Press 1987.

———. Lake Trout Angler and Author. Kentfield, California. Personal telephone conference (April 13, 1998).

Rowe, Rob. Owner/Operator. Snake Falls Camp and Airways, Pakwash Lake, Ontario. Personal telephone conference (March 29 and November 29, 1998).

Rutter, N. W. "Glaciation." *The Canadian Encyclopedia.* Vol. 2. Edmonton, Alberta: Hurtig 1985.

Saskatchewan Angler's Guide. Saskatchewan Natural Resources, Regina, Saskatchewan 1993–94. 18.

Schneidervin, Roger. Project Fisheries Biologist. Division of Wildlife Resources, Flaming Gorge, Dutch John, Utah. Personal telephone conference (May 21 and June 2, 1992; March 29, 1993).

Schoch, Bill. Senior Aquatic Biologist. Department of Environmental Conservation, Saranak Lake, New York. Personal telephone conference (June 30, 1998).

Scott, W. B., and E. J. Crossman. *Freshwater Fishes of Canada*. Ottawa: Fisheries Research Board of Canada. Bulletin 184, 1985.

Scrivener, A. "Hofschneider Corporation Story." *Hardware Trade* (February 1964): 8–9.

"Snowbird Lake Lodge—Housekeeping in Style." *North of Sixty News*. Vol. I, no. 1 (January 1988): 3.

Speckerman, W. J. Correspondence to Hofschneider Corporation (August 3, 1962).

Sport Fishing Guide. Department of Renewable Resources. Government of the Northwest Territories, Yellowknife (1992): 8–9.

Stanton, Charles R. "Forest Regions." *The Canadian Encyclopedia*. Vol. 2. Edmonton, Alberta: Hurtig 1985.

———. "Forestry." *The Canadian Encyclopedia*. Vol. 2. Edmonton, Alberta: Hurtig 1985.

Straw, Matt. "Ice Line Choices (Simplified?)" *Ice Fishing Guide 1999*. In-Fisherman/Primedia (November 1998): 46–47.

———. "Ice Rods: Cutting Edge Gear for Today." *Ice Fishing Guide 1999.* In-Fisherman/Primedia (November 1998): 28–30.

Sura, Dan, Ron Lindner, and James Lindner. "Stout Trout." *In-Fisherman* (March 1995): 142–144, 146, 148–150.

Tech Bulletin. "Flaming Gorge." Luhr Jensen & Sons, Hood River, Oregon 1991.

Technology Report No. 5: Lake Trolling Techniques for Trout. Luhr Jensen & Sons, Hood River, Oregon 1983: 1–8.

Thomas, Rex. "Fish Lake Lakers." *Outdoor Life* (June 1992): 92.

Thompson, Bill. "Nature's Nasties." *Ontario Out of Doors* (May 1996): 23–26, 28, 30, 33, 80.

Thompson, Susan. Fisheries Technician Supervisor. Department of Renewable Resources, Whitehorse, Yukon Territory. Facsimile transmission (April 28, 1993).

Tindall, George Brown, and David E. Shi. *America: A Narrative History.* 2 Vols. New York: Norton 1996.

"Treeline Lodge." *Nueltin News.* Vol. 12, no. 1 (1993): 3.

Trewartha, Glenn T. *An Introduction to Climate.* New York: McGraw-Hill 1954.

Trophy Lake Trout Tactics. Videocassette recording No. SLT01. Brainerd, Minnesota: In-Fisherman 1990.

Trudel, Marcel. "Champlain, Samuel de." *The Canadian Encyclopedia.* Vol. 1. Edmonton, Alberta: Hurtig 1985.

"Ultimate Ice-Fishing Trip, The." *Nueltin Notes.* Nueltin Fly-In Lodges, Manitoba/Northwest Territories (May 1993).

Vladykov, Vadim D. "Lamprey." *The Canadian Encyclopedia.* Vol. 2. Edmonton, Alberta: Hurtig 1985.

Walsh, Mary Williams. "The Great Canadian Diamond Rush." *Los Angeles Times* (October 4, 1992): D1, D10.

Weber, Ron. "The Lure Fish Can't Pass Up." *Rapala Fishing Guide.* Normark Corporation 1981: 2–11.

Webster, Dwight A. "Thermal Stratification." *McClane's New Standard Fishing Encyclopedia.* New York: Holt 1974.

Welch, Paul S. *Limnology.* New York: McGraw-Hill 1952.

Welcome to Trout Lake Lodge Ltd. Red Lake, Ontario. Brochure 1996.

Wharton, Tom. "Angler Glows After Record Catch." *Salt Lake City Tribune* (June 9, 1988).

Williams Catalog. Breck's International, Sherbrooke, Quebec 1997.

Williams, Glyndwr. "Exploration." *The Canadian Encyclopedia.* Vol. 1. Edmonton, Alberta: Hurtig 1985.

Williams, Tom. *Flaming Gorge*. Dutch John, Utah: Flaming Gorge Natural History Association 1981.

Wilson, Kevin. "Making a Point: If You're Looking for Exotic Fishing, Look North." *Canadian Sportfishing* (March 1999): 56–57.

Woodland Caribou Provincial Park. Ontario Ministry of Natural Resources. Brochure and Canoe Route Map (no date).

Woodland Caribou Provincial Park: Background Information. Ontario Ministry of Natural Resources. Toronto: Queen's Printer 1986.

"Woodland Caribou Provincial Park: Lakes and Fins" (no date).

Woodman, David C. *Unravelling the Franklin Mystery: Inuit Testimony.* Montreal and Kingston: McGill-Queen's University Press 1992.

Worden's Lures/Yakima Bait Company Catalog. Granger, Washington 1992.

World Record Game Fishes. Pompano Beach, Florida: International Game Fish Association 1997, 1998, and 1999 eds.

Zoltai, Stephen C. "Dubawnt Lake." *The Canadian Encyclopedia.* Vol. 1. Edmonton, Alberta: Hurtig 1985.

INDEX

ABOUT THE AUTHORS

Ed Eveland, originally from Plainfield, Iowa, moved with his family to southern California at the beginning of World War II. Following wartime service with the United States Navy, he earned a bachelor's degree with a pre-legal major from the University of Oregon. Later he completed his master's degree at California State University, Long Beach, majoring in English. A long and distinguished career with the Long Beach Unified School District included positions as high school English teacher and department head, junior high and high school principal, and assistant superintendent, secondary division. Retiring as an administrator in 1990, he was elected two years later to the Board of Education in Long Beach, the third largest school system in California with over 92,000 students. He has published several novels and written a cookbook, *Real Men Cook on Sundays*. In addition to plying northwestern Ontario's lakes for lake trout, he has fished extensively California's coastal and inland waters for many years.

Ross Shickler was born in Buffalo, a family gateway to Canada's great angling, first passaged by his grandfather in the 1920s. He grew up on the shores of western New York's beautiful Chautauqua Lake, where fledgling fishing skills were honed. He finished bachelor's and master's degrees at the Fredonia campus of the State University of New York, majoring in science education and minoring in history. In 1983 he received a doctorate in educational administration from the University of Southern California. He taught science at junior high and high school levels in the Long Beach Unified School District before assuming administrative positions there. Currently, he is a high school principal in Long Beach. He is a member of the International Game Fish Association, National Fresh Water Fishing Hall of Fame, Ontario Federation of Anglers and Hunters, National Fishing Lure Collectors Club, and Canada's National History Society. Since co-writing this book, he has fished Nueltin and Great Bear Lakes, outstanding lake trout water bodies in northern Canada.